Personal Skills
in Public Speech

STAFFORD H. THOMAS
University of Illinois, Urbana-Champaign

PRENTICE-HALL, INC., Englewood Cliffs, N.J. 07632

Library of Congress Cataloging in Publication Data

THOMAS, STAFFORD H.
    Personal skills in public speech.

    Includes bibliographies and index.
    1. Public speaking. I. Title.
PN4121.T48 1985   808.5'1   84-14382
ISBN 0-13-658576-0

Editorial/production supervision and
    interior design: Colleen Brosnan
Cover design: Whitman Studios, Inc.
Cover photo: Alpha
Manufacturing buyer: Barbara Kelly Kittle

Printed in the United States of America

10 9 8 7 6 5 4 3 2 1

ISBN 0-13-658576-0 01

Prentice-Hall International, Inc., *London*
Prentice-Hall of Australia Pty. Limited, *Sydney*
Editora Prentice-Hall do Brasil, Ltda., *Rio de Janeiro*
Prentice-Hall Canada Inc., *Toronto*
Prentice-Hall of India Private Limited, *New Delhi*
Prentice-Hall of Japan, Inc., *Tokyo*
Prentice-Hall of Southeast Asia Pte. Ltd., *Singapore*
Whitehall Books Limited, *Wellington, New Zealand*

Contents

9   STRATEGIES OF PERSUASION   170

Part 4   *Specialized Forms of Speaking*

10   PROBLEM SOLVING IN SMALL GROUP DISCUSSIONS   188

Preface

This book presents a body of useful information and advice about public-speaking skills. Although the primary audience for this book is college and university students, men and women in the professions and the business world may find it useful as well. College students are at most a few years from entry into the competitive, vigorous, and challenging world of commerce and labor. Some of them will, within a few months, enter that marketplace and be called upon to present a perplexing variety of technical presentations, status reports, sales pitches, policy announcements, training seminars, and the like. The number and variety of occasions to present more or less formal talks before discerning audiences often surprises students as they undertake careers. Some students have already launched their vocations and may have discovered the value of public-speaking skills in the marketplace. As increasing numbers of workers and retired people come back to school, numerous courses and workshops in public-speaking skills are being offered. The author recognizes the needs and interests of these students as well as those of the typical undergraduates.

The first chapter of this book presents an overview of the major decisions surrounding the preparation and presentation of a speech and suggests in brief form what speakers ought to concern themselves with and what they should dismiss. The work of preparing a speech is extensive; emphasis in Chapter 1 is on the personal strengths that any individual can and should develop toward this end. An underlying assumption of this book is that presenting a speech for colleagues, fellow students, or managerial personnel should be a positive, stimulating, and zestful experience. That ideal can be realized when you are well informed, confident, and organized. This book is intended to help you develop those attitudes and skills useful for your career and for your own personal satisfaction.

Chapter 2 addresses questions about the allied skill of listening, the complement of speaking. Chapter 3 introduces a major unit on the most common speaking task: informing others. It begins with the pervasive task of developing a sense of purpose and focus in every speech. Chapter 4 concerns structuring and developing the ideas chosen for a specific occasion, and Chapter 5 shows how you can develop a talk with details which bring ideas to life. Chapter 6 details how to use your introductory remarks to prepare the audience for your ideas and shows how to conclude a speech in a satisfying, decisive manner. Chapter 7 treats matters of delivery, which apply just as much to other kinds of speech as they do to information giving.

Chapter 8 outlines some fundamental ideas behind persuasive discourse, and Chapter 9 presents some strategies for giving persuasive and argumentative talks, probably the second most common kind of public-speaking activity.

Because so much of adult speech behavior takes the form of group and committee effort, Chapter 10 develops some rudiments of small-group discussion. The forms that discussion may take, the types of leadership, the common expectations and pitfalls of group discussions, and time-tested patterns of issue development are all discussed. Similarly, because of their frequency in the workaday world, skills necessary for competent interviewing and a limited number of typical, realistic forms of interview are discussed in Appendix A. Although interviews are not usually thought of as forms of public speaking, many modern public-speaking courses include some direct instruction in interviewing because it is such a useful related skill.

This book stresses the individual nature of speech skills and the necessity for speech makers to develop ongoing programs of improvement. The book describes and reviews those matters that individuals can control in their speech. It also suggests specific exercises to reinforce speaking skills and to strengthen any weaknesses. It presents a self-assessment test to aid this process.

ACKNOWLEDGMENTS

A book is always a joint effort of many dedicated colleagues. The author must bear final responsibility for shortcomings and claims, but the merits of a book must be credited to those who helped to shape it. The author therefore wishes to acknowledge here the work of many colleagues and editorial consultants who immeasurably aided this production.

The author owes thanks to editors Steve Dalphin, Gert Glassen, and Colleen Brosnan, all of whom offered patient and helpful guidance. Suggestions for the chapters on persuasion were made by Meredith Cargill and Paul Lisnek. Tracy Kaplan kindly assisted in reproducing her classroom presentation of a speech on handgun control, which appears in manuscript form in Appendix B.

The support of my wife, Susan, and of our children, Alan and Virginia, was invaluable. Their understanding and sensitive comments at various stages of the manuscript were crucially important.

Finally, the contribution of many colleagues is acknowledged. An early draft was reviewed by Richard Thomas, who made many constructive suggestions. Professor David Bartine patiently moderated some of the inevitable clashes of opinion among reviewers and offered many useful suggestions.

chapter 1

An Overview of Speaking and Listening

THE NATURE OF PUBLIC SPEECH

The desire to speak well and earn the regard and cooperation of our fellows has been a human dream well documented from the earliest recorded times. A wealth of sophisticated, thoughtful, and detailed advice has come down to us from the fifth century B.C., and we have fragments of treatises on the subject written in even earlier times. Roman, medieval, and modern views have been preserved and integrated into our knowledge of the oldest continuously studied liberal art: rhetoric.

The Ethical Basis of Speech Study

The art and science we call rhetoric grew out of the enduring human striving for justice and equity. Greek citizens deprived of their land and seeking to regain it engaged skillful, sophisticated speakers to plead before the early courts for redress of injustice. Unsure of their own skill and fearful of char-latans, they sought out reputable pleaders whose demonstrated art would give the best chance of success. These orators were studied, copied, and questioned. Their craft was taught systematically, and often the orators wrote down their principles and philosophies. Thus a sense of right and wrong grew alongside the science of learning about what would succeed and what would fail. That

1

sense of responsibility has continued through every age and is no less insistent for today's students than for those of 2000 years ago. The wisdom, logic, and presentation skill of lawyers and judges who can see through crafty, dishonest ploys in argument have tended to triumph and survive. But even dishonest speakers taught us much over the centuries, for their deceits and all the means by which those deceits were successful lie before us in history. We know, thus, not only what is desirable and effective, but also what is dishonest, unethical, and specious. Inherent in our study is a concern for values, honesty, ethics, and equity.

Although success is one measure of a person's individual skill, it is not the only one. History records many examples of successful speakers who blighted the lives and fortunes of millions of people around them. Thus the student of effective speaking always needs to recall the element of personal responsibility for each utterance, a concern for its effects on others, and the moral implications of the success for which we all naturally strive. Even for mundane speeches in which no great principle is at stake, we can learn and then apply the guidelines for good speech so that we habitually speak well. Once the habit is established, we can rise to those rare, more profound demands on us as speakers.

PURPOSES OF SPEAKING

Public speaking can be considered as an effort of one person, acting either alone or in consultation with others, to influence a group of other people. It is helpful to consider the usual purposes of speaking in order to focus our attention on matters of immediate personal needs. It may happen that the very purpose of a given speech is the source of the speaker's difficulty with it. For example, if a speaker is strong in explaining difficult ideas but weak in persuasive skills, then probably just that one particular kind of speech will need most attention and practice. This book deals with speaking as a reasoned, purposeful act. Every speech act fits into some context, a social situation which requires it and is later modified by it. Thus, a speech is not a thing, but a dynamic event taking place in an ever-changing scene. When a speech produces no desired change in that scene, it may have been ineffectual. However, we cannot always judge it so. Some speaking situations are ceremonial and require no obvious change. In other words, many speeches that have no far-reaching consequences can be quite successful. For example, a graduation speech might delight an audience with its dignity and ceremony without anyone's recalling much about the content of the talk. Purposes can be grandiose or humble, international in scope, or localized within a community or classroom. Similarly, a speech that fails in one way can be immensely successful in other ways. Former President Nixon's "Checkers" speech, regarded as a relatively weak presentation of evidence, was nevertheless important in securing for him visibility and eventually the presidential nomination. Critics might have judged it poor as an artistic effort, yet in a practical sense it was highly successful. Critical judgment of speeches and speaking, we might observe, is a complex and tricky undertaking, but an interesting and rewarding effort. A later section deals with criticism.

A discussion of the common purposes for speaking in public follows. It is usually desirable to make one of these purposes clearly dominant. When two or three purposes are equally evident to listeners, there is a strong likelihood that the speech is scattered, incoherent, or trivial sounding to the audience. It is possible, however, to combine more than one purpose so long as one of them is clearly more important than the others.

Information giving. A common intent of a speaker is simply to impart information to others. How a job is to be done, how much progress has been made in solving a problem, or what has to be considered in coping with a new tax law—these are questions whose answers might constitute an informative speech.

Persuasion. When we not only want to inform others about some topic, but we also wish them to act in a certain predictable fashion, we are persuading. We have to assume when our purpose is persuasive that others may resist our plans, our recommendations, and even the information we give to support our claims. The task of persuading listeners is thus much more complicated than just relaying information to them.

Convincing. Although we often speak quite compellingly to others about matters we feel strongly about, or on which we expect some objection or resistance, in some of these cases we do not want any particular action as the outcome of our speeches. We seek only general agreement with our positions. For example, if we urge people to accept some general value rather than a policy, we are trying to convince them. We might persuade them to buy stock in a company, but if we merely wanted them to believe that holding stocks and bonds is a prudent, productive way of saving for retirement, we would be trying to convince them. In such a case, belief in our position, not the purchase of stocks and bonds, would be our desired outcome. The distinction between persuading and convincing is a fine one, and as far as actual differences in preparing and delivering one or the other kind are concerned, we can almost ignore them. The main difference is in outcome; in persuading we want a change in behavior, whereas in convincing, we seek only a change in attitude or belief. Many professors make no distinction between the acts of persuading and convincing. According to one view, when audiences believe a speaker's claims, those listeners are both convinced and persuaded. This author, however, finds the discrimination useful sometimes. Suppose a speaker persuades listeners to vote or give blood; that same speaker might choose to convince listeners that voting, in general, is useful and that donating blood is humane without expecting anyone present to actually perform the acts described.

Entertaining. When we wish only to amuse listeners and have no intent of changing their beliefs or actions, we present satirical, imaginary, or deliberately distorted information. There are not many occasions for which the sole purpose is entertainment. Perhaps at conventions, club meetings, or after-dinner presentations we might encounter a speaker whose reputation as an entertainer makes businesspeople want to hear him or her, but purely entertaining speeches are more the province of professional actors, night-club comedians, and lecture-circuit specialists. For our purposes, however, the desire to amuse and charm our listeners sometimes occurs in addition to the desire to inform or persuade. In such cases the one main caution is that perspective must be maintained so that the audience has no confusion about our main intents.

To allow amusement to dominate a serious speech can backfire on us. We may seem to be trying to con the audience, trivialize a serious matter, or insult someone who feels time is wasted in gratuitous foolishness. When our secondary purpose is to amuse, we must consider very carefully any satire, jokes, or amusing content of the presentation to prevent alienating a sizable portion of our audience.

Inspiring. Members of the clergy and teachers commonly assume the duty of motivating their flocks to higher performance or offering hope and comfort in a generalized way. In the business world inspirational talks are often given to motivate salespeople to new heights of activity, to encourage higher productivity among workers, and to brighten gloomy business prospects or career outlooks. The characteristic device of such talks is directness, personal involvement, and dependence upon striking anecdotal illustrations. Somewhat less common than informative or persuasive talks, inspirational speeches often result from especially effective speeches of other kinds. A particular type of inspirational speech, that to *actuate*, is given when everyone knows all the pertinent information in a case but when no decisive action has yet occurred. The plea to undertake the contemplated action makes the speech to actuate somewhat like the persuasive speech, but because new evidence and authority are not so important, it is sometimes given separate status as a purpose for speaking. A typical example is a speech calling for a staff to pick one of several previously explored health-care plans by a certain deadline. (Earlier persuasive speeches would have advocated buying various plans offered by competing suppliers, whereas the present speech to actuate merely calls for choosing one of the plans without preferring any one of them.)

Although other general purposes might be imagined, almost all public presentations have one of the just-named intents underlying them. Some authorities say that there is no essential difference between informative and persuasive speech since persuasion occurs whenever listeners believe the speaker.[1] Thus, trying to inform someone who does not trust us enough to attend to what we say is a failure to persuade that person to hear us. Similarly, if someone believes everything we say and still refuses to act in a way advocated in the speech, either the listener is irrational or our speech did not call for realistic, feasible behavior from the audience. For example, if smokers hearing a horrifying speech on lung cancer are asked never to smoke again, the speaker has little chance of success. As soon as the audience leaves the place where they heard the speech, they tend not only to move back to a former attitude,[2] but also to discount the unwelcome, unpleasant, and upsetting new information. The smokers do not quit smoking partially because too much was asked of them[3] and partially because belief is sometimes a temporary state.[4] We have all heard striking speeches which we believed for a time, but subsequent conflicting data and testimony from equally appealing authority weakened our beliefs.

A current example of this kind of conflict is the well-known belief of Linus Pauling, Nobel Prize-winning scientist, that massive daily doses of vitamin C will prevent colds and help maintain robust health. Repeated efforts to prove and disprove Pauling's contentions leave us confused and unsure whether a gram or more per day of the vitamin will help or endanger our well-beings, and whether Pauling or his opponents are the more credible authors.[5] Pauling's supporters see no reason to suspect his intentions in promoting the inexpensive and readily available vitamin. Meanwhile, his detractors claim that vitamin C is valueless in preventing or curing colds and that in fact too much of the chemical can be harmful. To decide, we strive to discover motives and purposes for the claims.

Another controversial topic—weight reduction—may further illustrate the difficulty of deciding on credibility of persuaders. For years a claim has been made in some quarters that weight is dependent solely upon caloric intake in food versus caloric consumption in exercise. It has been supposed that when intake exceeds consumption, weight gain will occur. NOVA, a scientific TV series, presented the disturbing notion that previous ideas about dieting might be wrong. Maybe some individuals react differently from the majority of dieters, and maybe exercise and dieting yield markedly different results for some than for others. One person might lose weight on 1800 calories a day, while another might not lose even at the near-starvation level of 500 calories per day.[6] One of the sad realities of the human condition is that we do not know what evidence, what person, or what group to believe and what to discount. NOVA's producers evidently intended their program to inform viewers, but some of them considered the presentation to have been persuasive because its content was not always consistent with what authorities on dieting have traditionally claimed. When conflicting claims seem about equally plausible, no one is infallible in deciding what to believe. Tragically often, the most plausible claim turns out to be wrong. In any case, the intention of a speaker is of concern to students of public speaking for at least two reasons. First, listeners are so sensitive to it that speakers want to be sure not to alienate their listeners by revealing indecisive, confused purpose statements. Second, intention can be a useful unifying device for the structure of a speech itself.

Clearly, one of the first concerns of any speaker is to imagine as exactly as possible what his or her dominant purpose in every speech is. From this decision comes the form of the talk, the strategy of organization, and, to some extent, the choice of points one will include. Sometimes, the specific purpose will also dictate what is to be left out of a speech. Now reasons for our earlier advice to make one purpose dominant and not to mix several purposes equally should become clear: Having too many purposes allows ambiguity in all of the matters just named; multiple purposes may invite confusing and conflicting choices in the content. Clarity of the thesis or central idea may be compromised because the speaker overqualifies it in an attempt to work in numerous purposes. The more dominant the single purpose and the more direct and forceful the thesis, the less muddled and ambiguous a talk is likely to be.

FORMS OF PRESENTATION

There are relatively few ways in which someone might choose to give a public presentation. Nearly every speech is clearly in one or the other of these modes. Sometimes a part within a speech is presented in a form different from the main one.

Manuscript Speaking

When exact wording is very important, no departure or personal comment is desirable, or significant outcomes of a speech could result, this form of speaking may be consciously chosen. For example, when the fate of the world economy might be at stake, a presidential foreign-policy statement cannot safely be trusted to either memory or impromptu styles. In manuscript speaking, the speaker depends on a printed version, which is read to the audience. Such speeches tend to lack animation and spontaneity, qualities which are desirable but usually considered less crucial in most manuscript speeches. Students are generally advised to avoid this form of presentation unless it is specifically assigned.

Memorized Speaking

Although memorizing a speech would appear to be the safest way to ensure effective delivery, in general this method is not very reliable. First, the speaker may lack involvement, vivid delivery, or animation. Second, there is a high risk of forgetting, and subsequent attempts to recapture the ideas may embarrass both the speaker and the auditors. Listeners tend to distrust speakers who memorize, and they resent the "canned" sound that such speeches often have. The form works well in plays or professional comic routines, because actors spend 6 weeks or more in laborious rehearsal. In public speeches, however, the usual effect is an unnatural, struggling, or insincere impression. Students are advised to avoid this pattern because of the time it requires to acquire good polish and smooth presentation. Once popular, memorized speeches are now considered an inefficient use of time and talent.

Impromptu Speaking

Sometimes no preparation other than brief organization of some general information is possible. Some group might call on someone to present a spur-of-the-moment talk. At a PTA meeting, for example, without any warning that a talk is expected, a chairperson might be called on to report on the progress of a fund-raising project. General awareness of progress, personnel, and problems involved in the undertaking are all that person has as content. Although someone with a good sense of organization and much knowledge might bring off such a talk, impromptu speeches tend to be halting, disorganized, incomplete, formless, and sometimes embarrassing. Students should avoid trying to throw something together at the last moment when given a speaking assignment. Even with a gift of gab—the ability to keep talking under pressure—students are likely to create a much weaker impression using this form of speaking than using the next one.

Extemporaneous Speaking

The most common speaking situations require us to prepare information for some specific occasion and audience. Even if we have days or weeks for preparation, we are not expected to memorize or read the information. In this form the essentials are careful research, organization into an intelligent form listeners can follow, and strategic planning for the people, place, and occasion. Most of this book is built on the assumption that extemporaneous speeches are the primary type required in the classroom. In industry, business, social clubs, and religious institutions, this is the most common pattern for speeches. It is not memorized, but it is rehearsed. It is not written out, but it requires plenty of information. The speaker may or may not use notes, an outline on the platform, or visual aids.

PREPARING A SPEECH

As a speaker, you will face some real problems in preparing a speech. You will also confront some peripheral matters which waste time and annoy you but are not really worth your concern every time you speak. The following suggestions can help you overcome these obstacles.

1. State a strong central purpose, your intent as just discussed. Say it aloud or write it down as precisely and bluntly as possible. You do not have to say it bluntly to the audience, just to yourself.

2. Make a single sentence statement of the proposed *content* of your talk. The preceding item was about intent; the thesis or central idea of your speech is about content. For example, "My purpose is to persuade the listeners to give to the United Fund drive. The content of my talk is that each employee present will directly benefit from the activities that the various agencies perform with donated money."

3. After deciding about the purpose and overview of the content, turn attention to the best *form* for you to use to be clear to listeners and to succeed in your purpose. Stated another way, you must achieve your intent with your content. You may have to alter your thesis statement as you find out more about the subject and your audience. But be aware constantly that you need a working thesis to guide you in selecting and wording your main ideas. The optimum form or pattern for presenting your material may spring from the subject matter itself or from your purpose. Among these common forms are time order, spatial order, problem-solution order, and so on. This step is *choosing a pattern of development*. It is treated in detail in Chapter 3.

4. As you gather more and more ideas and jot them down in whatever order they occur to you, you will discover that some naturally group together logically and that some are more important than others. Decide which are the three or four absolutely most important ideas you have to say. These are the main points. Group any others that logically support these together. You might have perhaps 20 ideas which form three or four clusters. Each cluster consists of one main idea and several supporting ones. You may find gaps and inconsistencies in the clusters. These gaps suggest that you may need to do a bit of research to fill in the gaps and to make each main idea comparable to the others in depth of support and illustration. All of this activity is directed toward your *choosing several main points*. Do not pick over four or five, or your audience simply will not remember them. You may become confused yourself when you have more main ideas. You can easily lose sight of what is very important and what is of only peripheral importance.

5. After choosing main points, you must decide how to support and develop them. *Development* consists of testimony, statistics, opinions, illustrations, details, and many other factors. Some of the support will come from the preceding step, and statements that were rejected as main points may well become support points.

6. With your thesis, main, and subordinate ideas chosen, you must then decide on the best *arrangement of the main points* and form an outline of the gathered material.

7. All during the process of preparation, you should be thinking about who the listeners are going to be and how you can best appeal to them. This concern is called *audience analysis and adaptation*. It is one of the most important matters in the whole process, and many technically good talks fail because of inadequate attention to the audience and its probable reaction to the various ideas of the talk. Some adjustment of the actual talk may be necessary to tailor it to a specific audience.

Figure 1-1   "...Today we begin our speeches on significant historical events...."

PLANNING FOR THE ACTUAL PRESENTATION

After you decide what is to go into a speech, you must decide how to present the chosen information most effectively. *Delivery* of the speech is dependent upon various physical factors, the place where the speech will occur, and adequate rehearsal to determine whether the effects will be both predictable and desirable.

Sometimes a presentation is more effective with various *audio* or *visual aids*, such as blackboards, flip charts, overhead-projection devices, movie equipment, amplifiers, and so on. Choosing the best aids, ensuring that they will operate, and rehearsing with the actual devices are important preparations for all speakers.

A final concern is not a single one, but a complex set of matters you, as a speaker, should consider. Study and be prepared to deal with contingencies, probable questions from the audience, hecklers, failure of equipment and readjustments if it does occur, and any unique circumstances that could arise during your talk.

COMMON FEARS OF SPEECHMAKING

Everyone has some anxiety regarding speechmaking. In this section we list and briefly comment on some of the most common fears which, like ghosts, are not very likely to pounce on you. Later in the text is a more detailed discussion of some of these needlessly intimidating matters.

"I will disgrace myself in public and never be able to face my coworkers and associates again." This situation practically never occurs, but at times you may dread a presentation so much that it seems to be a risk. We tend to distrust our own preparations and self-mastery, and, at a distance, audiences seem so cold and critical that we tend to imagine conditions much worse than they are. Although the author has seen some painful and comic performances, he can recall no outcome as strong as "disgrace" ever occurring as a result of a speech. Acute embarrassment is not disgrace. Neither is incomplete presentation. You can easily avoid ineptness and do much to prevent embarrassment by carefully preparing and envisioning probable responses in the audience. Remember that even when an audience is hostile to the ideas of a speaker, it has a deep sympathy for anyone in a vulnerable spot, and its sense of fair play usually prevents its inflicting outright cruelties on a speaker. We speak later of dissociating personalities from ideas, a process that further helps protect our feelings.

"I will forget everything I know when I see all those eyes staring at me." Again, this bugaboo is so unlikely that you can almost dismiss it. The fear of forgetting can, however, be so intense that you indeed block mentally for a moment. The secret is not to panic, lose your self-possession, or give up if momentary forgetting does occur. If you take the precaution of bringing an outline with you, or note cards if you prefer them, there is practically no danger of really ruining the speech. In the worst case—imagine for a moment that you forgot the whole point of your speech—you need only look at your outline, take time to read it, and the whole point will probably come back to you. The fear of forgetting is worse than the act itself, because the audience is not as impatient as the speaker is. What seems like an eternity to a speaker is quite a short time to the listeners, and they are quite tolerant and sympathetic. If you go blank in the middle of a talk, a quick look at your notes is all it takes to renew the thread of your talk. Sometimes even very experienced speakers go dry on material they have presented many times. If you watch Johnny Carson and other talk-show hosts, you will note occasionally that they momentarily lose their trains of thought and retrieve them quickly, usually with little fuss.

"I am afraid hecklers will bother me." Again, this spook is rare. Although in tense situations heckling occurs occasionally, audiences usually side with the speaker and put pressure on the big-mouth heckler to stop. Further, the speaker is usually so much better prepared on the topic than the listeners that heckling is unlikely. The later section on resistant audiences deals with those rare occasions during which audiences do harass the speaker.

"I am afraid I will get my points out of order." If you follow the advice concerning the design of your speeches, this fear can be dispelled. First, it usually does little harm to invert the order of a couple of points. In many speeches the sequence of main points is not crucial. For instance, if an actuary is talking about the impact of a new policy on three segments of a company—the employees, the management, and the stockholders—reversing the first two items is unlikely to be noticed unless something dependent on an earlier idea is omitted. Even if you should botch the intended order and, in fact, leave awkward questions in the minds of the audience, you can go back and straighten them out. There is no harm is using a

transition like this: "I ought to mention that if you are not familiar with our daily procedures in the machine shop, you should know that we operate under 'Flextime.' This term means that we do not have shifts like other companies, but we have employees begin their work days at every hour of the morning." If such a point should have been mentioned earlier, but it was not, the statement will clear up any others dependent on that knowledge. Audiences tolerate some disorganization, although you should do a careful job to be safe.

"I am embarrassed about the sound of my voice." Do not be. You do not hear yourself the same way others do, and you are probably being hard on yourself because your imagination sets a standard for you that may be unrealistic. If you believe your voice is inadequate and you are seriously concerned that the sound of your voice will alienate others or impede your effectiveness, every metropolitan area and most medium-sized communities offer help at low cost and with little trauma. Your voice is a part of your personality and image, of course, but any unique quality of it is not necessarily a defect. Many an actor has made a career on a raspy, husky, or harsh voice, and some have become beloved by their fans. Actors Peter Lorre, Humphrey Bogart, Boris Karloff, the popular pianist Liberace, the novelist and actor Truman Capote, the news commentator Barbara Walters, to name only a few media personalities, all have or had striking vocal qualities or outright speech impediments which they have overcome or exploited. Anyone can use unique personal vocal attributes to produce the sonic component of what we loosely call "personality."

Further, you may indeed have an undesirable quality of voice that worries you, but it may be readily corrected by a few sessions with a speech therapist. Finally, even if you do have a defect which is not responsive to treatment, all is not lost: Some of the greatest speakers had severe speech impediments but so compensated for them that listeners, in their eagerness to consider the speakers' ideas, paid no attention to the flaws.

"My vocabulary is limited and colorless." First, of course, you can do something about that fact if it is true, and you should attack the problem. Second, it does not require a large, impressive vocabulary to speak directly and well to even the most well-educated audiences. The trick is to speak accurately, not pompously. Third, the vocabulary peculiar to your profession or trade is likely to be shared with your listeners. You will seem more a part of the group if you speak their language than if you try to impress them. A useful activity is to constantly expand your working vocabulary, not to create an extraordinary variety of language, but to help you choose precisely the right word. Consider carefully Mark Twain's idea that the difference between the right word and almost the right word is the difference between "lightning" and "lightning bug."

Keeping in mind that our educational system rarely provides comprehensive speech training comparable to that available in mathematics, history, or science, it is no wonder that the study of public speaking is permeated with misinformation, patchy understanding, and unbalanced views. Because public speaking is a skill akin to all oral communication, many people suffer from the illusion that good conversational ability, quick wit, wide general knowledge, and a gift of gab will suffice. Indeed, they will do so, but only in the same sense that an inner tube will suffice as a boat. Something more sophisticated is much more versatile and useful, especially if you plan to go very far.

FEEDBACK

The public speaker uses information from the audience in much the same way that technical systems such as audio amplifiers use feedback. *Feedback*, a widely used term in many sciences and professions, refers to relatively slight but very significant responses from one part of a system to another part. The speech act can be considered as a system consisting of speaker, message, language signals, and listeners. The group of people interacting is in many ways analogous to a complex electrical, mechanical, or hydraulic system in both form and functions. The idea is that a small portion of electrical power is sent back from the final output (loudspeakers) to the input of that same system, where it is used to control the overall fidelity of the whole system. In engineering and mechanics the same concept occurs. Although it might seem to be stretching a point, a comparable effect occurs in speech. The audience "feeds back" a subtle response which can be detected and interpreted by the speaker, who is able to make adjustments in content, manner of delivery, or style. For example, noticing some members of the audience straining, leaning forward and frowning, you might conclude that louder speech is needed. Looks of boredom, raised eyebrows, shifting in seats, or dozing are quite definite examples of feedback that tell you that either manner or content are not going over well and that major adjustments need to be made to improve the "fidelity" of the message.

As has been mentioned, some speakers so dread the stares of the audience that they do not wish to endure pain from negative feedback. They may even feel that they do not want to know how people are responding to them—no news, they think, is good news. Rather than looking at their audiences they look out the window or up at the ceiling, or stare at their notes exclusively. For some struggling speakers, simply overcoming those bad habits will constitute a major breakthrough in their speech skills.

When you cannot see the audience, you cannot detect their responses, at least visual ones. Many people are quite startled at the revelation which comes to them when they really look at their audiences for the first time. Assume that you are very well prepared, not dependent on your notes, and not intimidated by the audience, and that your lack of eye contact has been purely habit. Looking directly into the eyes of your listeners may be a delightful surprise if you realize how much you can learn about the state of the audience and how responsive and supportive they can be. Unhappily, the opposite reaction is just as visible. Your looking at the audience can indeed reveal their confusion, disinterest, or rejection of the message. No doubt many speakers count on their own obliviousness of the audience to make the speech an endurable experience. In short, they simply refuse to see and consider feedback because it is too painful to do so. If you look at the audience, at least they have a basis to respond meaningfully. That fact is what the whole feedback concept is all about: If things are not going as planned, you can first be notified and then make some adjustments on the spot.

How to Recognize Various Forms of Feedback

Sometimes the audience sends signals which the speaker misses altogether or misinterprets. Following is a list of some of the common forms that feedback takes, the specific signals and their probable meanings. This list is meant to be helpful toward understanding the countless possible responses. Above all, do not take these descriptions as infallible interpretations and overreact to them. For example, someone frowning may like what you say just fine; he or she may have just misplaced glasses and is squinting to see your face.

SOME COMMON FORMS OF FEEDBACK

Facial signals: Frowns, heads turned sideways, heads wagging, or fingers across mouths may indicate trouble. Usually these visible body signals tell the speaker that the audience doubts or even contradicts what they hear. Occasionally a frown is merely a sign of deep concentration and inward comparison of the speaker's data with what the listener already knows.

Failure to laugh or smile at a humorous sally: This signal can suggest either that some listeners have become wary and doubtful or it can mean that the respondents either did not get the point or did not like it. Sometimes people get and enjoy a jest without showing any response, although they may have a tremendous inward response of mirth. The signal may also mean, "Yes, I get it. Move on with the substances."

Shifting in seats as if restless: This sign is generally taken as a negative signal, as if to say that the presentation is going on too long or contains much irrelevant material. If only one or two people are shifting, they probably itch. If several people about the room are doing so, consider accelerating the talk. In the future, also try to time and proportion your talk quite accurately. Although that task added to all your others may seem burdensome, remember that the talk is for the audience, not your pleasure alone. Sometimes you can, with the best of intentions, overelaborate your points and assume your listeners do not understand when in fact they do. They become restless at needless explanation or repetition.

A tight-lipped, blank look: This indication usually tells a speaker that listeners are becoming tired or bored. Some may not be listening, even when almost everyone else is. Some people may have heard the data before, may be preoccupied with personal concerns, or may just be tired.

Audience looking to one side of you or beyond you: Sometimes a distraction or potential threat is visible to the audience but not to you. Do the natural thing and look to see whether the screen for visual aids is about to fall over or something else is amiss.

Audible signs: Audible signs such as groans, snoring, catcalls, unwanted laughter, and muttering are so obvious that they do not warrant comment. Rarely, an audience will actually approve a speaker and playfully show mock criticism, but you can usually tell the genuine response from teasing.

People leaving the room: This disconcerting activity is usually not rude behavior directed at the speaker. Sometimes people have to excuse themselves for previous commitments, rest-room visits, and even sudden realizations that they are in the wrong place. Professors often have students stay in their classes for 20 minutes before they discover that they are not in their course on surgery or Swahili. Speakers wonder what goes on in such students' minds as they listen, and what has happened to their own proud mastery of clarity in utterance.

Poised pencils, gestures, or motions arrested in midexecution: This is one of the best possible indications you can receive from an audience. A state called *involuntary attention* is occasionally produced by a speaker's presenting very compelling or striking information and the audience cannot help but give its attention. In this state, the listeners have no sense of time, place, or will. They are quietly swept away by the talk. Much sought by actors and speakers, this state is rarely sustained very long, but real spellbinders can produce it.

Dead-pan listeners: Dead-pan, very still people with no discernible emotions at all are usually cooperative, attentive, and responsive. The lack of any apparent emotion is not to be read as hostility or indifference. When people in the audience appear so, they are usually expending their effort and concentrating on what they hear. Contrast their behavior with the occasional smiling, nodding listeners who flatter you until you learn that they are almost mesmerized and do not understand or retain a word you say. Students learn to please their teachers by such feigned behavior, which allows them to retreat into the recesses of their minds. Adults pull the stunt on speakers, too, especially if they are not very interested but want to impress the speaker or others.

Change of attitude: A sudden production of a pencil to take notes, a change from placid to a "businesslike" attitude, or a change of expression from a blank smile to an air of concentration—all these signs suggest that the speaker has begun well, has captured attention, and has led the audience from the attention-getting part of the talk to the deeper substance of it. Do not misinterpret the change as *loss* of attention, when in fact it is usually a desirable indication of sustained focus on your message.

Smiles and nodding the head: Among the more positive kinds of feedback, these motions indicate approval, identification with the speaker, and some degree of involvement. Rarely are the smiles a sign of derision. Although few positive signs of feedback are described here, they are in fact often detected. People just have more ways of showing their displeasure than their approval. No news is sometimes good news, after all, and lack of smiles does not imply failure to enjoy a talk.

CONSTRUCTIVE CRITICISM

A necessary part of growth is guidance by others with experience or at least an objective, detached viewpoint. When you seek the help of another to point out flaws in your presentation or the structure of your speeches, you are asking for criticism. That word strikes fear into many people because of the negative connotations it often has. To avoid those negative, destructive implications, we use the term *constructive criticism*. Henceforth in this book, the word *criticism* is used to mean helpful comments to correct weaknesses and reinforce strengths.

Constructive criticism is the logical extension of feedback. While a speech is in progress the audience can give only relatively subtle signs about its degree of approval and understanding, but after the speech a critic can give as elaborate and complete a judgment of the presentation as the speaker desires. Because it is explicit and direct, there is less ambiguity in criticism than there is in feedback during the presentation.

Constructive criticism is defined as objective, detached, and positive guidance toward improvement. It does not mean that the critic withholds comments about the bad features of a speech, but it does mean that all such comments are directed to guide the speaker away from errors. This kind of criticism has various qualities, discussed next. First, useful criticism is positive; it includes observations about what was good in a talk as well as what was bad. It includes comments about choices a speaker has to make and admits that in some situations the bad effect created might have been even worse had a different choice been made. In other words, criticism is not fault finding. It is a friendly, cooperative effort toward better practice later.

Good criticism is also pointed. It is not evasive to protect the speaker's feelings, but frankly confronts real problems in the most direct and precise wording. Often speakers become so involved in the message or presentation that they are quite unconscious of some very annoying habit. If a critic hems and haws about observations and advice, the speaker has to guess, and may guess wrong about any effect on others. Of course, if a speaker has some problem about which he or she can do absolutely nothing, there is no point in calling attention to it. For instance, if the speaker obviously has a medical condition such as palsy or spastic tics, no constructive purpose is served by reminding the speaker of the problem. If advice is sought, however, and the affected person brings up the issue, one must be honest and as supportive as possible in an effort to minimize the bad effects.

Third, criticism should be balanced. It should present comments to the speaker in a way that reveals what were the major faults and what were the more trivial points. It should reveal to the speaker what needs merely some polishing and what needs structural overhaul.

In addition, criticism should be thorough and searching, but not so overwhelming that it discourages the speaker. There should be enough specific detail that the speaker is challenged to deal with the most severe problems. Once the first ones are mastered, later additional ones can be brought up.

Next, criticism should be systematic. Some overview, however simple in format, should guide the comments. For example, dividing comments into those about content of the speech, delivery by the speaker, and audience analysis and adaptation is a useful pattern for criticism. In later speeches critical comments in each of these categories will allow the speaker to compare various speeches and learn whether he or she has improved in some respects.

Good criticism is dispassionate but not depersonalized. Everyone runs some ego risks in speaking, because the speech act is highly personal and an integral part of the self. A speaker whose habits are held up to scrutiny is therefore in an emotionally vulnerable position and may tend to resent and discount criticism. If you reject a critique, then it follows that the purpose of the critic is thwarted and little useful has been accomplished. Add to that failure the likelihood that the feelings of both the speaker and the critic are likely to be bruised, and it is evident that a critic has a difficult responsibility and needs careful, superior language control in order to be helpful. It goes without saying that gratuitous comments to injure the ego of another, comments designed for the critic's own self-aggrandizement, and projection of personal pet peeves (often one's own shortcomings) onto the person criticized should all be avoided.

Accepting Constructive Criticism

Although most of the comments made so far refer to the critic of a speech, and emphasis is on criteria for criticism of others, there is another side of the coin. Every speaker needs to be a graceful recipient of criticism. Sometimes this attitude of open, willing reception of comments is hard to maintain. There is no shortage of half-baked criticism. Some people may seek opportunities to make comments for some reasons other than to help the speaker. In these cases, the best thing a speaker can do is to establish emotional control, hear out the comments, and if they happen to be useful—use them. If they are specious and unfair, reject them and consider the source's biases and limitations.

Even when criticism is sought or perhaps hired, many people cannot bring themselves to accept it. Their feelings of security are so fragile, perhaps from earlier humiliations—real or imagined—that they automatically set up unconscious barricades of excuses, rejections, and rationalizations.

The public speaker is in a high-risk occupation if ego protection is the chief concern. If you are overly protective of your feelings and are unable to take criticism without hurt and resentment, probably the first revision in your behavior should be to discover how to accept well-intended, if sometimes clumsily worded, advice from other fallible creatures like yourself. A certain toughness, even amused detachment, seems to be desirable to use critical comments productively. Those who are genuinely "detached" from the criticism can examine the comments thoroughly and dispassionately as if they applied to someone far away, and yet familiar. Any merits a critique may have are useful, somewhat like a $5 bill you find on the street: You can use it in any way you wish. You can put it in the bank and make productive use of it, or you can throw it away if it seems to be counterfeit.

In contrast to ego-protective persons, detached receivers of criticism can take or reject critical comments. They have options. Self-protective, vulnerable speakers have no options. They can only defend against comments. They may, ironically, sop up compliments greedily to feed injured egos and shore up any emotional defenses. This habit of selectively screening comments so that the compliments are accepted as gospel and the negative opinions are rejected as hostile fault finding should be avoided if possible. A person who cannot use criticism might ask a trusted intimate friend with some speaking experience how he or she learned to accept useful criticism. After all, critical comments are aimed not at the speaker but rather at how well a set of values is exemplified in a speech. The overly defensive person considers all criticism as an attack by natural enemies, the critics. A less defensive, more secure person considers criticism as a convenient, useful, and even unexpected boost of career goals.

REALISTIC SELF-ASSESSMENT

One of the ironies of modern educational practice is that we spend hundreds of hours teaching students how to write English and only a very few hours, if any, on how to speak it. Recent reports on the generally low mastery of English and mathematics among high school and college graduates have redirected attention to basic instruction. This nation cannot afford widespread illiteracy among its potential leaders. Part of one's preparation for a life of social participation and work is mastery of language. Our failure to produce skill in its use is, of course, partly individual shortsightedness and immaturity. Another cause, however, is the lack of relish for the hard work and practice necessary for success during the school years. Fellow students and teachers who have settled for careless, hazy language habits and have exhibited them in their own classrooms and social encounters also help to explain the plight. Another factor to consider is the phenomenon of timely learning: Children who do not learn language skills when they are optimally ready to learn may never master the skills. Although adults retain much capacity to learn, feelings of inadequacy can inhibit later learning. Much of this weakness to command our language is revealed during adult speaking performances, such as delivering public speeches, giving reports, instructing workers, interviewing, and selling.

In the world of business and industry, where most of our lives are occupied, we spend far more time speaking than we do writing. Of course, no one begrudges educational efforts toward mastering written English, but the result of our neglect of speech training in the lower grades is that effective, lucid speech is rare within the work force and inadequate at the entry level of management. Further, it is often minimal at the middle levels, and may need improvement even at the top levels. Certainly one of the criteria for advancement to higher levels of responsibility nowadays is excellence in speaking skills.

When it dawns on young professionals and managers that they need to pay attention to their communication skills, they quickly discover that no one can help them during the actual delivery of a speech. A secretary can proofread letters and remove spelling and syntax blunders, but no one can cover for a floundering speaker. Even a speech writer hired to produce an impressive talk can do only so much. Sooner or later people face the need for personal mastery of the art of public speech. No erasers can remove an oral mistake, and whatever impression it creates can only be modified, not deleted.

This fact is sobering. The momentary irritation that leads us to utter a sharp word, insult someone, or reveal a brief lapse in attention can have far-reaching consequences. Former Secretary of Defense Haig's well-intentioned remark that he was "in charge" after President Reagan had been shot and hospitalized was widely misinterpreted. Doubtless trying to reassure the press and public that our government was proceeding smoothly, Haig seemed to be saying that he had seized power or that he was hazy on the order of succession required by the Constitution. Nothing he could say thereafter quite erased the unfortunate image created by just three words. Similarly, minor errors in language can have major effects on our images, respect for our ideas, and friendship of our associates. Whatever we say and do affects somebody. Consequently, the problem of improving our speaking skills is twofold: We have to *do* some things better, and we have to *avoid* other things we presently do badly. In fact, you may discover that more apparent improvement occurs as a result of dropping your annoying behaviors than by adding new ones. Do you know anyone who could quickly improve the impact of every oral presentation by simply omitting "Uhs"?

One severe complication of learning to become a better speaker is the force of habit on our behavior. We come to a program of improvement with years of training, good or bad. That training is just as powerfully rooted when our backgrounds include only random imitations of family and associates as it would be with the most meticulous professional training. In other words, we are "trained" whether we like it or not. To revise our habits is a major undertaking and may cause much discouragement when the power of habit becomes evident. Just try to leave out the "you know" that punctuates many people's speech today. It is difficult to stop saying anything we repeat quite often. We hardly notice extraneous words and phrases. The person who begins each sentence with "Like" is probably talking in fragments, thinking hazily, and impressing others with a lack of mental discipline. Meanwhile, the error becomes more firmly entrenched with each repetition, and that speaker is probably unaware of the impression being created.

However, the prospects for improvement are excellent. College students have several advantages over the beginning speaker in the lower grades, where scant formal training in public speaking may occur. First of all, young adults enjoy a unique status. They have lived long enough to sort out the real and the probable from the fictional and the unlikely. They have learned through school, family, and social contacts a great deal of information about the world. In short, they have a gigantic store of information that younger students do not have. Just living has given college students a lot to talk about. As we mature, our lives and careers diverge, and we become more heterogeneous in tastes, experiences, reactions, and perceptions. All of these are interesting to other people, who naturally like to compare their experiences and inner lives with other peoples'.

Adults are also generally freer of unreasonable fears because experience has shown them that they are competent to deal with life's problems. Children are likely to fear speaking because they lack experience. Their imaginations may create worse situations than really exist when they are called on to speak. Nevertheless, many adults have held onto earlier fears and have systematically avoided having to speak in public so that a residual anxiety may remain. Happily, a few successes in their presentations can quickly turn their normal reticence and concern into a positive force: They may come to look forward to opportunities to speak.

Many people feel that they make "all the mistakes in the book." The truth is that most people are likely to make five or six mistakes over and over rather than thirty or forty different mistakes. A speaker's task becomes, then, the discovery and repair of a few faults rather than wholesale reformation of habits.

It is actually quite rare for a speaker to be really disgraced, even though many people have the impression that they run the risk every time they speak. A few dramatic and perhaps painful experiences create an inordinate fear and an illusion that debacles are frequent. One might draw an analogy to the airline industry's bad press when a plane crashes. Few wrecks occur, but news of the ones that do happen is so dramatically and thoroughly circulated that one thinks that millions of people must have been killed over the history of aviation, when in fact relatively few have been. Comparison with other forms of transport invariably shows air travel to be much safer statistically, but worried travelers do not care about statistics on stormy days. Similarly, telling an anxious speaker that he or she is unlikely to botch a presentation is not really much help. Some speakers say fatalistically, "I'll probably find a way

Figure 1-2 "You usually look better than you feel."

to foul up." Nevertheless, it should help you to realize that outright failures are quite rare, although unsatisfying partial successes are plentiful. An insight here is that you know how you feel, but you do not know what you look like to others. In fact, you probably look much better than you think you do. When pressured, struggling to field a question, or deeply concerned over the importance of your subject, you may think you look as disconcerted as you feel. Most of the time you simply do not.

To prove this point to yourself, arrange to give a taped TV speech and during the playback look for the good points. The chances are that you will look better to yourself than you expected, although TV may tend to accentuate minor problems you do have. Even if this test is inconclusive, and in your judgment you look *worse* than you expected to, all is not lost. You may just have an unrealistic, inflated notion of aesthetics in the situation. The point remains that most people look better than they think they do, and minor errors that feel just terrible to the speaker sometimes do not even register with the audience. Even if they do, the effect does not damage either the message or the speaker's credibility.

Audiences are forgiving, too. They can see themselves in a speaker. When someone flounders, audience members suffer. Similarly, when listeners see someone handle a speech masterfully, they rejoice inwardly and admire the speaker. Because of this identification with a speaker's performance, auditors do not like to hear a speaker apologize for minor flubs. The apology calls attention to the weakness, which would be suppressed or forgotten quickly in the normal course of the talk. When the speaker insists on repeatedly reminding listeners of defects, it is impossible to ignore them—they become part of the message the speaker is imparting. Of course, if explanation of a raspy voice is needed, tell listeners once and then credit them with enough memory power to recall the reason for an occasional cough or gulp.

No one expects us to look and act like movie stars. It is as bad to set unrealistically high standards as it is to set excessively low ones. In the momentary euphoria and satisfaction with compliments given them and genuine awareness of their own improvement, some students overreact and set further goals for themselves which are a fantasy. We cannot be someone else. We are accepted and respected for what we are, faults and all. Efforts to improve ourselves should not be to fool anyone, to give us whole new identities, nor to flee from the mistakes and responsibilities of our pasts. To keep perspective, remember that the speaker's task in a program of self-improvement is to realize full potential and to present clearly the real self to others in a controlled, deliberate way.

Most audiences are open, hopeful for a speaker's success, and quite forgiving. Still, you should not pressure them too much with chaotic organization, irritating mannerisms, inaudible or unintelligible sounds, or incompetent reasoning and facts. They will tolerate considerable minor transgressions and a few outright blunders before they turn against a speaker. You should never presume their tolerance to justify careless habits, but you can be reassured to know that most audiences are not hostile to anyone addressing them until they have just cause. The listeners would prefer you to succeed, to enlighten or amuse them, and to look good. Some exceptional circumstances are described in Chapter 8, but meanwhile do not expect the worst. To give you courage, use the knowledge that people are generally favorable toward competence, clarity, and commitment.

Most people who have occasion to speak in public have been asked to do so because they have specific expertise or knowledge on a topic of interest to the audience. Thus, there is built into the occasion a tremendous advantage for the speaker. People come to the presentation for a reason, and, therefore, until it is shown otherwise, they expect something of interest or value. From the standpoint of the speaker, then, the problem is how to avoid losing the audience rather than how to gain their attention in the first place. Even if the presentation is purely ceremonial, such as a retirement speech for someone everybody else is glad to be rid of, common decency and the wish to break cleanly with the past is a bond between audience and speaker, after a fashion. Ceremonial occasions are those which must be faced, whether there is any real communication to be shared or not. To conclude the relationship with civility, to acknowledge early contributions, to cite any outstanding achievements, and to say farewell are all probable functions of such a speech. To do so gracefully is itself a striking achievement for the speaker.

QUALITIES OF EFFECTIVE SPEAKERS

One of the curiosities of the speech discipline is that no one has ever produced an indisputable list of behaviors that everyone will agree constitute "good speech"; however, everyone has a more or less agreed-upon list of minimum standards. Because so much leeway in describing a speaker's objectives is unfortunate, it is to our advantage here to make our own list. Note first, however, that what is a question of taste cannot be made into a firm rule very well. For example, extreme pitch slides which might sound appropriate in one person's presentation might sound affected and artificial in someone else's. Similarly, what appears to be quite excessive gesturing by one person might be about right for someone else. What seems to be static, unmoving posture in one person's judgment might seem to be superlative self-control to another. None of the following qualities, then, is an absolute, but each one is a guide toward suitable actions speakers must consider when they begin a program of self-improvement.

1. Adequate loudness is an obvious requirement, but less obvious is the necessity to project the voice to all parts of a room. A common shortcoming is to speak to the front half of an assembly and ignore the rear. Do not force listeners to call out, "Speak up," or "We can't hear you!"

2. Animation is one of the most sought-for qualities in speakers. You do not have to move much, gesture often, or raise your voice to particularly dramatic levels in order to achieve desirable animation. The sense of inner compulsion to share your ideas with others, the urge to say things just right, and a mood of eager relish to speak can create the quality. Most audiences say they want their speakers to have interest, liveliness, and dynamism. Observations of effective speakers reveal that they seem to have more of a mental brightness than any particular set of physical behaviors.

3. Visual contact with members of the audience seems to be an important source of effectiveness. Most of the time you ought to be looking at your listeners. You should spend only a small part of the time examining notes, looking away into space, or reading the outline. Your gaze ought to be shifted so that everyone has some direct eye contact. Ideally, everyone, not just a few people, should have the illusion that you are talking directly to them. Naturally, a fair-sized audience contains so many people that you cannot really look individually at each person very long or very often. Nevertheless, attempting to do so creates an impression that you spent some effort to talk directly to the listeners. There is also a major benefit of using decisive eye contact: It permits rapid perception of feedback from the audience, which can warn you of unclear points, disapproval, need for further development, or reveal approval and understanding by the listeners.

4. If in every speech you give, you appear to know exactly what you are talking about, believe in it yourself, and then articulate it clearly to others, you will come as close to assured success as anyone can. Audiences appreciate the good sense and prudence of the speakers addressing them. When they hear a sincere, direct, well-researched presentation, audiences will listen and appreciate the message and presenter, even if they do not fully agree with them.

5. When audiences hear a zealot, they are wary, even when they more or less agree with the message. For instance, if a nondrinker hears someone violently condemn a single beer as the devil's poison, even the teetotaler may be embarrassed at the immoderate denunciation. Likewise, a devout Christian may be put off by another's denunciation of someone else's faith. In summary, avoid extremism. Audiences normally look for balanced, tolerant views on most subjects. Heavy-handed, caustic, or insulting remarks about others, even people who are unpopular with the listeners, are likely to backfire on the speaker using them. This is not to say that you should be wishy-washy, indecisive, or free of strong opinions. Harmony and consideration for others may simply require you to forbear imposing your opinions at times, or to temper your expression of them. You can limit the number of crises in your life by moderation, thoughtfulness, and restraint.

DISCOVERING YOUR SPEECH PERSONALITY

So far we have discussed those advantages that any speaker has but which most people in their anxiety overlook. Now you should turn attention to those skills and thought processes which constitute your individual speech style, paying particular attention to those which are positive. The purpose of this exercise is to isolate the component parts of your speech personality and to examine your strengths and weaknesses.

In the list which follows, various behaviors are described. Go through the list and score yourself as follows: If you always exhibit the "good" version of the behavior under discussion, give yourself 4 points. If you usually exhibit it, but occasionally forget or neglect to consider the behavior, give yourself 3 points. If you are quite hazy on the issue, and you think and act on it only sometimes, give yourself 2 points. If you never think about the action discussed or feel yourself weak in that matter, give yourself 1 point. Do the same if you cannot tell for each item which behavior is the desirable one and which is the undesirable one. Consider the first sentence the question, and answer it. The sentences and phrases which follow it are further explanation or elaboration.

1. Can you be heard clearly in a small room? A medium or large room? Can you gauge how loud a voice level is appropriate in a variety of sites?

2. Do you have a fairly accurate idea of how loudly you speak? If people ask you to repeat things often, you may be lowering your voice to what you regard as a comfortable level, only to find that others do not hear you as you hear yourself. Be sure not to confuse loudness of voice with clarity of articulation: either can cause lack of understanding, and listeners frequently mistake one for the other.

3. Do you articulate each sound clearly? Do you slur or mumble? Do you say "limted libilty compny" for "limited liability company"?

4. Do you talk at a rate of speed comfortable for others to attend? Do people frequently ask you to slow down or repeat ideas?

5. Do you breathe deeply and effortlessly when you speak? Do you run out of air, swallow in the middle of sentences, or gasp suddenly at odd places in a talk? Even in large rooms, do you find that you can project your voice, raising the volume level to accommodate the size of the audience?

6. Do you move nervously, or can you stand still comfortably without feeling compelled to move about?

7. Do you slump or slouch when you stand up to speak? Do you stand up straight without seeming tense or rigid?

8. Do you put your hands in your pockets in a bid to seem relaxed? Do you put them in and out of pockets as if hunting for a convenient place to store them for the duration of the speech?

9. Do you put your hands on your hips to get rid of them, or do you wrap your arms around your abdomen for the same reason?

10. Can you use gestures smoothly without their seeming jerky, awkward, or mistimed?

11. Do you vary your gestures or tend to use the same one or two over and over?

12. Do you look directly at your audience's eyes? When speaking, are you aware of individuals or just a hazy mass of indistinct faces? Can you, in the midst of talking, also pick up responses from individuals in the audience and determine accurately the meaning of their responses?

13. Do you project a positive, friendly, and interested air when you talk? Do others seem to regard you as severe, gloomy, grim, too serious, or unfriendly (regardless of whether you feel such emotions)?

14. Can you consciously achieve various emotional tones appropriate to different occasions and subjects? Can you project a neutral tone?

15. Do you think before a speech occasion about the best way to dress for the occasion and the audience?

16. Do you try to think about who is going to be in an audience you must address and how best to present your message for those whose opinion you value?

17. Have you badly misjudged an audience's attitudes on some issue and been badly embarrassed by insulting or offending listeners? If so, was the incident unavoidable or could you have conveniently found out enough about the audience to prevent the misstep?

18. Do you inquire about the place in which you are to give a talk before you give it, or do you just accept whatever the locale has to offer without investigating its size, acoustic properties, arrangement of the room, audio-visual aids available, and so on?

19. Do you know how to use any necessary visual aids such as an overhead projector or slide projector without distraction and delay? Do you practice with strange machines before using them in a presentation? Do you set up focus, visibility level, and angles of viewing properly before using such aids?

20. Do you deliberately include a wide variety of visual aids, vocabulary, illustrations, and examples when you prepare a speech?

21. Are you conscious of structuring a speech for maximum intelligibility among audience members? Do you work into the design of your talk a definitely perceptible sense of form, including a well-marked introduction, body, and conclusion?

22. Do you have a feeling, during presentations, of where you need to inject transitions? Do you know what a transition is, why it is needed, and how to use numerous kinds of transitions?

23. Do people smile, sit up attentively, laugh easily, and seem relaxed when you speak, or do they tend to look glassy-eyed, bored, and impatient? During serious speeches, do your auditors listen intently and show concern for your topic?

24. Has anyone ever complimented you for your talks? Have they done so when you thought you had performed very badly?

25. During preparation, are you constantly striving to cut down the number of main points to three or four, meanwhile attempting to organize all the important information into subordinate points under those three or four main points?

26. Do listeners accuse you of using too much or not enough illustrative material? Do you have a knack for choosing pertinent, directly applicable illustrations and examples?

If you score at least 55 points on this self-test, you are "normal," and radical surgery will not be necessary. If you score below 35 points, you may need a careful assessment by a professional speech teacher or some directed activity such as a night class or club where speeches are routinely expected of you. Being a toastmaster or joining a civic club or service organization can furnish you with the atmosphere and good motivation to practice speaking without calling attention to your need and desire to practice often. The worst thing is to regard yourself as a "case" or some kind of oddity. Nearly everyone has some shortcomings and can profit by occasional reassessment. Much of this book is concerned with specific exercises and objectives for those who wish to maintain and polish their skills.

COMMON PITFALLS IN PUBLIC SPEAKING

Now that you have an idea of your strengths in speaking, a preliminary warning of common pitfalls to avoid is in order. Do not think negatively; these shortcomings are generalizations about frequently committed crimes against audiences. A speech is for the audience, not for the speaker. These pitfalls do not comprise an exhaustive list, and even unimaginative speakers can create many more abuses of the audience. However, within these few violations are the roots of many others: disorganization, mistiming, and diffidence.

Develop the habit of thinking in useful patterns for speech. Avoid fearing that the obvious structure is boring to the listeners. During preparation of a speech, some people tire of going over and over material in an effort to group information into strict form such as introduction, body of main points, and conclusion. They feel after a time that the obvious and belabored information is dull. But remember, the audience gets to hear it all just once, even though you may have hashed it over again and again. Make the structure absolutely clear, even if it seems painfully obvious. Remember, too, that if the speech really is blatantly obvious to everyone, maybe you ought not to give it at all, or at least you ought to give it a major overhaul before delivery.

Control time effectively. Time is used in several ways in a speech. First, the whole event occurs in real time. Next, some ideas have to occur in a certain precise order for clarity. Then, some ideas need more time than others for internalization. It takes more time to understand complex, unfamiliar concepts than more common ones. Consequently, time must be manipulated in another way—namely, time of silence for ideas to sink in. Pauses for ideas to sink in, for variety, for emphasis, for transitional effects, and for gathering your thoughts are all powerful manipulations of time. Misunderstanding of time's uses is the root of numerous public-speaking errors. Mastery of it opens unexpected possibilities for improving your impact on others. For example, having a sense of timing allows you to place points or illustrations at the optimum point in a speech not only for lucidity but also for pleasing dramatic effect.

Present your best energetic self before your listeners. Do not hide from the audience. They are your best friend, not the fearsome enemy that lore and horror stories make them out to be. If you think in terms of conversing with a few of them and letting the others overhear the conversation, the atmosphere for improvement is established. Hiding from the audience includes standing behind a lectern without moving, as if you were in a fortress, "hiding" metaphorically behind your manuscript or notes, and minimizing self-exposure by speaking in a low, fast, monotonous voice as if to escape quickly the ordeal of speech. Obviously, this "hiding" is psychological; in a speaking situation, you naturally feel exposed to public scrutiny with some risk of disapproval. But if you think of listeners as friends, then even if the worst happens and you are acutely embarrassed—if your notes spill or the lectern falls, for example—you are in on the joke, too. Audiences do not relish seeing anyone in pain, and their laughter will turn to applause if you keep your composure. Most of the terrors of speaking are imaginary, but even imagining some of the things that can go wrong can be painful. They are less so when you are among friends.

EXERCISES

1. State to your class members what your probable profession or occupation will be and think of three or four specific kinds of public-speaking tasks that are common in that field. If you cannot think of several such occasions, interview someone actually in that profession and find out the types of speaking situations that are common in your chosen field.

2. Discuss to what extent giving a speech is merely labeling a given behavior, which, if not so labeled, would seem to be conversation or discussion. Try to decide where one should draw the line in calling oral discourse "a speech" or just "talking."

3. Select some field of work and investigate how the concept of feedback has any application to it. Then state what form feedback takes in that field. In what ways is feedback in that field comparable to that used in communication? In what ways is it different? Present your findings to the class.

4. The author states that feedback is a constructive process. Is there any evidence that it can be destructive in a common situation? Discuss.

5. State specifically how people can avoid feedback from an audience. What behaviors and reasons for avoiding feedback are there?

6. Have a volunteer give a short speech before the class, and have the members of the audience studiedly try to hold back all feedback. Is it possible to give utterly none? What effect does withholding feedback have on the speaker's performance as reported by the class members? What does the speaker report concerning any perception of "withheld" cues?

SELECTED READINGS

DAVID K. BERLO, *The Process of Communication* (New York: Holt, Rinehart & Winston, 1976).

LLOYD BITZER, "The Rhetorical Situation," *Philosophy and Rhetoric,* 1 (January 1968), 1–14.

JOSEPH A. DE VITO, ed., *Communication: Concepts and Processes,* 3rd ed. (Englewood Cliffs, N.J.: Prentice-Hall, 1981).

LEONARD HAWES, "Elements of a Model for Communication Processes," *Quarterly Journal of Speech,* 59 (1973), 11–21.

JAMES C. MCCROSKEY, *An Introduction to Rhetorical Communication* (Englewood Cliffs, N.J.: Prentice-Hall, 1983), Chapter 1, pp. 3–22.

C. DAVID MORTENSEN, *Communication: The Study of Human Interaction* (New York: McGraw Hill, 1972).

RAYMOND S. ROSS, *Speech Communication,* 5th ed. (Englewood Cliffs, N.J.: Prentice-Hall, 1980), Chapter 1.

RICHARD F. WHITMAN AND PAUL H. BOASE, *Speech Communication: Principles and Contexts* (New York: Macmillan, 1983), pp. 3–34.

chapter 2

Effective Listening Habits

THE IMPORTANCE OF LISTENING

All the effort to present clearly spoken and reasoned speech is wasted when listeners fail to carry their share of the communication burden. Unfortunately, many attempts to communicate are unsatisfactory because of the widespread existence of poor listening habits. Thus, one of the keys to your overall communication skill is knowledge about listening habits. First, to be a good communicator you must realize that other people are likely to have poor listening habits. Next, you should consider all methods to improve the chances of getting messages across to people who are not particularly good listeners. Finally, your being alert to the importance of good listening logically means doing everything possible to improve your personal competence in this important communication skill.

Because so much speech is a response to prior information in the form of conversation, other formal speeches, and interviews, good speakers cannot afford to begin their own presentations with hazy, inaccurate information. The world of business and the professions, which we all enter in one way or another, has learned the value of precise information. Anyone who habitually misunderstands, misses information altogether, or strikes others as inattentive is not likely to succeed in either professional or social life.

Some people suppose that because of its effortlessness, listening is easily sharpened by merely "paying attention" as other people talk. However, that supposition is quite wrong. The ability to hear is not the same as the ability to listen, and considerably more effort is involved in listening. Although physical effort is obviously minimal, the psychological discipline required for efficient listening is quite demanding. Moreover, constant earnest practice in new habits is a price that must be paid if good listening is to become a normal, everyday pattern. As numerous studies have shown, most people do not listen very well.[1]

People listen poorly in several ways. They miss a great deal of information, they bias whatever they hear so much that it is recalled inaccurately, and they even add information consistent with their beliefs[2] to the point that what they remember bears little resemblance to what was really said. Further, they may think they are listening intently when in fact they are responding to unimportant parts of the message and missing the essence of it. They may miss transitions, modifications, or very important limitations on some point and take their first impressions of it as the essence. They may confuse an example with the point it is intended to illustrate, or they may dwell on a bit of humor too long. Sadly, poor listening habits are both widespread and extreme.

RESPONSIBILITY FOR COMMUNICATION

Now suppose, as often occurs, that an important message is sent to you by one who is unskilled, boring, and inarticulate. Whose responsibility is the impending failure of communication? It is easy to conclude that all who speak must bear the responsibility for their communications. Yet, those who listen have nearly absolute power to prevent communication, no matter how clear, complete, and reasonable a speaker's message might be. Conversely, listeners can turn a failure into success by their efforts. We should realize that responsibility for communication must be shared by both the speaker and the listeners, for either party can be the source of miscommunication. Such a view means that we must try to improve the conditions for others and to go beyond the minimum effort to listen closely when they speak. We may require a great deal more work on our listening habits. At the same time, we should examine in detail the process of listening itself and consider why it seems so easy but yet proves so difficult.

Studies of listening behavior indicate that poor habits are indeed widespread. In experiments in which the subjects knew they were being tested for listening, the average score of retained information immediately after hearing a lecture was about 50 percent. The subjects varied widely in their skills, and some of them retained very little of the information at all. Most of them scored poorly. The subjects were again tested two weeks later and their retention had dropped to 25 percent.[3] When we realize that most of the communication an individual conducts in a day is listening,[4] the implications of that study are depressing. For instance, if we extend the findings to college lectures, then most students will retain only half of what they hear for a short term and only about half of that amount for two weeks. No doubt repetition and reading the textbooks accounts for students' abilities to master a subject eventually. Even so, the apparent waste of effort by the lecturers and the attendant cost are striking.

Another implication is that many transactions conducted orally are riddled with errors and costly misunderstandings. The usual outcome is that all parties to the misunderstanding are sure that they were right and that the other individuals did not hear correctly. Still another implication is that training students in good listening habits, whether at home or in schools or colleges, is inadequate. On this matter, there is little doubt that systematic instruction has been almost absent for generations, although some schools are now making progress and are offering either separate courses or modules within courses in speech to improve listening performance. One final implication may be that we are suffering from too much communication, or rather attempted communication. The sales representatives and advertisers who shout at us to buy their wares may do us all a disservice as they try to improve their sales. As their advertisements grow shriller, we seek to avoid them. But then, more and more imaginative advertisements attract our attention. Soon, in the effort to turn off the overload of messages, we begin to turn off the wrong messages— namely, those which are important to our mental growth and health. In other words, we quit listening because of overstimulation. We might then become dominated by a procession of incoherent but attractive and stimulating messages and less attentive to drab but essential ones.

A common thread in all the implications just listed is each individual's emotional self-mastery. If we put our minds to the task, we could surely reject or accept sensibly from all the messages loaded onto us daily. Or could we? Few of us are saintly enough or disciplined enough to act on what rationality tells us is best for us. Then, too, our guard is down much of the time, and advertisers in particular are able to appeal to us cleverly by indirect and unexpected means. Although every person certainly ought to cultivate self-control, it may be unrealistic to expect people to constantly beware of everything in the media. What is needed, then, is not a defensive attitude but a receptive one. But to be receptive does not mean that one is unselective. On the contrary, sharp listeners understand fully what they hear, put it into a real perspective, and act on it or reject it when its value is judged low. Listeners need to practice habits of analysis. When these habits are truly automatic, they need little defense against the illogic of empty claims, for such illogic stands out quickly to the good listener.

TYPES OF LISTENING

Not all listening is intense, purposive concentration on a speaker. Some kinds of listening require much less attention than others. Listed next are some of the kinds of listening and a brief commentary about how each one is distinctive.

Phatic listening. Just as there is a socially acceptable body of speaking with nothing other than greeting and recognition intended, so there is a kind of listening to match it. The listener nods and catches the drift of the conversation, but may not turn full attention away from whatever is of immediate concern. For example, two riders watching their commuter train pull into a station might exclaim about how late the train is, how icy the weather is, and how hectic holiday travel is. Neither party learns anything new, each one exchanges polite greetings, and each one comments mildly on the shared situation. Little is demanded of either respondent. Main attention is focused on boarding the train. This kind of casual exchange eases the strains of everyday living, facilitates social encounters, and maintains etiquette.

Conversational listening. Conversational listening is slightly more involving. In it each respondent concentrates on what the other is saying, but typically neither person intends any profound, searching exploration of ideas. This is not to say that conversational listening is inaccurate or half-hearted. It is usually easy, brief, undemanding, and pleasant. Of course, it can sometimes be quite deep and important.

Appreciative listening. Appreciative listening to some idea, work, or person also requires stronger attention among listeners to the speaker's message. You might, for example, listen closely to a description of a friend's trip to the art museum to compare opinions of great works of art and to enjoy another person's account of familiar works. Similarly, you might listen to reminiscenses of a retiring employee just to appreciate the retiree's viewpoints on familiar shared experiences and on fellow workers. Introspection, not information, is the aim. We listen to music this way. We pay attention fairly closely and allow our emotions free play, even to the point of making ouselves vulnerable to illogic. For instance, in listening to Wagner we allow ourselves to believe in magic fire, gods, spells, and the like. We do not *really* believe in them, but we suspend our disbelief long enough to enter the imaginative world of composers and artists and to appreciate their visions. Appreciation might be diminished if we insisted upon absolutely objective, logical listening in such cases.

Analytic listening. Analytic listening is devoted to examining in detail someone else's statements and logic. Often it is directed toward revealing the assumptions and hidden implications of speech. If a disc jockey on an FM station says repeatedly, "All calls are recorded and may be used on the air," analytic listeners may examine the statement to determine whether the station has had so many profane or obscene callers that the station's personnel hopes to discourage such calls by implying a threat in recording all calls. Or the policy might mean only that the station is obeying some legal obligation to inform listeners before they are recorded. Or the width of the station's appeal might be the issue—the number of recorded calls is a measure of listeners and thus a marketing tool for the station. Discovering full meaning and implication is the purpose of analytic listening.

Critical listening. Critical listening, perhaps the most demanding type, requires intense concentration upon accurate perception, memory, and analysis of what is heard. Implied in it is the possibility of response or rejection of what one hears. Applied to each statement is a kind of test or challenge. The listener may pose such questions as these: Can this be true? Is that statement consistent with what you said earlier? Does it match what I know? Where do you get your evidence? Are you and your sources biased? Do you have anything to gain by claiming this or that? Is your logic sound? Critical listening is analytical listening carried one step beyond discovery of implications. It envisions a direct response, evaluation, or control of some kind. For example, the critical listener may reject, for explicit reasons, a plan of action proposed or he or she may offer a counterproposal.

Creative or sympathetic listening. Creative or sympathetic listening is a form of attending to others with a view toward helping or comforting them. Perhaps a friend with a severe personal problem needs your ear, and you may be asked to suggest some escape or aid in solving the problem. A sympathetic listener has to be creative and go beyond decoding just the words said. Such a listener perceives from a detached and calm perspective what the speaker cannot because of emotional involvement. This kind of listening can also take the form of joint creativity, such as actors' trying to solve the problems in a play production, or a chairperson's getting a committee member to abandon an uncooperative attitude about the purchase of a new piece of equipment, or a conductor's attempting to discover and correct some sour notes during the rehearsal of a symphony. Someone has to have a sympathetic, broad view and not take action until all issues are aired. The creative listener is thus not only a receiver, but also a clearing house and classifier of information. New ideas and approaches to a problem are the intended product of this kind of listening.

No doubt there are other specific kinds of listening, but those listed here cover most of the occasions you have to consider. Because life does not depend on textbooks, but rather the books depend on trying to describe life, combinations or variations of the listed types of listening do occur. In any given situation, you might think one form appropriate when in fact circumstances beyond your knowledge might make another form more appropriate. Imagine a young employee called in to meet with a supervisor, who worries aloud about a problem in the division. The young employee may perceive that advice is being sought during this "sympathetic" hearing, when in fact the session was really intended to determine how critical and analytic the young employee is. The meeting may actually be a screening for promotion as the supervisor observes the candidate's responses. In other cases, listeners could imagine themselves to be in critical listening situations when all that is expected of them is appreciative listening. For instance, a middle manager might announce that top management had adopted some pet scheme for reorganization. In a staff meeting, lower employees who oppose the change might feel threatened and defensive when all the speaker wishes to do is announce the change and put it in motion smoothly.

REASONS FOR LISTENING

There are several good reasons for actively cultivating listening skills. Following is a discussion of some of these reasons. Above all, we listen to acquire knowledge. Information is most commonly heard, and sometimes overheard. We are usually listening all day long, even when we make no particular effort. If someone exclaims "Fire!" or "What a beautiful sunset!" we are likely to look up effortlessly from our work, and divert our attention to what seems more insistent and interesting. By contrast, we have to make an effort to seek out reading material. The best reason to listen, then, is to learn.

We also listen to increase our attentiveness. All skills improve with practice. When we listen consciously and test our listening skill from time to time, we improve our acuity. We discover that much more happens to us and around us when we exert ourselves to respond to the environment.

We listen to develop our language skills. As we become more critical of our own listening, we discover flaws in our language. We may, for example, find that we misunderstand vocabularly words and idioms. Because we do not have any particular reaction from friends when we take the word "peculiar" to mean "unpleasant," we may assume we understand it correctly. But when we listen critically, we might discover that such a meaning is not correct. The increased attention and discrimination may have revealed that this definition does not accurately fit into many contexts of the word. Consider the following examples and substitute your own synonyms for "peculiar" to determine whether you really understand the word: He noticed a peculiar odor. He had a peculiar facial tic. She wore a peculiar perfume. This pronunciation is peculiar to New England. Now look up the word. Did you have all the meanings clearly in mind?

Figure 2-1

We sometimes listen for personal reasons, including emotional relaxation, entertainment, and mental health. When the daily grind gets on our nerves, we often find solace in listening to music, to comedians, to inspiring sermons, or to lectures far removed from our usual experiences. We may go to an aquarium or planetarium to escape our mundane, tiresome worlds and to enter into another devoid of our problems. There is nothing like a learned speech on the solar system to put one's personal problems into perspective.

We also listen to increase out understanding of ourselves and others. As we grow, we constantly add to our stock of comparisons with other people. We are curious about them, but good taste often prevents our probing into questions which deeply trouble us. We may hesitate to ask even close friends how they feel about the issues of race, religion, sex, and grooming. Sometimes we are startled upon discovering how closely we agree in attitudes with people we earlier regarded as entirely uncongenial. It is often through listening that we learn how provincial some of our ideas are, as seen through others' eyes. Similarly, through listening we learn more and more accurately about the human condition, its weaknesses and strengths, its foibles and nobility, and its infinite variety.

FACTORS INVOLVED IN LISTENING EFFICIENCY

Fortunately, much can be done to improve listening behavior. Evidence shows that our potential listening efficiency is very high, in spite of the very low physical effort involved.[5] Assuming that someone has normal hearing, or even marginal hearing correctable with aids, a conservative estimate is that that person could be trained to listen well enough to understand and recall most of the content in a lecture. The reasons why listeners retain very little of the facts and data in a talk are examined in some detail here. Later in the chapter, methods of overcoming bad habits and replacing them with better ones are presented.

Poor Listening Habits

A variety of poor listening habits can interfere with listening. A first step in improving listening efficiency, then, is being familiar with the following poor listening habits you could develop:

1. The tendency to confuse personality, appearance, or manner with ideas is a frequent and destructve habit.

2. The temptation to refute speakers as they proceed because of unpleasant voice, delivery, or unwelcome message is a distraction from full and complete reception.

3. Idle overextension of one point to the detriment of others is a common fault. You may miss ideas because you dwell on what you think to be a weak or incorrect claim and you spend too much time analyzing that claim while the speaker has gone on to other points.

4. Allowing distractions to divide your attention is a frequent trap. Noise, heat, fatigue, overeating at lunch, or any number of other causes for wandering attention may make it easy for you to let your attention wander away from the business at hand.

5. Pretending to listen when you really are not paying attention is a very destructive habit. Faking attention not only results in your losing information, but it also misleads a speaker into thinking that you are listening and understanding. Sometimes a speaker counts on listeners' understanding of an earlier presentation, only to discover later that crucial information was never heard. In many situations, such as jobs, college courses, or technical training, faking attention can lead to serious problems.

6. Depending on striking effects, spectacular anecdotes or jokes, and entertainment when serious work is appropriate is a common weakness.

7. Sometimes, trying to take elaborate notes can defeat your listening so occupying you that you lose important and subtle relationships of ideas. Often it is better to just concentrate carefully on an oral presentation and to jot down notes after it is over to refresh your memory about the main ideas. You cannot immediately outline everything without sometimes losing the thread of the talk.

8. Mental laziness—unwillingness to deal with an idea or even a difficult vocabulary word—accounts for much poor listening. Giving up too soon, a lazy listener fails to work with the speaker and to note subordinate relationships, transitions, and tedious but important information. This fault usually accompanies dependence on entertainment.

Combinations of several of these flaws are probably familiar to each of you. Recall a tedious class conducted on a warm, spring day, just after lunch, when students are getting ready to go home for a weekend. Dutiful listening was probably hard.

Before we examine suggestions for improving listening, we first explore a few more ideas. The preceding list of poor listening habits implies that listeners are guilty of various sloppy, lazy habits which account for poor communication. However, remember that the responsibility is shared. Furthermore, some physical facts complicate the listening process. It would be very simple and straightforward to improve listening if all that were necessary was to *avoid* the flaws just listed. But other forces act against improvement. We need to understand what they are, how to cope with them, and how to cultivate personal habits of attentive and courteous listening.

PHYSICAL FACTORS AND LISTENING

The first fact that should be always on your mind is that the act of listening attentively cannot be sustained very long. In other words, most people's span of attention is quite short. Very early investigations revealed that it was usually only five to eight seconds long. Later investigations indicated that the span of acute attention was even shorter, perhaps less than two seconds.[6] The implication is that listening is not one sustained effort but a series of peaks and valleys of attention. If a crucial point comes during a lull, we might miss it or grasp it imperfectly. Further, if a speaker does little to regain interest again and again, attention can suffer. Because listeners can hear and process information faster than a speaker can comfortably say it, they tend to get ahead of the speaker and build their own version of what is about to be said before the speaker can say it. Of course, they often miss the intended point. This act is called *overextension*. It is, needless to say, a very bad habit for listeners to have. A better use of the listeners' time between parts of a talk is summarizing and mentally repeating what has already been established. This habit allows listeners to keep more accurate views of the presentation. Remember that listening is limited by certain physical and psychological facts. Speaking rates are so much slower than audiences' listening rates that listeners may become impatient and start to get ahead of the speaker. They may guess wrongly about what is to come next and become confused. They need variety and emphasis to maintain their attention as a speech unfolds. Everyone has a recurrent and brief span of attention. There is no guarantee that audience members are all focusing attention at the same time or that they perceive the same statements correctly as the main ideas of a speech. To compensate, speakers have learned to use interest-arousing details, to repeat ideas, to make careful transitions, and to summarize. Even so, there is still a high risk of poor listening efficiency.

LISTENING AND RATE OF SPEAKING

For decades it has been supposed that poor listening has resulted from several faults of the speaker, which are easy to identify. Most teachers, including the author, have urged speakers to slow down their rates of speech to aid comprehension and attention among listeners. Common sense indicates that messages delivered too fast will be missed. However, some experiments tend to contradict what we have all believed. A study of rates of speaking and efficient listening reveal some startling information. Many people speak at a "normal" rate of about 125 words per minute (WPM), and a given individual tends to vary little from a typical or characteristic rate. What is normal for one person is not normal for another, however, and some people speak 150 to 180 WPM habitually. What is confusing is that listeners may find those who speak at 180 WPM clear and comprehensible but those whose rate is slower harder to understand. Indeed, radio and TV newscasters tend to speak at 150 to 225 WPM, whereas college debaters (anxious to cram in all possible evidence in support of their claims) often speak at rates from 350 to 500 WPM, two or three times the rate of ordinary speech. The debaters are still comprehensible. A study by Foulke found that rates of 175, 225, 275, 325, and 375 WPM were all understandable, but optimum intelligibility of the messages seemed to occur around 275 WPM, almost twice the so-called normal rate.[7] In fact, there is some reason to believe that too slow a rate creates the effect of great tedium and decreases audience comprehension of messages. It seems likely that commonly encountered speeds of delivery have little to do with comprehension except insofar as they blur speech or create some extra commentary on the speaker's attitude toward message or audience, or both.[8] For example, listeners might perceive fast and careless pronunciation as an effort by the speaker to be rid of the burden of speaking, or as defensiveness or furtiveness. A slow rate might be regarded as evidence of boredom, lack of expertise, or pedantry. An extremely fast rate might be perceived as nervousness, extremism, or just flightiness. In any case, you must be wary of imputing too much to speakers because of their chosen rate—you may misjudge them and miss important information.

Just as "common sense" about rate and other vocal qualities can lead to wrong conclusions about a person, they can also mislead about a message. As early as 300 B.C. rhetoricians warned against dull, lifeless, monotonous delivery. However, twentieth-century experimenters were unable to demonstrate under rigorous laboratory conditions any loss of intelligibility in monotonous presentations, at least as they defined intelligibility. They defined monotony as absolutely unvarying pitch or inflection in the voice. However, not even the dullest speaker has *no* variation. Absolutely unvarying monopitch is unearthly, machinelike, and consequently attention commanding by its bizarre sound. It is by no means comparable to the speech of a person who is not interested in the topic, the audience, or the occasion. Thus, you should take with a grain of salt any conclusion that monotony does not damage compre-hension of a message.[9]

Some experiments, in any case, have supported the ancient, sensible view that bored, uninterested, and lackluster delivery can damage the perception of a message, whether the mechanism is physical or emotional. It does not much matter whether listeners are unable or unwilling to hear a message if they fail to get it. A study by Thomas, in which three kinds of delivery were pitted, against each other—namely, "varied and flexible," "monopitch," and "bored, uninterested, and monotonous" delivery—indicated that the ancients were probably right after all. A bored speaker produces bored, uninterested listeners. Varied and flexible presentation helps to maintain listener attention and interest, assuming the same message in both cases. The study concerned intelligibility, essential to reception and comprehension of information.[10]

Still more information about how delivery affects listening is presented by Addington[11] who suggests that speed in delivery indicates to listeners some-thing about the animation and extroversion of the speaker, whereas variations in pitch suggest the degree of dynamism. Extremes should be avoided, for excessive speed or pitch range can suggest insincerity or pose, which can be just as destructive as those qualities suggested by too slow a rate and too constricted a pitch range.

PSYCHOLOGICAL FACTORS
AND LISTENING

When the studies are long forgotten, the speaker and listener still share certain tasks. Both contribute energy to those tasks, which are:

1. Gaining the listeners' attention.
2. Holding that attention.
3. Making the speaker's ideas clear.
4. Causing listeners to remember the ideas.

Working against the accomplishment of these tasks are the limitations of all audiences, which are composed of fallible creatures.

1. Audiences have limited attention spans. They cannot or will not focus very long on one idea, and they need variety to renew their attention.
2. Audiences have limited interest. Listeners do not have the same experience with concepts that the speaker addressing them has. The person talking to the audience may be fascinated by growing orchids and may be surprised and even hurt to learn that most of the audience cares little or nothing for the topic.

3. Audiences have limited emotional control, especially in groups. Much has been written on the nature of large groups of people assembled. They are thought to be less perceptive, more guided by peer-group norms than by civilized standards of behavior, and more anonymous because of the inevitable immersion of individuals in a faceless crowd.[12] In any case, crowds do indeed behave differently from the individuals that compose them, and some of their responses are inclined toward emotional rather than rational behavior. They may be slow to respond to reason or quick to react to some idiosyncrasy they perceive in the speaker. Although we do not need to conclude that audiences act worse than they would as individuals, still a speaker and student of listening should realize that crowd phenomena do exist and should be considered.

4. Audiences have limited language skill. Speakers court trouble if they talk over the heads of their listeners. A sesquipedalian vocabulary may presage vituperation. It is just as risky to talk down to listeners. A condescending attitude will alienate listeners: "Although few of you have eaten in Paris, surely some of you have had decent imitations of French dishes." "During the time I was special assistant to the President, I thought of such as you." "Even though most of you here today do not share my Harvard education, surely some of you can understand this."

5. Audiences have widely different backgrounds. To predict how they will hear and react to specific information can be difficult. You may think your listeners share a great deal when in fact some of them can react violently to what others find amusing or unimportant. The old saying that religion and politics are taboo subjects, though not literally true, is a warning of the perils of assuming too much about the backgrounds of your listeners.

SUGGESTIONS FOR IMPROVING LISTENING

There is no question that conscious attention to listening skills can improve your performance.[13] The greater problem is ensuring that you hold onto the improvement once it is gained. Like unused muscles, listening habits will gradually weaken unless you make an effort to maintain them. The habits described next are of little use if you allow them to degenerate to occasional efforts. A good plan is to try at least once a day to consciously practice two or more of the named habits to keep them active and fresh in your awareness.

First, seek active involvement in speech presentations. Do not expect the speaker to do all the work. Try to accept the talk on its own terms and allow yourself to be immersed in the views presented, as long as they are not obviously false or harmful. For instance, if someone speaks on "encouraging ballet training" in a hostile community, listeners should try not to be defensive but rather to put themselves wholeheartedly into the receptive, open frame of mind of potential supporters. To allow fears about "sissy dancers," temperamental ballerinas, and unfamiliar music to control how they hear the talk is to unfairly and inaccurately perceive what is happening. The effort to become wholly involved gives the listeners the best chance of capturing the vision and message of the speaker but does not hinder each listener's chance to form sober, reflective opinions on the talk after it is over. Thus, a listener can become fully engaged while listening and then make a reasoned judgment afterward.

You should also try to suspend your judgment of a speaker until you hear the whole speech. Maintain emotional control and try to turn off your defense mechanisms until you hear the message. Of course, there are occasions when early in a talk you become aware that some speaker is just ranting. Just be sure you do not dismiss unwelcome ideas too soon or reject a person because the ideas presented are unfamiliar or unpalatable.

Fight the temptation to mentally argue with the speaker as the talk progresses. It is usually best to hear an entire rationale before attacking the component parts of it. Often what seems outlandish in detail takes on a unity and coherence as a whole. For example, Americans trained in Judeo-Christian ideas at first find Japanese Shinto belief in many gods to be sacrilegious. When the Shinto ideas are examined in detail, however, the student may be surprised to find an unexpected reverence for nature and religion which is quite consistent with Western beliefs. The Oriental's ability to be committed to Christian and Shinto principles at the same time often mystifies Occidentals. The whole rationale makes sense even though parts of it seem farfetched. (For a sensitive exploration of this subject, read James Clavell's novel *Shogun,* in which the heroine becomes a devout Catholic without abandoning her Japanese beliefs.)

Another helpful listening tool is to control distractions. Do not give up too quickly if noise, heat, hunger, sleepiness assail you. Move your place if possible, or do something to maintain your link with the speaker. Wait out the noise from jet airplanes, lawn mowers, loud talking in hallways, or other distractions. Sometimes the speaker can be given a signal requesting some adjustment to interference. Merely raising your hand, cupping a hand to the ear, or otherwise indicating difficulty in hearing will usually suffice.

If you are taking notes, it is sometimes a good idea to outline the main ideas and chief supporting points of a speech. Do not try to record every anecdote or illustration. If the information is flowing by quickly, then only record the bold promontories. If handouts accompany a presentation, as they often do in business settings, then no outline or note taking at all may be necessary.

Review the talk afterward. This is the hardest, and at the same time the most useful, habit a student can adopt. Spend 15 minutes reflecting on the notes, correcting them, filling in key phrases or ideas you could not jot down during the speech, and then examine the notes for overall fidelity to the meaning of the talk. In miniature, the speech will thus be repeated and reinforced. This effort to follow up on a talk will do much to give you an extraordinarily clear, precise record of what occurred. Concentrate on the thesis and main ideas above all. Remember that once you leave the lecture site you can never again quite recapture the total effect of the speech, and if you can firmly set in your mind all the main ideas and flavor of the talk, you can think about its implications at your leisure.

The preceding general suggestions should be accompanied by some cautions about what to avoid. Old habits die hard, and the effort to replace them with better practices may be exasperating. The following cautions about what to avoid are intended to complement the constructive behaviors just described.

Avoid refuting the speaker point-by-point during the speech.

Avoid confusing the speaker's voice, manner, dress, or physical appearance with ideas presented. Some brilliant, constructive people happen to be unpleasant in appearance, but prudent listeners will avoid losing valuable insights through thoughtless dismissal of sound ideas presented by less-than-ideal speakers.

Avoid mental laziness, the unwillingness to search through an idea and its implications just because the idea is not familiar.

Avoid the temptation to fake attention, to present a blank, smiling, and even nodding visage to the speaker while really thinking about something entirely different. Fish-eyed, half-attentive poses are destructive in that they may fool the speaker into thinking you understand when you do not.

Avoid trying to take notes on everything.

Avoid idly extending the speaker's remarks beyond what was intended. It is easy to mistake claims because of your own overapplication of some point. This habit of adding steps not intended by the speaker and then reacting to our own extensions as if they were claims in the speech is called *inductive leaping*. For example, suppose a speaker says that our library will be remodeled. We jump to the conclusion that the speaker is demanding new taxes, because taxation is the usual way of financing such projects. Then we challenge the speaker with some such question as this: "How can you argue to increase property taxes when they are already too high?" It may happen that property tax was not at all the source of funding the speaker had in mind, if financing was to be mentioned at all during this particular speech.

Avoid demanding of speakers constant entertainment, striking effects, and anecdotes to hold your attention. Much of the communication of the world is serious, hard effort to solve problems, and the juvenile habit of expecting speakers to motivate listeners is unrealistic. Of course, shrewd speakers will try to keep their material interesting, but it is unreasonable to expect them to do all the work.

EXERCISES

1. Record in a lecture by means of some convenient symbol the number of times a speaker seems to be using a deliberate appeal to audience attention. A joke, anecdote, extended example, or striking illustration would count as a bid for attention.

2. During a student speech, take notes very carefully. Then give the notes to the speaker for analysis. Does the speaker agree that the notes are a fair outline of the talk? If not, where did the worst faults in listening lie? Too much emphasis on the wrong things? Too much emphasis on details? Misunderstanding of theses? Misunderstanding of the main points? Totally missed main ideas? Inability to know what was major and what was minor information?

3. During a student speech have one person listen only for the speaker's transitions and jot them down. Compare the list with the speaker's. In a variation, have two students note the transitions and then compare their perceptions about what constitutes a transition.

4. Bring to class cassette recordings of TV ads or radio spots which clamor for attention but offer very little of substance. Analyze the degree to which these ads aid or hinder good listening habits.

5. Bring to class recordings of advertisements which you believe *depend* on careless listening so that consumers will think claims are being made when, in fact, legally speaking, the advertiser has only triggered wishful thinking or "overextension" in listeners. (For example, many publishers heavily advertise magazine sales as contests with what seems like an explicit promise: "We want you to become our next millionaire, and to guarantee you a chance, send in your. . . .")

SELECTED READINGS

LARRY BARKER, *Listening Behavior* (Englewood Cliffs, N.J.: Prentice-Hall, 1971).

C. WILLIAM COLBURN AND SANFORD B. WEINBERG, *An Orientation to Listening and Audience Analysis* (Palo Alto, Calif.: SRA, 1976).

RALPH G. NICHOLS AND LEONARD A. STEVENS, *Are You Listening?* (New York: McGraw Hill, 1957).

GARY T. HUNT, *Public Speaking* (Englewood Cliffs, N.J.: Prentice-Hall, 1981), pp. 11–32.

CARL H. WEAVER, *Human Listening: Processes and Behavior* (Indianapolis: Bobbs Merrill, 1972).

ANDREW D. WOLVIN AND CAROLYN GWINN COAKLEY, *Listening* (Dubuque, Iowa: Wm. C. Brown, 1982).

Pertinent Experimental Studies

D. W. ADDINGTON, "The Relationship of Selected Vocal Characteristics to Personality Perception," *Speech Monographs,* 35 (1968), 492, 503.

CHARLES DIEHL, RICHARD WHITE, AND P. SATZ, "Pitch Change and Comprehension," *Speech Monographs,* 28 (1961), 65–68.

C. H. ERNEST, "Listening Comprehension as a Function of Type of Material and Rate of Presentation," *Speech Monographs,* 35 (1968), 154–158.

EMERSON FOULKE, ed., *Proceedings of the Louisville Conference on Time-Compressed Speech,* Louisville, Kentucky, 1966, Chapters 2 and 3.

S. H. THOMAS, "Effects of Monotonous Delivery on Intelligibility," *Speech Monographs,* 36 (1969), 110–113.

chapter 3

Developing the Focus of Informative Speeches

CHOOSING A TOPIC

Your first task in preparing a speech is selecting a topic. Whether for a class assignment or for another occasion, you may have difficulty choosing a topic for a speech. Assuming that you have not been assigned a specific topic and that you are armed only with an imperfect idea of the audience and occasion, you have a difficult task. You must pick a subject consistent with your skills and knowledge and the needs and expectations of the audience. You probably have a body of favorite topics on which you can speak comfortably and authoritatively. If something in that collection of subjects seems to be appropriate and challenging for the audience, then you are all set. However, that happy coincidence is rare. You usually have to dig around and explore topics with which you are not so familiar. A beginning step if you are fairly desperate for a good topic is to sit down with pencil and paper and jot down every topic you can think of, no matter how preposterous the topics look to you. The idea is that when you begin to put something on paper, it is before you for comparison and it is not in your mind for a moment and then gone. Something else that you write down later might chance to fit with something you wrote hastily early in the process. A relationship between two quite different ideas might furnish a good topic. Think of as many topics as you can. Do not trust yourself to remember them; write them down. You may be able to eliminate some right away, but at this stage you are mostly trying to dig into your experiences, your attitudes, and your skills for key words to trigger a good topic and treat it in a fresh way. A wise professor once said that once you make up your mind firmly about what you are to speak on, your preparation is about one-third finished.

Now, let us assume that you have written down about 30 topics, none of which seems appealing to you, or if they appeal to you, they still do not seem right for the audience. The only recourse is to go to the library, where you can discover some interesting, appealing materials that did not occur to you on your own. If out of your own experience or the nature of the occasion you have not yet found a topic, the choice may have to be arbitrary. Perhaps you can pick a subject which is of current interest in the news media. Simply apply your own expertise to the topic, and expect to field a variety of questions after the talk. Some speakers customarily allow considerable time for queries, but if you do and the audience does not cooperate and ask for further elaboration, you may be left standing awkwardly with nothing more to say.

Some writers on the subject say that the key to choosing a topic and appropriate treatment is to imagine some way to get the audience members directly and personally involved. The trend away from formal speeches to group encounters no doubt influenced this pattern. However, even though this style is usually easy on the speaker and involving for the listeners, excessive informality and a feeling that the speaker did not give enough value may result. Most people think that a public speaker knows a great deal about a subject— far more than the audience. Their discovery that the speaker has much the same information that they do comes as a shock and disappointment. To avoid these, as a speaker you should at least try to be the dominant figure in any "simulation games" or group activities. The great variety of such games is beyond the scope of this treatise on public speaking, and is not pursued here.

Several lists of potential topics appear at the end of this chapter. Refer to them if you need help choosing a stimulating topic for a speech.

SHAPING THE MESSAGE

It is amazing how many people get up to give a speech and reveal such a hazy purpose for giving it that no one knows just what they intend to communicate. This section tries to help you shape the content of the message itself after you have chosen a suitable topic. The first step is to decide on your general purpose, as discussed in Chapter 1. Say it out loud to ensure unambiguous intent: "I want primarily to inform this audience on the new tax withholding instructions. I do not want the listeners to think I am persuading them. I merely want to explain the new laws and make sure everyone understands that I am *informing, not dictating* policy." Such an explicit statement to yourself need not be stated so crudely to your listeners, although if there is any

Figure 3-1 Even familiar experiences can furnish interesting speech topics.

risk that they will misunderstand, it would not hurt to state your purpose in addition to your central idea. You should state clearly *intent* and *content*. The first is your purpose, and the second is your thesis or central idea. If you do not vocalize your exact purpose, you may find that you get lost in the details of the talk and lose perspective. Then, neither you nor your listeners will know just what your purpose is and where you are leading them in the talk. It is easy to confuse your *purpose* with your *thesis*. In order to make a truly informative speech, you must clearly distinguish between your purpose and your thesis.

FOCUSING THE CENTRAL IDEA

One of the most common complaints of listeners if that speakers do not focus their speeches around a central important idea which those who attend can grasp readily and recall clearly. "He said something about some kind of new safety regulations that the school board wants." Such a report of a speech indicates that the listeners did not feel the talk applied to them, did not recall the central idea, and did not realize what the speaker expected them to remember. When listeners recall only the subject and have a confused, partial recall of the talk, the fault is often the speaker's failure to focus (or concentrate all attention) on a controlling theme, or *thesis*. In the example just noted, the speaker might choose to focus the speech on the theme that safety rules apply to everyone in the plant, not just to those who wield tools. The larger the group addressed, the more chance there is for the theme to go astray and be misperceived. That the master phrase is worded in such a way that the speaker's purpose can be realized is of the utmost importance. Look at the following thesis statements or master phrases and decide which one in each pair is the superior one. Is *A* or *B* the more focused central idea?

A. Fire regulations imposed by the city require us to prohibit smoking in all offices except for one designated as a lounge area.
B. There are going to be some changes in smoking rules in the company.
A. Everybody around here is overweight and needs exercise.
B. The company will sponsor a new on-the-job exercise plan for those who are overweight.
A. There is something new under the sun with regard to investment opportunities.
B. The company will offer stock options beginning in January.
A. Parking in lot *A* will be restricted to faculty only after March 15.
B. Some bad news about free parking anywhere on the school grounds will be announced, and it will affect nearly everybody.

Note that in these pairs of thesis statement one is vague and hazy and the other is directed. Some, such as the statement about vague changes in parking policy, are downright misleading. As an outgrowth of your observations of these contrasting thesis statements, you should conclude that there are ways to test the effectiveness of thesis statements.

THE TESTS OF A GOOD THESIS (CENTRAL IDEA)

Every thesis should be about just one idea. Avoid dual or triple theses. "We will reinvest more of our capital in bonds and refurbish the stockholders' room before we offer the new interest rate" is sure to lead the speaker into giving two speeches at the same time, with resulting disorganization. A thesis such as this one communicates confusion of purpose as well as lack of focus of the central idea, which seems to be that redoing the meeting room might somehow disarm stockholders and help them accept the proposal to reinvest rather than pay dividends. Give either one speech or another; do not give two at the same time.

Every thesis should be exactly worded. It is hard work to force yourself to prune and reword again and again, but this process is necessary to arrive at the very best wording of your thesis. For example, if you want to stress certain specific qualifications applying to some thesis, you should word them in subordinate form, not coordinate form. The following example illustrates this point. If a bank official were explaining a new plan to all of the personnel, the thesis might be worded in several ways:

> Good: Our bank's interest pay periods for passbook accounts become quarterly beginning in January, 1987.
> Poor: Our bank will change over on the first of the year, 1987, from semiannual to quarterly payments and the new rules will apply to passbook accounts.

Note that the wording of the second version leaves unclear whether other accounts than passbook types will receive quarterly payments. The word "and" makes the second clause coordinate (equally important) with the first clause, as if two things are going to happen. In fact, only one thing is going to happen—namely, that passbook accounts alone are going to the quarterly dividend pay periods.

A good thesis should be limited in scope. Avoid world-embracing statements if you can narrow the applicability to just exactly the area or group of individuals covered by the statement. "Everybody in the warehouse is too fat" is probably a loose, indefensible statement. It is less likely to embarrass individuals than is a more precise statement, but if there is a single person in the office who is of normal weight, then the statement is false and perhaps offensive. Just as loose claims are evidence of sloppy thought, so are loosely worded thesis statements.

When a speaker plans to explain a plan of action or describe some event, the thesis may contain some value statement that may help listeners understand why the speech is being given. Again, that statement should not be vague, either. For example, to avoid the dull thesis "There are nine steps in making aluminum," a speaker could add some life by saying "All nine steps in producing aluminum require much expensive electric power." Avoid flat statements such as "Making plywood is interesting" or "Investing in futures markets is complicated." Do not say as a thesis "The Mount St. Helens eruption caused widespread destruction" because the audience already knows that. Try "The Mount St. Helens eruption demonstrates the vulnerability of the Pacific Northwest cities." A talk on that topic appeals more directly to human concerns (safety) than does a discussion of dollar amount showing past damage. Note that much of the same research data can be used in a speech descriptive either of the devastation or of what may lie in store for the future. Informative thesis statements should inform—that is, they should tell the audience something it probably does not already know.

SOURCES OF INFORMATION

Your main challenge in constructing an informative speech is to gather information which most of the listeners do not already know and which will benefit your purpose. If you are already familiar with a topic, then the problem of constructing and focusing a speech is greatly simplified. For example, if you grew up on a pig farm and had cared for pigs for many years, your expertise might approach that of a competent veterinarian in certain limited ways. You might know a great deal about nutrition, health, sanitation, and marketing of pigs from personal experience. If the audience is composed of similar students, all from pig farms, a speech on raising a champion sow is likely to be a dud, for everyone else knows the same information as you. However, if you are the sole farmer in a class, the expertise you bring to bear on agricultural topics can be powerful. Similarly, other students planning interesting, unusual careers may draw quite good topics for the speeches from their professional courses and experiences.

However, most of the time, even if you have an excellent background in the topic you have chosen for a speech, you will need to look up further details from authoritative sources. For most speeches the research step is indispensable and must be assumed as part of the burden of preparing a public speech.

Personal Experience

Students often overlook their own expertise as a source of good information on a topic. For example, an ardent stamp collector can very quickly develop a surprising degree of expertise in detecting valuable stamps or detecting forgeries. College students often have rich backgrounds which amaze other students even though they themselves may not regard their own competence as particularly exceptional. One student in a basic speech class became interested in collecting Nazi ceremonial daggers and astounded the audience when he talked with great authority on the in-fighting and symbolic "upsmanship" practiced within the Nazi party as represented by a great variety of costume daggers. The first source of expertise, then, should be yourself. What experience, no matter how ordinary, have you had? Is there in a job or hobby some fact or insight which, although you long ago accepted it as ordinary, is still for most listeners exceptional and extraordinary? Search your background for unusual events, experiences, and acquaintances. By contrast, do not dismiss very familiar topics as useless for informative speeches, for within even the most familiar and common experiences may lie fascinating personal experiences which others will find interesting.

Library Sources

Other sources of information must usually be consulted, however, to furnish current, accurate information. The best friend of the public speaker is, therefore, the library. A great variety of aids and services are available in most college libraries. If you are not already familiar with these from your writing classes or other basic courses, you should learn what facilities are available. One of the supreme ironies in education is that libraries are full of excellent information and willing, even eager, personnel to help students, yet the students often feel unwelcome and inhibited in the libraries. A very important part of education is to learn how and where to find information. Go to your library and determine to master its local services. Perhaps your catalogue is computerized, and the machines intimidate you. About 10 minutes' worth of experimenting and sympathetic instruction can open up a world of aids and services to you. If your library has only a card catalogue, as most libraries do, with minimal effort and strain you may still find a wealth of aids for your speech research.

The card catalogue is the first place to search, especially if you are seeking information by or about a well-known person. If you look under "Steinbeck," for example, in most catalogue systems you will find both books and essays *by* Steinbeck and *about* him. You must consult your librarian to determine the local policies and details of the system. Most card catalogues, however, are useful if you know any one of three pieces of information—namely, the *author*, the *subject*, or the *title* of some particular work. Thus, if you look under "Einstein," "Relativity," or "General Theory of Relativity, A," in most catalogues you will find the same information about Einstein.

A variety of other specialized aids is almost equally valuable. Encyclopedias of all sorts are commonly kept in an area of the library called the reference room, and you can go directly there to seek information on topics that seem promising for a speech. The encyclopedia is particularly valuable because it furnishes brief and economical overviews of many topics. Often it saves you time by revealing that some tentative speech topic is *not* very appealing after all, or that the topic needs extreme narrowing, or that it is so technical that listeners may not like it, and so on. Most encyclopedias contain brief but authoritative lists of readings which you can examine further for more information.

Among the valuable encyclopedias likely to be found in even modest libraries are the following standard works:

1. *Encyclopedia Americana*
2. *Encyclopedia Britannica*
3. *Grove's Dictionary of Music and Musicians*
4. *Encyclopedia of Education*
5. *Encyclopedia of World Art*
6. *Encyclopedia of Philosophy*
7. *Encyclopedia of Psychology*
8. *Encyclopedia of Science and Technology, McGraw-Hill*

Many other reference works are also useful. Index and bibliographic col-

Figure 3-2   "I don't see why I need books. This is supposed to be a speech class."

lections on a wide variety of subjects may be found in most college libraries. Do not overlook city libraries, even when the college library is distinguished. Some towns have excellent facilities and holdings which students never think to examine. Often a public library is in less demand, has complementary holdings, or has certain specialized collections which the college does not have. Still another possibility for finding very rare or specialized works is to use interlibrary loan facilities. Of course, this service is relatively slow, but it does open the possibility of finding some of the rarest, most unique works in the nation.

Yearbooks, such as the *World Almanac* and *Book of Facts, The Facts on File Yearbook*, and addenda to encyclopedias are useful for acquiring very recent information not found in standard encyclopedias. Also, do not overlook the newspaper and periodical indexes. The most useful and widely available are *The Reader's Guide to Periodical Literature*, a current index of what is contained in nearly 200 magazines, and *The New York Times Index*. The first dates back to 1900 and the latter is available back to 1913. Thus, if you wanted to know what the newspapers were saying about President Wilson's position on the League of Nations in 1918, you could find both an index and perhaps copies of the actual newspapers of the time in large libraries.

Some libraries cannot stock the enormous bulk of periodicals in actual size, so they subscribe to microfilm or microfiche editions of books and periodicals. Readers need an index to such holdings as well as guidance on how to use the card and film readers in the library.

Following is a list of other specialized index collections:

1. Art Index
2. Business Periodicals Index
3. Education Index
4. Humanities Index
5. Social Science Index

The best way to discover rapidly what aids are available in your own libraries is to go to the reference rooms, look around, and then ask the librarians if you have specific questions. The more precise your inquiry, the more likely you will be to get help. If you ask what the library has on term-paper topics, you will probably not get much help, but if you ask where you can find journals of medicine or engineering, you are likely to get instant assistance. Just remember that most libraries contain far more information than even the most astute investigator can digest, and the more specific the questions you ask the librarian, the greater your chance of expert, quick aid.

Many topics concern the operation and foibles of the government. You should be aware of the *Congressional Record*, a pulp paper record of speeches and transactions in Congress. In fact, it contains much more, including speeches attributed to Senators and Representatives who directed the publisher to include not only speeches that they actually gave on the floor but also speeches by other persons, editorials, and idealized speeches on current topics. *Idealized speeches* are actual speeches which are edited after presentation to reflect what the Senators and Representatives wish they had said rather than what they actually said. Nevertheless, the *Record* is a fascinating, valuable, and unique source of information. The *Congressional Index* is valuable in assisting you to find current topics in the enormous bulk of verbiage the *Record* necessarily contains.

Another broad category of aids is the biographical holdings of a library. The earliest such aid is *Who's Who*, published since 1849. It is a record of prestigious families of the British Empire and the royal family. It is a model on which later biographical collections are modeled. *Who's Who in America*, published since 1899, contains sketches on the lives of prominent Americans. A recent work is *Current Biography*, which was begun in 1940. Kept up to date by being published annually, it has longer articles about people in the news. The *Dictionary of American Biography* (abbreviated as *DAB*) contains brief summaries on the lives of deceased Americans of some distinction. Its British equivalent is the *Dictionary of National Biography* (*DNB*), which contains sketches on the lives of over 30,000 distinguished figures in English history. These two works are useful for historical research.

For more recent biographical data, consult either the *Reader's Guide* or *Biography Index*, which will guide you to sources of modern periodicals. The *Biography Index* does not contain biography, but directs the reader to current publications about living people. *Notable American Women* is modeled on the

DAB, and *Who's Who of American Women* has information about prominent American women today. This latter source began in 1958, and is hence valuable as a source of data on recent history in women's studies, topics of particular interest to women, and biographical facts about prominent women.

Interviews

You can also gather much useful information on nearly any conceivable speech topic from experts on campus. Although students must be considerate of the time demands on professors, most teachers are glad to inform others on their specialties. Class lectures, notes from courses, and comments by other students can suggest to you who might be a good candidate for an interview. In the interest of conserving time and good will, before you conduct an interview you should prepare a limited number of very specific questions, whose answers will directly support main ideas in your proposed speech. You should take notes, try to let the person interviewed do most of the talking, and be alert for striking details or up-to-date commentary on your chosen topic.

When the interview is completed, you should thank the person interviewed for the time devoted to the interview and ask for permission to quote any notable remarks. In the speech outline, you should record the interview with the name of the person consulted, the date and place, and if your instructor so desires, some identifying code such as "Professor Wilkes is chairperson of Microbiology and Clinical Medicine." This information helps bring the evidence to life and make it credible. If the data are from a class lecture, say so. "Lecture notes, Microbiology 177, lecture by A. J. Floyd, M.D., January 19, 1984." You must accurately document the essential information gathered and completely identify the source of that information, just as specifically as you do published information.

RECORDING DETAILS AND SOURCES

Most students learn in their written composition classes that full documentation of major papers is required. It is wise to offer the same backing for a speech. If you apply the footnote and bibliography styles you learned in composition classes to your speeches, the instructor will perceive you as careful, intellectually honest and rigorous, and anxious to secure support. Although sources are extremely important in persuasive and argumentative speaking, it is wise to assume that they are needed in informative speaking as well. Following is a brief description of a practical way of retaining information gathered in the library, in lectures, and in interviews.

The key to efficient utilization of time and energy is to use 3″ × 5″ note cards (or some other size if more convenient). Some people like to use half sheets of paper. Take an ample supply, of say 20 or 30 cards, to the lecture, library, or office. On each card, enter *just one idea or concept*. There is a strong temptation to save the cost of cards by cramming more than one idea onto each card. This is false economy. The whole point of the card is to insert one idea, which can then represent one entry in the eventual outline. If you make, say 30 cards, and if each card genuinely contains only one idea, you can then shift these cards about on a table top until they are arranged into an outline. You can indicate indentation by pushing some cards to the right of others. The cards at the extreme left then indicate main ideas, while those pushed to the right become subordinate ideas in the outline. The farther to the right the cards are pushed, the less significant details they are.

The information you gather tends not to fall conveniently into a mold upon which you have already decided. Instead, it emerges in words conditioned by the views of many people. You have to match up material from diverse sources and shape it into a convincing and coherent plan for a speech. To make that process easier, remember to put *just one idea on a card*. In addition, you should also put some identifier in one corner of each card. For example, all cards recorded from an interview with a resource person we will call Professor Ross, interviewed as an expert source, might contain the word "Ross" or the letter "R." You might also add an arbitrary number to show the order of ideas from the interview, if that order matters to you. To illustrate further, suppose that during the interview with Professor Ross, you found nine ideas worth recalling for your speech. Then you would take at least nine notes and have nine or more cards. Each card then has on it the quoted information, plus the symbol *Ross*, and a number representing the original order of ideas from Ross.

Similarly, if you go to the library, check out a book for perhaps an hour or two, and take notes in the library, each card ought to have either a single idea or perhaps a table of data on it, a symbol indicating the author or a shortened title, and the page number on which the ideas or table is found. If you can follow this simple discipline, you may save many hours of preparation time. Each note card then contains one idea, an identifying symbol to remind you of the exact source quoted, and the page number. Figure 3–3 is an example of a *note card*.

You may end up with many note cards representing many different books consulted, interviews, and the like. To avoid confusion, you should also fill out another kind of card—a *bibliography card*—which contains only the complete information for a single book or interview or magazine article. The point of this kind of card is to furnish you with a ready-made bibliography (list of sources consulted). Every source consulted should have just one card, filled out completely. Essential to record on the bibliography card are the author of the book, the title of the book, the city of publication, the publisher, and the date. (Remember that you already entered the page numbers and an identifying symbol on the note cards.) Figure 3–4 is an example of a bibliography card.

Now let us review briefly. Suppose you go to the library and read three books. You should immediately write down full information for each book that

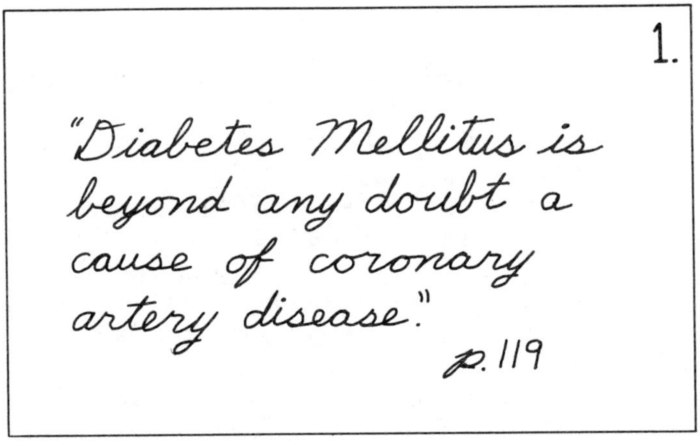
1.
"Diabetes Mellitus is beyond any doubt a cause of coronary artery disease."
p. 119

Figure 3-3

you find useful. You enter the author, title, city, publisher, and date on a card for each book. You now have three cards. Let the first book of the three be numbered source 1, the second one source 2, and the third source 3. Every time you take notes from book number 1, put that number on a corner of your *note cards*. For example, assume that you are reading source 1 and that you find a valuable idea on page 77 of that book. Your note card should have the idea or a quotation, the symbol 1 or an abbreviation of the source, and the page number (see Figure 3–5).

So far, then, you have three bibliography cards and one note card, which contains an idea from source number 1, page 77. *Every additional note card from source 1 should have the same symbol*, plus the page number. If you follow

Figure 3-4

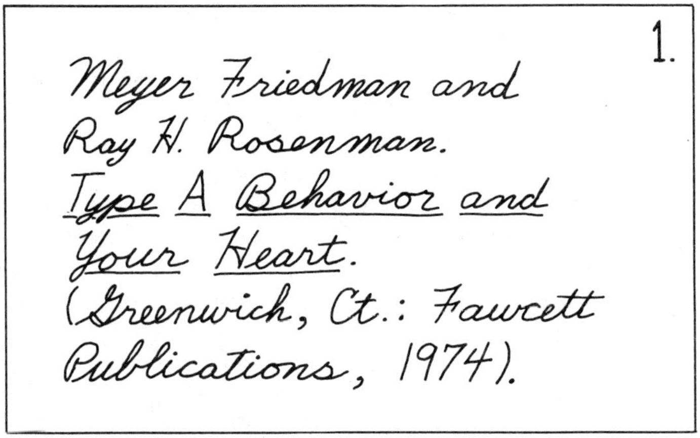
1.
Meyer Friedman and Ray H. Rosenman. Type A Behavior and Your Heart. (Greenwich, Ct.: Fawcett Publications, 1974).

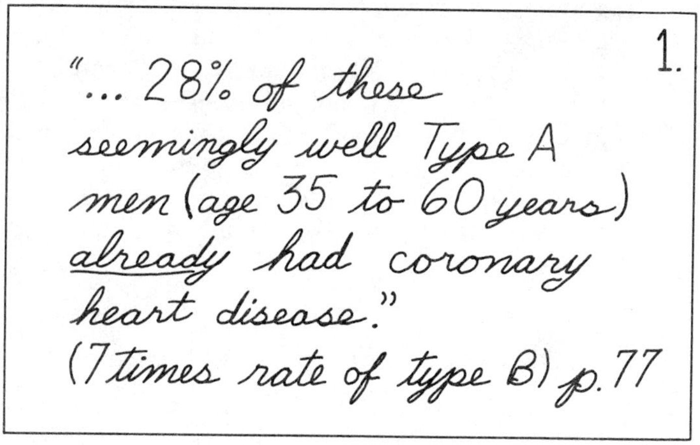

"... 28% of these seemingly well Type A men (age 35 to 60 years) already had coronary heart disease." (7 times rate of type B) p. 77   1.

Figure 3-5

this pattern on every note card, you will not have to go back to the library to verify sources. You have complete information for every source you used on the bibliography cards and you have a note card for every idea you plan to use. In addition, if your teacher wants you to use footnotes to document each idea, all you need to do is look back at your note cards and the information is readily available. The note cards give exact page numbers and the bibliography card shows all other information.

Although this method might seem time consuming and fussy, it is actually very time saving. Once complete, you have in effect a complete bibliography and all the information for your outline. It remains necessary only to shift the cards about until you have produced a cogent outline. Simply copy the outline from the arranged cards. Alphabetize the bibliography cards and copy them onto a single sheet of paper. This sheet will then comprise a formal bibliography which you can attach to your outline.

Another advantage of preparing your outline in this manner is that you might readily see that your table-top outline is incomplete—that it shows major gaps in essential information. You might realize that a single session in the library is not enough to get all your needed information. You may need to reinforce your own ideas with expert opinions. Thus, you may need to make another trip to the library, record new information and new bibliography cards, and fill in the gaps in your trial outline.

COMMON PATTERNS OF DEVELOPMENT

When your purpose and thesis are absolutely clear, you are ready to turn your attention to the message *structure*—that is, the exact choice of form or pattern your speech will follow in order for you to achieve your purpose. You have quite a wide range of choices of how to develop your chosen topic. Not every pattern is appropriate for all topics, however, and common sense will dictate which ones you can eliminate. The following discussion of some types of patterns presents some options to help you choose just the right pattern for a given purpose and topic. Often, choosing an unusual and unexpected approach to a topic will credit you with greater skill and creativity than most people would display, and at the same time will motivate listeners to attend to your talk with greater interest. In all cases, however, it is wise to ensure clarity above all.

Time Order or Chronological Pattern

This familiar pattern has the advantage of leading listeners along a train of thought with a built-in coherence that some other patterns lack. It is adaptable to many situations and even though often used, it is durable and safe for a wide range of topics. The central plan is merely to report and develop each main idea as events occurred in real time. An example of an historical speech delivered in a chronological pattern follows: "First, there was not enough money to pay for war expenses in 1918. To pay its debts, Germany imposed high taxes and devalued its currency. Next, because everything was inflated in price, a depression set in during the 1920s. Then, as inflation, depression, and unemployment grew, the Germans grew desperate. At the peak of the Depression, in 1932, conditions were just right for the rise of Adolph Hitler and the Nazi party. At last, Hitler took over and launched the Second World War with the cooperation of his demoralized people, who at last saw hope."

Cause-Effect Patterns

Careful examination of the preceding example reveals that simultaneously with the chronological development there is a superimposed pattern of stating a situation (cause) which leads to another subsequent situation (effect). The defeated, demoralized, and bankrupt Germans (situation 1, or cause) accepted the diabolical leader Hitler in their desperation and launched a terrible world war (situation 2, or effect). As in this case, a cause-effect pattern may go through several stages, wherein one cause leads to an effect, which in turn causes another effect and is its cause, and so on. As you might infer, it is quite possible to begin a speech with an effect and trace that effect out to its cause or causes, or vice versa. If you begin with the question, for example, "How could an intelligent, industrious, and productive Christian nation such as Germany launch a cruel, cynical, and destructive scourge on humanity as they did in the Second World War?" the pattern is inverted: It becomes an effect-cause pattern which can be equally effective. To use such a pattern, you would state the description of the effect and then give its causes.

Problem-Solution Order

The problem-solution order is a variant of the chronological pattern. In this pattern, you would present a problem, perhaps describe its origin and symptoms, and then show what attempts to solve it are under way. A description of the present status of the problem then leads to a statement of an actual or proposed solution. For instance, if your purpose is to inform listeners on the new withholding laws for income tax applied to your staff, you might want to choose a problem-solution order rather than the more obvious chronological order. Following, in brief tabular form, is a contrast of the two patterns:

CHRONOLOGICAL ORDER

1. First main point: For several years, we have held out tax according to a formula to which you have grown accustomed.

2. Second main point: This formula has resulted in the taxes being withheld ending up quite close to the actual tax you owe at the end of the year.

3. Third main point: The new tax table may result in our underestimating your tax and forcing you to produce a large tax payment and penalty.

4. Fourth main point: You can prevent this awkward demand by individually checking with the payroll division and filing a new W-4 form.

PROBLEM-SOLUTION ORDER

1. First main point: The new tax laws you have read about will produce a large income-tax deficit which you may find hard to pay.

2. Second main point: The company is bound by a formula for withholding your tax, and we expect that you will owe a larger tax than our tables will allow us to withhold.

3. Third main point: Because a sudden large tax bill may be painful or impossible for you to pay at tax time, we have a plan you might wish to use so that your taxes due will be small, as in past years.

4. Fourth main point: To use the plan I have described, see the payroll officer on an individual basis within the next three weeks.

Note that the two patterns permit use of exactly the same facts, but the second outline stresses the company's innocence in creating the problem and offers a direct redress of the problem. It would be possible to use either structure in presenting a speech on the topic, of course, and the choice of the best one might depend upon how much emphasis you wished to put on the company's apparent concern for its employees.

The problem-solution pattern is a typical way in which speakers can "adapt information" to particular audiences. There is nothing shady or dishonest in this kind of adaptation, for there is no intent to deceive anyone or to misrepresent ideas. The great educator and philosopher John Dewey spelled out this pattern in detail in his book, *How We Think*. Dewey's model is so important for problem solving that a digest of it is included in Chapter 10.

Spatial Order

Spatial order, or arrangement by place, is a less frequently used pattern which can add freshness to some topics. Rather than describe events in the order that they happened in time, you might choose to report them by geographical position. For example, in a talk on the effects of the Six-Day War, rather than reporting what happened on day 1, then on day 2, then on day 3, and so on, you might choose to say that on day 1 the following event occurred. In Haifa, this reaction occurred. In Egypt, that reaction followed. Meanwhile in London, another significant result happened. As London reacted in a given way, Paris behaved in another. Washington took such and such a position, while Moscow denounced the warlike Capitalists again. Time becomes subsidiary to place when you present such an arrangement of events. Often you create quite a dramatic effect by using the space orientation instead of the more obvious time order.

Topical Order

Topical order, or arrangement by natural divisions of a topic, is another common pattern which is quite useful when neither time sequence nor space arrangement is particularly important. For example, a speech on a concept or abstraction would not require any reference to time or space orientation. In fact, speeches on topics such as "parity," "indemnification," "balloon mortgages," or "variable annuities" would probably not utilize time or space order effectively. The topics might be divided into logical components, each of which would be discussed in turn. For example, balloon mortgages as a topic might be discussed under three or four headings, such as: (1) comparison with conventional mortgages; (2) effects of short-term, high interest rates; (3) effects of large balance-due at end of loan term; and (4) effects of refinancing at unpredictable interest rates.

The central issue in choosing the topical-order pattern over other alternatives is whether clarity and precision of statement can be better served by removing considerations of time and space or by using one (or even both) of them.

Free Association

Free association, or a stream-of-consciousness pattern, is not very useful for informative and persuasive speech. It is mentioned here only because you might occasionally encounter it. In free association, a person says something to catch attention. Then, whatever was said suggests something else, which is also said. That idea, in turn, brings to mind yet something else, and so on. The ideas may have nothing in common, and the result is a very incoherent speech. Occasionally this pattern is used when understanding is likely to be intuitive, if it occurs at all. Sometimes—in speeches to entertain, for example—this pattern can be useful for satirical effect. It can also be used for serious commentary on matters which, if treated by other patterns, would command little attention. The very outlandish nature of the incoherence makes it temporarily appealing.

Note, however, that using free association is sometimes risky; someone listening might easily conclude that the speaker is demented or drunk. Nevertheless, writers such as Ionesco, Kafka, and James Joyce have artistically developed such apparent incoherence in plays and stories which do reach high levels of expressiveness.

DETERMINANTS OF FORM

Having chosen your topic, your thesis statement, your general purpose, and an appropriate pattern of development, you probably realize that all of the decisions you have made are interdependent. That is, you have to know what to say before you can structure it, but you also have to know whom you are addressing before you choose a topic and form. Thus, even though your own personal skills and limitations are important factors when you are preparing a speech, your choice of a topic and a pattern of development also depend on the particular audience and situation.

A speech, then, is the outcome of considerations made from a multitude of possible choices. The final presentation is the result of many estimates and predictions. You have to imagine what outcome you desire and take a series of steps to make the real outcome match the desired, predicted one. With experience you can come closer to predicting the likely outcome of all the choices you make for a presentation.

Let us now consider some further details about speakers and their audiences, particularly some differences between classroom speeches and speakers and real-life talks and speakers.

Student Speakers and "Real" Speakers

In the classroom situation, students usually have an advantage that they do not appreciate: they receive directions on what formal type of speech they are to give and how long it is to be. A typical assignment might be to give an informative speech six minutes long on some significant event or process. The time limit and the description of the task save the student perhaps hours of painful struggle in deciding on the exact nature of the talk. The purpose, the most likely pattern of development (such as chronological order), and even the probable thesis may be suggested by the assignment. For example, if a student is to speak on Safe Disposal of Atomic Waste, a limited number of choices have to be made and the research necessary to prepare the talk is definite and limited. But speeches expected in real job-related or social situations may be considerably more difficult because little specific direction is given for the talks.

However, even though college students' speech assignments specify definite lengths, purposes, and audience, and thus solve some problems, these speakers, as all others, must still conduct an audience analysis. Fortunately, students are in the classroom every day and thus furnish opportunities for potential speakers to discover the audience members' likes and moods, their prejudices, the distribution of various majors, and obvious factors such as sex, age, and race. If you are planning a speech, you should still try to find out everything possible about the particular classroom audience you are to address, artificial as it may seem to be. The members still have differences in tastes, senses of humor, skills, interests, and hobbies, all of which may help you choose ideas and examples that will appeal to the listeners and make your speech successful. Addressing a class is in some ways artificial, but you ought not to dismiss it too quickly as such, for it furnishes a unique opportunity to study a group over time. It, like each student speaker, is constantly changing. Its members get to know each other and each person may establish expectations about the other speakers' abilities, skills, tastes, hobbies, and likely success. The opportunity to study one audience in great depth over time is valuable, and the "captive" nature of the same listeners for each successive speech in a course is a small price to pay for the depth of audience study possible in the classroom. By contrast, even the most strenuous efforts to learn about another audience in the "real world" may produce very little information.

AUDIENCE ANALYSIS

Because each speech is unique and its specific audience dictates to some extent what must be said, an effective speaker is sensitive to each audience he or she faces. Rarely is there occasion for you to speak to a truly universal audience, one which includes all kinds of people, evenly distributed by age, sex, politics, religion, race, and interests. Most commonly you will address an audience that shares much in common. A college classroom, while it does contain both sexes and perhaps many religions, is still unified by what it has in common. The students are all likely to be more liberal, more affluent, more uniform in age, and more critical then a general audience. Even within so limited an audience as a classroom of 20 students, however, there may be significant differences in religion, politics, background, and hobbies to furnish an alert speaker with both warnings and opportunities concerning the speaking situation. You do not want to offend, insult, or ignore anyone. At the same time you do want to talk about matters that will interest and challenge your listeners. The examples you choose to illustrate the main ideas should appeal to several of the specific audience's probable interests. Similarly, the introduction and conclusion should gain attention and end the talk in a satisfying manner.

The Ethics of Speechmaking

As a speaker, you should first consider your audience carefully, and then you can select the best wording and style to maximize the impact of the speech you are preparing. Some listeners may not immediately like what you think they ought to hear. You have a duty to adjust the message, in consideration of the audience's needs and feelings, and to gradually lead the audience into a more receptive frame of mind that will give the message the fair hearing and best chance of success that it merits.

Some people object that "adjusting" ideas and people are offensive and dishonest tactics. This argument has raged in the pages of history and books on rhetoric for 2500 years. Plato complained that rhetoric was akin to cookery: One puts together different ingredients each time an occasion to speak (or cook) arises. Plato felt that rhetoric was too often used to make bad cases look good and to make one's opponents look bad when their ideas were good.[1] To come to terms with this objection, you have to consider the art a tool, like a knife or gun which can furnish us game to eat, protect us from criminals, or help us commit crimes ourselves. It is not the rhetoric or the knife that is good or evil; it is the use to which each is put. When we talk about adjusting ideas or people, we are talking about acting ethically in the best interests of the audience. As a simple example, imagine a doctor visiting a high school classroom to speak on The Dangers of Smoking. The students who smoke know from past experience that many doctors oppose smoking, and they do not want to hear any dreary advice. Suppose that the speaker prepares the students by beginning with an unexpected, indirect approach and charms them with his or her personal style. The speaker can adjust the message that smoking increases risks of disease by taking the unexpected emphasis that smoking drives away smart men and women, and appealing just to teenagers' vanity instead of their fear of disease. The speaker has not lied, distorted the facts, nor withheld essential truths on the other side of the argument. However, to make up statistics, threaten loss of masculinity, or make claims beyond medical knowledge would all be unethical. Even though it would be exerting pressure in the best interests of students, such a speech would still be dishonest. The borderline between explanation and "pressure" is unclear. The whole issue of ethics is a complicated one, and although we do not wish to evade its issues, we are concerned here with describing strategies. It should suffice to say that everyone knows that a skill can be turned to illegal or immoral ends, but ideally that tactic should be avoided. Of course, we hope you will use your persuasion skills for the public good, for the advancement of society, and for your deserved speaking success. Some of the exercises at the end of this chapter help to explore this difficult and tricky matter of determining the limits of ethical speech strategy.

Dimensions of an Audience

When you are preparing a speech, you need to know several facts about who is to attend and how the listeners will *probably* respond. This notion of probable response is the heart of audience analysis. Following is a list of some terms descriptive of audiences and some common assumptions about what they mean:

Age: Young people tend to be more liberal, open-minded, open to experimentation, optimistic, and physically active. They seem to like humor, adventure, sports, and activity.

Sex: The chief issue here is persuasibility. Conventional findings of the experimental literature and personal observation indicate that women are more easily persuaded by men than by other women. Men are not highly persuasible by people they regard as their peers or inferiors, but both men and women tend to be persuaded by their superiors. The issue of persuasibility is not clear, however. A mixed audience of men and women will usually behave differently from one composed of just men or just women. For example, a mixed audience is generally more neutral than one composed of all men or all women. Note, however, that this depends a great deal on the topic of the particular speech. That is, an all-female audience might react quite differently from an all-male audience on such topics as punishment of rapists, abortion laws, or maternity leaves from jobs.[2]

Religion: Although we ordinarily do not pry into people's religious affiliations, sometimes the locale or volunteered information will tell us that a sizable portion of an audience is one or another preference. You should be aware if everyone in the audience is of the same religion, or if many religions are represented. Usually a speaker tries to avoid knowingly offending anyone or pitting one sect against another. If you stumble into an offensive statement or a stereotype, your whole case can be weakened even if the blunder had nothing to do with the issues of your speech. It is probably best to avoid religious jokes, stereotypes about various religions, or opinions on dogma because any conflicts are not going to be resolved by the speech. If you know that your listeners have no religious beliefs at all, that fact can be significant too.

Socioeconomic background: You should consider the social standing and apparent wealth of your listeners during speech preparation and during delivery. If the listeners are all poor, uneducated workers, you should adapt your examples and vocabulary to matters they can understand and relate to. If you address a relatively affluent, professional group, such as a reunion of Princeton graduates, you must make different vocabulary and topical adjustments. If the audience is all alike (*homogeneous*), your using in-jokes and references to shared experiences may enhance your reception. If, on the other hand, the audience is mixed (*het-*

erogeneous), and one part is well educated and another part is not, and some members are rich and others are poor, then for the best effect, you must tailor your vocabulary and images accordingly.

Size: A large audience is generally harder to address than a smaller one. All kinds of adjustments are necessary: you have to speak louder, use a wider pitch range, speak more slowly, pause more, and emphasize key ideas more pointedly than with a small audience. An audience of 15, compared with one of 100, is quicker to respond, gets ideas more clearly, expects a conversational quality, and likes close eye contact. Audiences of over 50 persons begin to show crowd behavior, including slower response, somewhat duller wits, and even unruliness. Much nonsense has been written about "bovine crowds" and how to control them. In this text we assume that you will rarely have occasion to address very large crowds. Consult the list of readings at the end of this chapter if you do have to speak to a group of over 100.[3]

Adapting to an Audience

All human beings share needs for essentials, such as water, food, clothing, shelter, and companionship. Less intense but still very important needs are those for achievement and recognition, sex gratification, adventure, and entertainment. Common sense tells us that individuals attend to their most pressing needs before they address less urgent ones. What may not be so obvious is that all of these needs are potent sources of appeal for our talks. No matter how trivial a topic or a speech situation might seem, if you can work into your talk appeals to people's basic needs (and fears that those needs might not be met), you are appealing to universals. Any audience, anywhere, any time, regardless of age, sex, religion, and race responds to such appeals, for they seem to command attention at a primitive level. If you can induce your audience to identify with the most fundamental, urgent needs of all people, it will apparently become more involved with your speech and with you as a speaker.

These universal needs were systematized into a convenient hierarchy by Maslow.[4] Maslow envisioned a pyramid whose wide base was animal needs such as self-preservation, on which stood higher-level needs such as comforts and, eventually, even higher-level needs such as social recognition and self-fulfillment. None of the higher-level needs is as insistent as those at the base, but once basic creature needs are met, then those at a higher level become more the focus of attention. When someone is starving to death, for example, completing a painting is less important than is finding food. After adequate food is located, however, the impulse to express art can again return intensely.

It is not difficult to find ways to work some reference to the many needs we all share into just about any speech. Such appeals can be quite forceful as examples, attention-gaining devices, analogies, or means of enhancing audience involvement. You might find thirst, for instance, hard to work into a speech urging listeners to give blood, but if you reflect for a moment you might realize how you could include another of the basic needs, such as the instinct for social approval or altruistic impulses. Similarly, you could use a conflict between two needs, such as self-preservation and honor, to create a stirring image in a speech.

Other, more subtle internal forces can also be called into play in an audience. People are not like blank pages onto which new information is written each time they encounter a persuader. People have enough stored experience from merely living that they tend to respond over and over in the same way every time a similar situation arises. Children afraid of snakes may carry the fear into adult life, and may scream in panic if they happen to encounter a Gaboon Viper or harmless garter snake. The same pattern of reaction can occur with abstractions such as language, concepts, or ideals. For example, every time someone says *Democrat*, an acquaintance might frown, mutter, or show signs of disapproval. Another might become angry and utter profanity every time a door-to-door sales representative comes around at dinnertime. Another might consistently "clam up" and say nothing whenever religion is brought into a conversation. When you are planning a speech, you must keep all these factors in mind, so you can adapt your talk to the audience appropriately.

Occasionally an audience's perception of *you* can operate as a disadvantage. Listeners may have such faith in you as a potential speaker, because of your reputation or past performance, that they give you little help and assume that you will take a decisive role in the presentation. They may even feel that it is insulting to give you a topic or helpful guidelines for the occasion. The following discussion can help you adapt to this difficult speechmaking situation.

Suppose that someone asks you to talk before a specific group at a specific time on anything you wish. This invitation is frightening because it gives you no direction about the expectations of the group or the topics that will appeal to that group. When this kind of request comes to you, assuming that you are willing or obligated to speak, you should immediately begin trying to get ideas for your talk. Find out all you possibly can about the group and the occasion. Then assess the group's expectations about you. Does the person who contacted you want a serious talk or an amusing after-dinner speech? Why were you asked? What is your relationship to the group or the occasion? Although it is not flattering to our egos, some invitations are desperate pleas to substitute us for some other unavailable speaker the group really wanted or to fill up lots of time on some occasion which was loosely planned or for which there is not really much of an agenda. If you are asked to fill in more than an hour and a half, you may be in difficulty. It is very hard to hold attention much longer than an hour, even with a fascinating topic.

After you find out why you have been chosen to speak, you should begin to think about whether the reason given is justified. Do you feel any particular identification with the group which would lead it to choose you? Has the group heard about you or enjoyed previous speeches of yours? If so, you probably have a tremendous advantage, for expectations will be high and you are a known quantity to at least some listeners. But beware of those occasions when only the haziest notion of your skills led some unfortunate program chairperson to grab the first soul willing to speak to the group. The audience will be civil, but it may find an unknown speaker too technical, or geared too high above its capacity to follow with enjoyment, or just the opposite—too simplistic or repetitious of what everyone already knows. Such a situation is embarrassing for everybody. Moral: Know as precisely as possible who is to hear you, what their probable interests and educational levels are, and what they probably want to hear from you. The chairperson's asking you to talk on *anything* might imply that you are so well regarded that your every word is precious; a more realistic assessment, however, is that the chairperson has no idea what would succeed with the particular audience and thereby passes the responsibility to choose on to you. Your only recourse in such a situation is to pump the contact person until you get an idea of who will be present, how many will attend, what the occasion is, and why listeners are present to hear you.

Attitudes

The tendency to repeat the same pattern of response each time a similar cue or stimulus is presented is called having an *attitude*. Everyone has attitudes about an immense variety of topics: We hold attitudes on religion, politics, or government. We also make judgments about numerous matters: We tend to compare new situations to the more or less ideal, consistent rules by which we have lived and we respond to other people and situations accordingly. These patterns are called *values*. If someone always dislikes profanity, never likes religious conversations, always turns off classical music, watches no X-rated films, or drinks cognac instead of brandy, we can say that we understand some of that person's values.

Values can be organized into a more or less consistent pattern called a *system of values*. Well-balanced, healthy people usually have such systems, whereas socially maladjusted people who are wildly inconsistent seem to be troubled by clashes among their values. For example, many wardens have reported that even the most violent and vicious criminals still exhibit codes of values; new prisoners known to have committed crimes against children, for example, are shunned, reviled, and denied places in the prison society. In fact, a given felon might be in most ways devoutly religious, a patriot, and a model parent and spouse, but some inconsistent value (such as disregard for an institution's money) might lead to embezzling large sums with no apparent qualms of conscience. Such a value system is said to be upset. Those values concerning honesty, usually demonstrated in dealings with friends and family, are not consistent with those held toward an impersonal entity, such as a bank or business. An embezzler might be angry with his or her boss and act out of revenge, or he or she may simply have a gap in maturation wherein all large companies are seen as fair game for fraud. We would not be surprised if such a person overstated insurance claims, for such behavior would be consistent with these sorts of opinions about companies.

As an alert speaker, you should try to fathom the value systems and attitudes of the members of your audience, who give many clues to what will be sacred to them and what will offend them. You must appeal to those needs, attitudes, and values which seem pertinent in some way to the topic of your presentation. Similarly, you should avoid addressing those matters known to be divisive, offensive, and unnecessarily provocative of hostility. This process of examining your audience, predicting their likely responses to your ideas, and eventually choosing and adjusting your ideas to match their shared legitimate needs and attitudes is a necessary step in thoughtful speech preparation.

Sometimes your profession or qualifications may make you attractive to an audience. If you are an attorney and your listeners are seeking someone to interpret new laws authoritatively, then your talk had best not be too humorous, for the listeners will not know what is serious and what is entertaining, and they might be resentful. If you are a banker and your inquiries reveal that a group wants an explanation of bond market fluctuations, your professional capability becomes a powerful device for you to satisfy the needs, appeal to the attitudes, and secure belief among members of the audience.

TOPIC LISTS

Following are seven lists of challenging, interesting topics for class use, grouped by broad professional interests. Refer to these when trying to choose an appropriate topic for a speech. The intention of these lists is to provoke thought, not simply to present you with pat topics. It is assumed that you will vary, contradict, or refine any topics you choose. The sometimes smart-alecky tone here is not necessarily desirable, but is used to show the range of tones and attitudes you might choose to adopt.

GENERAL INFORMATION

1. Learning a computer language and its uses.
2. Changing careers in midstream.
3. The New Right—its fundamental philosophy.
4. The ultimate do it yourselfer—building your own airplane.
5. Easy ways to become rich.
6. The UFO controversy, or do not touch the ET's.
7. Life on other planets.
8. What's a baronet (or the English peerage system)?

9. Returning to college after retirement.
10. The good life, or how to live well on peanuts.

FINANCIAL AND BANKING

1. Good opportunities for the small investor.
2. The crazy bond market.
3. Keep your money in your home town!
4. The future for new-home builders.
5. Futures investments you can trust.
6. Penny stocks for small-time investors.
7. Your friendly mutual fund—Dr. Jekyll or Mr. Hyde?
8. Junk metals, junk bonds, and junk stocks.
9. Gold and silver linings for your future?
10. U.S. Bonds and other U.S. obligations as investments.
11. Pesetas, Krugerrands, and other coins as opportunities.
12. Art objects, stamps, and coins as investment.
13. Real estate as an inflation hedge.
14. Profits sometimes grow on trees—Christmas trees.
15. How to succeed as a slum landlord, or rejuvenating old houses.
16. Famous financial traps for the unwary investor.

LEGAL AND MEDICAL TOPICS

1. Five ways to lengthen your life, beginning today.
2. What to do when somebody sues you.
3. The increase in the marriage rate, and what it means.
4. Terrorism and the medical profession.
5. How to reduce automobile insurance rates.
6. Why you should know all about CPR.
7. Dealing with common household emergencies.
8. Your legal rights and obligations when accidents occur.
9. How to write to the government and get something done.
10. Fifteen lawsuits about to fall on you in your home.
11. Unnecessary operations—facts and myths.
12. Your legal rights in the scam—the state of consumer protection.
13. Present trends in medical assistance for the aged.
14. What lawyers and courts do, and why.

MANUFACTURING

1. The outlook for (your favorite product) in the next 10 years.
2. Automation, unemployment, and industrial growth.
3. Competition from Japanese, German, and English technology.

4. The threat of third-world labor in high-technology manufacturing.
5. Trade unions as the conservative element in manufacturing.
6. Critical metals supply in the foreseeable future.
7. Recycling (paper, metal, oil) as a secondary supply by 1988.
8. Environmental impact of some local plant: the first 5 years.
9. Expansion of local employment in the next 10 years.
10. Benefits of the ____ plant for the community: the forgotten equation.

SERVICES AND UTILITIES

1. What Ma Bell is up to in your town: new equipment, new service.
2. Why power bills are so high, and what you can do to control them.
3. Gas or electricity? Advice to new-home builders.
4. Insulation in the attic—savings or ripoff?
5. Why you should not move to the sun belt.
6. Power savings: incentive plans available here and now.
7. New concepts in garbage disposal.
8. Why water costs two cents a gallon (or whatever the local cost).
9. How to use and use and use your travel agent—for free.
10. Why PBS radio stations ask for money every 6 months.
11. Cable TV for your town—soon and cheap.
12. What's left to tax? Some new ideas to build revenue.

RELIGION

1. Sin: yesterday and today.
2. The afterlife—is it still available?
3. Modern notions of Hell.
4. Has technology destroyed the prospects of salvation?
5. Modern common sense and biblical common sense.
6. Heaven as peaceful repose or dynamic fulfillment?
7. Marriage today within religious ideals.
8. Implications of scientific advances on dogma.
9. Reconciling our views on Saturn and Satan.
10. The ethical lifestyle, or what if religion was wrong?
11. A radical view of the afterlife, reincarnation, and Heaven.
12. How to help someone with a terminal illness.
13. Arming yourself against tragedy.
14. When life cheats you—how to seek help.
15. The ultimate conflagration: who and why?

16. Is a new religion timely?

17. War as a religious rite of purification and rebirth.

POLITICAL, CIVIC, OR PUBLIC SERVICE

1. How to initiate change in this state.

2. The intelligent person's guide to voting.

3. Why courts fail.

4. The five worst problems of your local police department.

5. What bail means.

6. How to spend a night in jail and keep your cool.

7. What you must tell your children about drugs.

8. The Kool Kat's Dope on Booze: 50,000 a year dead.

9. How you can save your school board half a million (etc.).

10. The forgotten gold mine—your public library.

11. That's right, your vote doesn't count, but . . .

12. Seven tips for your income tax return.

13. Support your local (theatre, playground, park district, pool)!

14. How to remove crooks from elective offices.

15. Using what's available—your (agricultural extension, forest district, park, public library, etc.)

16. How the police can help you or harass you, and why.

17. Extradition: expensive justice.

18. The scandal of unfunded retirement plans.

EXERCISES

1. List ten topics on which you would like to hear someone give a talk. Do not limit yourself to obvious topics but seek those which might answer definite questions such as this: Has recent space research produced any evidence *increasing* the probability of life on other planets?

2. For each of the following topics, first narrow the subject. Then narrow it again. Finally, choose three or four main points that might be appropriate to develop the topic into a speech.

    space exploration   economic growth   career planning

3. Present three topics to a fellow student, who in turn gives you three topics. See how many levels of specificity (narrowing) you can produce for each topic. Example: *Retirement:* Social Security; financing Social Security; alternatives to raising FICA taxes; gasoline taxes as support for Social Security.

4. Choose three of the topics you produced in exercise 1, and for each one state a specific purpose and three main points.

5. Bring to class and be prepared to briefly sketch two different methods of developing a topic such as Medicare. For example, you might give an historical survey of Medicare's problems leading up to the present crisis—the fear that the system may collapse. This would be chronological. You might also use a topical order, and begin with a discussion of the essence of the law, how it is financed, how it is vulnerable, and who is covered.

6. Search newspapers and magazines for stories in which you feel that some unethical information or distortions of truth occur. You might also find advertisements which seem to make claims using rhetorical strategies which encourage mistakes among readers. Bring to class stories and ads containing such strategies and state on what basis you think the claims are unethical.

7. We have discussed mainly distortions of information through assertion. Find or recall from your experience examples of information's being distorted by omission of details or description. Is withholding information just as unethical as faking it? Discuss.

8. Prepare a 3-minute talk on the nature of the ideal audience. Do not merely fantasize that this group would agree and approve anything you say. Try, rather, to: (1) describe a realistic situation; (2) state the topic and occasion; and (3) describe the nature of the audience in detail (sex, age, etc.).

9. Prepare a 3- to 5-minute talk on the responsibility of consumers to know how to protect themselves from evil rhetoric. Is there any such responsibility? In other words, does a member of society have a duty to learn logic, strategies, and fallacies which occur so often in politics, commerce, and even education?

SELECTED READINGS

THEODORE CLEVENGER, *Audience Analysis* (Indianapolis: Bobbs Merrill, 1969).

JAMES W. GIBSON AND MICHAEL S. HANNA, *Audience Analysis: A Programmed Approach to Receiver Behavior* (Englewood Cliffs, N.J.: Prentice-Hall, 1976).

RODERICK P. HART, GUSTAVE W. FRIEDRICH, AND BARRY BRUMMETT, *Public Communication*, 2nd ed. (New York: Harper & Row, 1983), Chapter 4, pp. 75–105.

PAUL D. HOLTZMAN, *Psychology of Speakers' Audiences* (Glenview, Ill.:. Scott, Foresman, 1970).

MICHAEL OSBORN, *Speaking in Public* (Boston: Houghton Mifflin, 1982), Chapters 7 and 8, pp. 141–181.

Topic Choice

JOSEPH A. DE VITO, *The Elements of Public Speaking* (New York: Harper & Row, 1981), Appendix A, pp. 359–368.

ALBERT J. VASILE AND HAROLD K. MINTZ, *Speak with Confidence*, 3rd ed. (Boston: Little, Brown, 1983), pp. 186–187.

chapter 4

Choosing
the Main Points
for Your Speech

Once you have chosen a topic that promises to appeal to the probable audience, the next step is to concentrate on the form or pattern of developing that subject. Of course, your choice of a topic is a major step and to some extent commits you to a limited variety of ways to develop the speech. For example, if you choose to speak on the importance of some major historical event such as The Nuremberg Trials or The First Moon Landing, you will have to make some decisions about structure, but you will also be more or less bound to explain what preceded the event, what it was all about, and what it led to. In other words, for these topics a time-oriented pattern of presentation would be most useful to keep listener attention and to enhance understanding. On the other hand, if your chosen topic is Photosynthesis or Ethnocentrism, the time-oriented pattern would be less useful, and you might find a topical-oriented pattern better. Further, if the topic is something best considered first in one place and then in others, a spatial-oriented pattern of development might be the best. For example, a speech on Hopes for a New Century: New Year's, 2000 might predict reactions to the beginning of the century first in Paris, then in New York, next in London, then in Berlin, and finally in Tokyo. Space or geography becomes the unifying element instead of time or divisions of a subject. In any case, choose a pattern that will keep your listeners continuously aware of your main ideas and thesis. For the just-described topic, you might be really astute and choose cities that will elicit dramatic reactions from the listeners. For instance, if you believe that more spectacular changes will occur in France than in China by the turn of the century, you might choose to omit the less interesting information or to deemphasize it. You might order the places where reactions are reported according to an increasingly violent, interesting, or colorful pattern. You should begin and end strongly. Put the most striking data early in the talk to gain attention and near the end to conclude strongly.

If you choose ideas poorly, your listeners can lose track of where your pattern is leading, what they are supposed to get out of the presentation, or what they should remember. Be aware of the power of organization to guide listeners in an orderly progression from the beginning to the end of your speeches. You have a responsibility to keep your audience clearly oriented, for by speaking to them, you are using up some of their valuable time. You should be considerate enough to use that time wisely.

STRUCTURING YOUR IDEAS

This book repeatedly emphasizes form and structure as devices to ease the stress on you as a speaker and to help listeners follow your speeches. There are two reasons for this emphasis. First, thinking about *Structure* in the abstract is important to help jostle you into the habit of always thinking of audience needs. Second, you might tend, as speakers often do, to get lost in details of the *content* after you choose a topic and concentrate on the actual wording of your speech. It is easy to lose sight of what is content and what is intent. If you become confused on this issue you are almost certain to confuse the listeners, who are using structure in order to understand the content in some particular set of relationships. In other words, the listeners subconsciously try to put a form or pattern onto whatever information they receive from a speaker in order to make sense of the presented ideas. The listeners expect certain cues or indicators of which ideas are most important, which ones need support before they can believe them, and how ideas presented in a speech are related to each other. The speaker's sense of structure or orderly relation of ideas is a crucial part of any effective public presentation. Be sure you guard against possible misunderstandings of your chosen purpose and thesis. Directly stating them early in the talk may seem blunt and obvious, yet omitting them and assuming the audience is sharp enough to figure out your specific purpose and thesis from subtle cues is an almost sure guarantee of misunderstanding. Good speakers make their intents and main ideas clear to listeners without boring them or assuming too much. If you are in doubt, it is better to be overly clear than not specific and direct in stating your purpose and thesis.

Making Strategic Choices

Imagine now a dynamic situation. Assume that you have been given or forced to choose a topic. Perhaps you used the topic lists in Chapter 3, thought up your own, or were constrained by the occasion to choose a locally hot topic. For example, if you are a police chief and you are asked to address a high-school assembly, your situation will dictate that you seek to build good will for members of the force with the people of the community. You will probably be channeled into a topic such as How You Can Help the Police Help You. In some cases you might be called in for a less pleasant talk on, say, drug laws' enforcement, student abuse of driving laws, and so on. The relationship you hold to the audience and occasion obviously narrows the possibilities for you somewhat. Experience with human nature and good judgment will probably prevent you from choosing a threatening or fear-based topic, such as You May Be Next—Auto Deaths in This County. Since the principle that fear appeals tend to backfire and fail to persuade others has been well-publicized, you as law officer know that the heavy hand is not likely to impress naive teenagers. The writer recalls witnessing several presentations to dissuade careless drivers by giving fear-inspiring talks with color slides of past accidents at various speeds. "Here is one victim in a head-on collision at 60 . . . ." The slide was impressive, but the audience reaction was so violent that the talk had little effect—listeners simply refused to accept anything so horrible as a reality in which they might be participants. At the same school, students were given an antismoking color film with built-in, none-too-gentle visual images of a complete surgical procedure for lung cancer performed at the Ochsner Clinic. The famous film caused fainting, screams, illness, withdrawal in horror, but had little effect on students toward dissuading them from smoking. In yet another school, students received a first lesson in their sex education by seeing the Army VD films, shown to shock recruits into restrained sexual activity by presenting visual details of venereal diseases in advanced stages. Nowadays we use more sophisticated and less disgusting means to persuade youth to look out for their own well-being.

Assuming that you will be more moderate in making strategic choices than these examples have illustrated, we turn now to some detailed steps for you to follow in choosing and wording the main points of a speech. Your main points should reveal the intent, the content, and the optimum pattern for your talk.

LIMITING THE NUMBER OF MAIN POINTS

One of the most easily demonstrated lessons is also one of the hardest to get across to speakers: A talk should contain from three to five main points, and *never* more, regardless of the length of the speech to be given. You might strenuously object that inherent in some topics is a distribution of genuine main points quite beyond these limits. If a topic is so constituted, then a speech may not be the best way to present it. A written report or even a manual may be better. *Audiences will not and cannot grasp exceedingly complex structures.* The overall structure of a speech is set by three considerations:

1. The decision of what goes into the introduction, body, and conclusion.
2. The choice of the optimum pattern of development.
3. The number of main points chosen to support the thesis.

Even if you meticulously observe the first two considerations, and then violate the third rule, sneaking in one or two extra points, you can quickly obfuscate your whole speech. Do not conclude that this is the same as claiming that audiences cannot grasp much. It is not. If there is much detail and a great deal of information packed into a speech, it simply has to be shaped and grouped into a pattern which the audience can grasp. If a complicated process is reduced to several arbitrary but sensible categories, then each main point itself can be reasonably complicated and still be remembered. When a speech has only a few main ideas, the audience is not likely to misperceive minor details as main points, as they might if there are too many main points.

Oddly enough, this is true whether a speech runs for an hour or for 5 minutes. Imagine a speech an hour long with five main ideas. Allowing time for the introduction and conclusion, you could expect to discuss each idea for about 10 to 12 minutes. In a five-minute talk, each idea has allotted to it probably not much more than a minute. If you double the number of main points, expecially in a short talk, a scant 30 seconds can be devoted to each point. Even in a long presentation, each point has only some 6 minutes for its consideration; if the talk is indeed complex, there is a high risk that listeners simply will not follow the talk as it progresses nor recall it when it is over.

A clever and ancient idea for dealing with this psychological fact of life is to consider a talk as a great pool of boxes containing many gifts. Suppose there are boxes of all sizes and colors and all shapes and weights. If there are fifty boxes in the pile, and these are to be distributed to all our family and friends, we need some organizing principle to deal with so many boxes. We obtain or invent bigger boxes to contain the small ones. For example, if nine of the small boxes are to go to Jan and her family in Omaha, we could get a box big enough to contain the nine gifts for Jan and her family. Another eleven boxes might go in another big box for Ted's family in Portland. Yet another dozen might be put in a box for Grandma and Uncle Bill in Fort Leavenworth, and so on. The point is that the "big boxes" are not just like the gifts themselves; they are bigger, more inclusive, and possibly invented just for this one task of shipping off a group of related gifts for specified addresses. Ideas can, by analogy, be treated somewhat the same way. When you have many tiny details which are still important to deliver, you must find a suitable main point as an appropriate container of just the right size and dimension to hold all the small ideas, like the packages.

A single extended illustration can reinforce this point: Suppose that you are explaining the advantages of a new office word processor to inexperienced workers who have never used a word processor before but who will be expected to learn to use the new one within a short time. Certain observations by users of the machine, certain comparisons with office typewriters, certain improvements in productivity, and certain changes in the attitudes of workers are known from past experience and furnish some of the ideas you want to use. You decide that the purpose of the talk is primarily to show the word processor as a benefit or reward to the office personnel and not as a mysterious new device to threaten anyone's job security. Fragmentary details begin to emerge: Not speedup. Not a threat to anyone's job. Easy for experienced typists to use. Permits more work, but with less effort and strain. Allows workers a new higher job class with incentive pay. Costs less than previous machines. Does require some learning. Is a computer, but not in the fear-inspiring sense. Typically can be mastered in three months. Pride builder, because it produces perfect copy without blots, smudges, erasures.

These details, of course, are not arranged in any coherent form as they stand. To form a speech, you must group them and use either naturally all-embracing statements to include many details or invent suitably broad statements. In this example, you might choose to say nothing at all about a possible threat: People not bright enough or adaptable enough to learn to use the machine might not find ready employment. This discordant detail is not consistent with any of the other listed details, and its omission is not treachery or a dissimulation. No company is committed to hiring the worst workers it can find. Any worker has to expect that a level of performance is defined and imposed on all employees, and fundamental leaps in level of skill are not implied by the new machine. (All this new detail, by the way, can be used should questions arise, or indeed, if you do choose to "lay it all on the line" in your basic talk.)

In any case, when grouping main points, you will discover many details that you can group together. One "package" might be the idea that within a few months the new machines will add to the pleasure and pride in each job. Having chosen this "big box" to contain subsidiary ideas, you can then talk about the details which support this assertion. When you have given details, illustrations, and reports of previous users, you are then ready to go to the next main point, or "big box." Listeners have little difficulty in understanding a talk structured in this way, with three to five main ideas, each of which includes numerous minor details. Some people actually imagine that instead of giving one big speech, they are going to give, say, four minispeeches, each complete in itself and linked together by transitions such as "Now that I have described the benefits for you, the users of word processors, I want to admit that the company expects to benefit, too, but not at your expense." Then, you can group numerous details within the broad main point. The final arrangement might look something like this, again whether for an hours' talk or a 5-minute one:

ADVANTAGES OF OUR NEW WORD PROCESSING EQUIPMENT

1. Five new *X* brand word-processor terminals and one line printer have been purchased for use in this office beginning June first.
2. All the new equipment will create an exciting, delightful revolution in accomplishing the routine tasks our secretaries have performed for years.
3. Though simple to learn and easy to use, the new equipment promises benefits for the company as well as for you, the users.
4. Long-range implications for all of us are better jobs, less drudgery, more pride, and better productivity throughout the company.

These four points are broad enough to embrace all the specific details envisioned previously, and even some more. Main points need only be general enough to embrace all the existing data, not more. For example, if point 2 were made more general, it might come out thus, with unfortunate consequences: The new equipment will revolutionize the work of the entire company. As you can see, such a point would be so general and all-embracing that it could easily be considered as a threat. Even though the statement is in fact just as true as the more specific one in the outline, it carries all kinds of implied threats in its deliberate vagueness.

In summary, choose absolutely without exception no more than five, and preferably fewer, main points, each worded so that it expresses accurately and yet broadly the conclusions a listener might reach from considering the details under it. With few main points and adequate rich detail to support each one, confusion in the audience will be minimized. As a bonus, you may find that you achieve coherence and a natural evolution of ideas. Having too many points forces you to compose a talk defensively, as if justifying every statement in a major battle. When details are grouped into a few main ideas, relatively fewer points of defense result—namely, the main points.

PRECISE WORDING OF EACH MAIN POINT

Although the preceding advice can help you to compose a speech, you still have some hard work and decision making before your speech is ready for presentation. Fortunately, overcoming each obstacle makes mastering all subsequent ones easier. The next step is to decide the exact wording of each main topic you have chosen. As hinted at previously, there is some risk of obscuring the main points by trying to include a great deal of detail under them. The task now is to so word each main point that it, taken with all the other main points, simultaneously meets several tests. First, it must be an accurate statement consistent with everything it embraces. If you say that new equipment will be a boon to the employees and a few moments later attach a qualification such as "if they see the handwriting on the wall and shape up," then you contradicted the main point by the threat in the qualification. There is nothing wrong with careful qualification, but you can qualify a statement until it is almost incomprehensible. Some advertising agencies specialize in mucking up statements so that they seem to say something, but in fact make hardly any claims at all. Consider all the qualifications of the following ad and ask yourself what exactly it promises:

> *Zot* pills can be of significant help in temporarily relieving the pain of simple headache for up to four hours when taken as directed.

Now, think about the ad. *Zot* pills *may* be of help, or they may not. This help is apparently not complete (the ad says it may be temporary) but it may be significant. Such possible, partial help is not likely to be present if there are any complications to a *simple* headache, whatever that is. In addition, any alleged help might last *an absolute maximum* of four hours, and could last anywhere from a minute or two *up to that maximum*. All this possible temporary relief from apparently trivial ills may or may not last as long as four hours and is likely *only* if you take the pills as directed; an extra one or half-dosage may result in utterly no reaction or unpredictable ones.

The purpose of the preceding discussion is not to ridicule advertisers nor to misread the claims, but rather to illustrate how clarity of thought can be muddled by artful wording. Most adults are probably so accustomed to such advertisement claims that they almost never take them seriously as medical guarantees. But the fuzziness of language and thought in such claims is communicable. We may unconsciously emulate such statements and by accident say things which simply are not true, even though the ideas seem clear and accurate as we utter them. Consider the following ambiguous statements, which can be understood in several ways depending on how they are said:

> *You can't catch a rabbit with a carrot.* Does the rabbit have a carrot or do you have a carrot as bait?
>
> *When the teacher caught Ann cheating she told her she was a failure.* Which of four events occurred? The preceding sentence could mean any one of the following:
> 1. Ann said that the teacher was a failure when the teacher caught Ann cheating on a test.
> 2. The teacher called Ann a failure for cheating.
> 3. The teacher confided that she had failed as a teacher because Ann was cheating.
> 4. Ann confessed that she was a failure when the teacher caught Ann cheating.

These sentences illustrate just a few of the traps inherent in language. People hear what we say, not always what we mean. In other words, it does not matter what you *mean* to mean; it is what people think you mean that influences them. Thus, good intentions often go unrewarded and people we mean to serve seem to turn on us. We can easily say something totally innocent in our own eyes, only to find that it appears offensive and aggressive to others. For example, imagine a management and union negotiating session. Someone says, "What are you arguing for?" intending to find out what policy the other negotiator requests. With suspicion and tempers often high in such negotiations, these words could easily be heard as equivalent to "Why are you so quarrelsome?" Either meaning is equally "true" and it might happen that both parties shared the same meaning. But if someone chose the "hostile" meaning, an unnecessary breakdown in negotiations could occur.

To ensure a precise fit between the wording of each main point and your intended ideas, you need to devote extra energy to stating ideas accurately. You must scrutinize what you state for ambiguity, unintended implications, and uncontrolled images. Often you can just write down the four or five main points, show them to people, and ask their opinions of them. If an outsider to your thoughts can see a chance of misunderstanding in the wording of the points, go back and revise the diction.

To help your listeners realize that the main points are just that, you should word them using parallel construction. This means that you should use similar grammatical construction for parallel ideas in each major point. Do not make your main points so dissimilar in wording that listeners have no way of realizing their coordinate (equally important) nature. Consider, for example, these four sentences: A new accident-insurance plan has been proposed. Medical costs are rising every year, and so are insurance rates. It is not yet clear who will be covered. There are two options if we choose the new plan.

Note that it is not clear what the relationships are among these various sentences. The second one seems to be unrelated, although the speaker probably wishes to contrast the costs of the present plan and the proposed new plan. However, we cannot be sure. In the third statement, we cannot tell to which plan the speaker is referring. The last idea opens up more questions than it answers. What options are there if we choose to stay with the old plan? Or, is one of the options to choose between the two plans? Parallel form would help clear up the confusion. As an exercise, formulate a simple plan for a speech using the preceding fragments of information and adding data as needed. At this stage, you need not develop an outline; just write four sentences which could improve the scattered, incoherent structure of the entries given.

Do not phrase the main ideas as questions, but as declarations of what you want the audience to believe or know. Do not, even in your private notes, make the mistake of thinking that a list of questions is an outline. "What insurance policy should we adopt?" is not a main point. It is a question. Even if you want to pose a hypothetical question to the audience and then answer it, do not confuse guiding questions with propositions you want listeners to accept. Certainly such questions can act as transitions between main points at the moment of delivery; consider them as part of your inward composition process, and not as expressions of your main points.

Read the following questions:

1.   What is the X company's financial strength? (You are to tell us!)
2.   What outstanding obligations does it have?
3.   What capital expenses must it finance this year?
4.   What major lawsuit for $3 million is facing it?

See what happens? When pursued to the point at which listeners must be given new and unexpected main points, the question form becomes awkward and illogical.

Finally, make sure that your main points do not overlap. If you are going to develop a body of information about a point, concentrate the relevant data under one main point, treat them fully, and then do not come back later with another main point that is simply some new development of the first idea. You are sure to lose your audience if you do.

OUTLINING A SPEECH

One of the best ways of ensuring that the purpose and thesis of your speech are clear, and that *you* understand what you would really like to say, is to prepare an outline from the main points you have carefully chosen and worded, as just explained. The following discussion details how to prepare a useful, concise outline for any speech.

Each main entry in an outline should correspond to a main point. Assign a number or letter to each one to clarify the exact relationship of idea to idea. The usual practice is to alternate letters and numbers, beginning with large or capital symbols and moving down to lower-case symbols. Lettered items are subdivisions of numbered items, and vice versa. Another system uses entirely numbers, with decimal subdivisions such as 1 for the first main point and 1.1 for the first subsidiary point. In turn, the symbol for the first entry to support point 1.1 would be 1.1.1, or some other convention. As long as the system you chose is consistent and clear, it does not matter which you use.

Note as you form your outline that to show subordination of a point, you should indent that point in the outline. If Assets is your main entry, and Money a major subdivision, indent money several spaces to the right. A subdivision of Money such as Coins would be indented further to the right. Dimes would be placed still further to the right, and Silver Dimes yet further. Test yourself: Where in the outline would Dollar Bills and Bonds go?

You should also indent ideas or objects of equal importance a comparable degree throughout the outline. By disciplining yourself to observe this convention you can ensure that either logical interrelationships or great gaps in information will emerge for the various points you plan to make. It is easy to overdevelop some points for which you have too much data and to neglect equally important points for which you do not have enough. Consistent outlining can help you avoid such possibilities.

As we discussed earlier, you should state parallel items in parallel ways, if possible. This helps the audience to realize when you have left one point and have gone on to another. It also reduces the necessity to use trite transitions such as "My second point is _____." Finally, it helps you focus on casting the points as equally important. For example, if one of your main points is that interest rates will remain high for years and another is that inflation will get much worse in the next five years, state these points in similar ways. You might help the process by choosing comparable time periods, say five years. Another way to encourage parallelism is to use similar sentence patterns: "Barring a major war, interest rates will continue high." "Barring a major change in world economies, inflation will remain high."

Although this kind of patterning might seem to lack variety and imagination, it can key the audience and become for them a subtle marker that you are leaving one point and going to another. If your topic is an abstract one, these additional markers are especially important to help the audience detect what is major and what is subordinate. One of the most common and unnecessary sources of haziness in speeches is the speaker's failure to let the audience know the hierarchy of ideas. Some of this can be accomplished by vocal inflection, pause, and variety in voice. Simultaneous use of transitions and parallel wording of similar ideas can help listeners see the skeleton of the speech sticking through the language chosen to clothe it.

For some speakers, dividing a main point is a major struggle. The general idea in dividing a main point is to produce two or more minor points which support or add up to the main point itself. Try to visualize the minor points as slices of a pie. Imagine a round pie, A. Take a knife and divide the pie into three pieces, 1, 2, and 3. If these three pieces are fitted back together on the plate, they constitute pie A. In an outline a main point A can be similarly divided into three or more "slices" or parts and labeled exactly as the pie was. Clear? All right, now cut pie A into two pieces. Call one piece 1 and the other 2. What was the name of this pair of pie slices? A, you say. Good. Now, take your knife and carefully cut the pie into just one piece. Careful, now: Cut it into only *one* piece. You cannot do it. Likewise, you rarely have just one subpoint in an outline. If you divide point A (or pie A) into just one piece, the piece is identical with the whole thing. You may, very rarely, have the occasion to subdivide a point into just one subpoint, but beware lest you confuse your audience. They will probably hear the subpoint as the next main point unless you clearly state your ideas to avoid that confusion.

TESTING YOUR MAIN POINTS
IN A PRELIMINARY OUTLINE

So far, you have delineated your main points; you have limited their number to no more than five, no matter how strong the temptation was to put in a few more; you have worded them clearly; and you have learned how to construct an outline. Now, you are ready to force yourself to group your ideas for your chosen subject and to discover what are truly your main ideas and what turn out to be supporting ones. In other words, you are ready to outline *this* speech. Remember the hierarchy of boxes within boxes.

Make all main points parallel in form to assist your listeners in identifying them. If you choose an action as the first point, then you should choose actions for the second and third points as well. If you choose descriptions, be consistent all the way through in the wording of your main points.

Word your main points with meticulous care to avoid any possible double meanings. Remember that our language plays tricks on us. Recall the Trucker's Oasis out West, with its neon sign for weary travelers, "Eat here and get gas." Then recall the newspaper story about a woman in a shower who was overcome by fumes from a leaking stove, but who was saved by a watchful janitor. To avoid such language problems, have someone else read your first working outline to search for ambiguity.

Avoid using questions as main points. A main point is a declaration of an idea, a conclusion, or an observation you want your listeners to accept. You will confuse them and yourself if you make your main points into questions. Again, rhetorical questions may be useful as transitions between points, but the main point is the answer to the question, not the question itself. You should never give a persuasive speech with a main conclusion like this:

> In view of these economies and convenience, when are we going to switch our payroll to computer records?

Such a statement should be phrased more like this: In view of these economies and convenience, we plan to switch our payroll to computer records next July.

Word your main points and arrange them so that there is no overlap in meaning from one topic to the next. Settle one point; then go on to the next. There is no harm in referring back to conclusions you reached in an earlier part of your speech, but do not assume that you can now use claims made earlier in a speech as proof of a new claim. Do not use a statement in one place as a main point and then later use it again as a minor point. Having a given statement appear as both major and minor will force the audience to consider it as one or the other. Using it both ways will, in other words, confuse your listeners.

Make sure that the points are arranged in the best order for your immediate purpose. Do the points add force as they are revealed? Do they have a discernible dramatic or logical pattern which brings the listener closer and closer to the conclusion you desire? Are the points in the optimum order for the intended effect? Try mentally changing the order and decide whether the new one is better or worse before you tinker too much with your outline.

When your outline can meet all of these tests to your satisfaction, it is probably ready to use as the foundation for a whole speech.

A Sample Preliminary Outline
(Based on a Speech by Alan S.)

This speech was given to fulfill a common assignment in public-speech classes—namely, to make a process speech. Each student was asked to prepare a 5-minute talk using visual aids to explain some step-by-step process. The student in this case illustrated with pictures, scissors, wool crepe hair, and adhesive how to make stage and cinema moustaches.

HOW TO MAKE YOUR OWN MACHO MOUSTACHE

I. (Introduction) Our community produces over forty plays a year, if we count the high school, college, church, and community theatre productions. (startling statement to gain attention)

    A. Many of you said you were interested in acting in plays when you gave your self-introductions. (link to auditors)

    B. Because so many plays portray older men, or men in period grooming, I want to narrow my talk today to one very useful and very common makeup device, the moustache. (exclusion of material, limitation of topic and purpose)

THESIS: Convincing moustaches in dramatics depend on rigorous control in selecting and applying makeup materials.

II. (Body: First main idea) The first absolutely essential step is to select the proper color of wool crepe hair from the makeup kit.

    A. The hair must be appropriate for the character.

    B. The hair must be consistent with the actor's hair, or at least believable with his total makeup.

    C. The hair must be chosen while viewed under intense stage lighting, not ordinary room lighting.

        1. Crepe hair is wool and lacks oil.

        2. Natural human hair is oily and looks different under stage lights, compared with daylight.

    D. If no stocked hair is quite right in color and sheen, several colors can be mixed together to create an intermediate color.

    E. In television, film, and close-up photography, the moustache can be made of human hair instead.

III. (Body: Second main idea) Once the hair is chosen, it must be prepared carefully well in advance.

    A. Stock hair is shipped in tight braids and cannot be used until it is straightened.
      1. Pull out of the braids enough hair to make the moustaches for dress rehearsal and all performances.
      2. Thoroughly wet the hair and then hang it up to dry overnight.
      3. Use a clamp on each end of the wet hair, in order to stretch it.
      4. When the hair is dry, it will be straight and manageable enough to make moustaches.
    B. Comb stock wool hair gently to remove any snags and knots.
    C. With sharp scissors cut the hair straight across to create an even line of individual hairs.

  IV. (Body: Third main idea) Once the hair is prepared, attach it onto the actor's face in bunches or tufts.
    A. If the production runs one or two nights, attach the moustache above the lip with a thin coat of spirit gum, which is the gum of an evergreen tree dissolved in ether.
    B. If the moustache is to be saved and used repeatedly, as in a long-running show, you can attach it the first time by liquid latex and then peel it off and save it for future use.
    C. In any case, attach the hair to the lip in irregular bunches or tufts just as the spirit or latex is starting to dry and become tacky.
    D. The secret to effective moustaches is to apply the hair vertically, not horizontally, for real hair grows out and downward on the lip, not sideways.

  V. (Body: Fourth main idea) Once the tufts of hair are firmly attached to the lip, as determined by gently combing or pulling on the moustache, the hairpiece is ready for the final step, trimming.
    A. It is essential for safety and appearance to trim the ragged moustache with sharp stainless-steel scissors.
      1. Dull scissors are dangerous, for they tend to slip.
      2. Sharp scissors make a neat, straight cut and are safer than dull ones, but all trimming is risky.
    B. Exercise great care to prevent cutting the actor.
      1. Many actors insist on making their own hairpieces.
      2. If makeup people create the pieces, they must warn the actor to keep still and fold his lips inward.

  VI. (Conclusion) The finished moustache on the actor will be both attractive and believable if you follow the steps of selection and application described here.
    A. (Restate thesis) Remember, no deviation from the order and carefulness described can be tolerated if you want to make an impressive, safe, and believable moustache.
    B. (Summarize) The choice of color, preparation of the hair, attachment, and trimming of moustaches can make the difference between satisfying and credible male characters and disappointing, ludicrous ones.

Remember that the outline is a tool for your own use, and no one else need see it. It should be serviceable to you and can be coded or worded in the most convenient way for you while you are actually speaking. An elaborately typed, detailed outline in a format too small for you to see is useless. If the outline has no meaning for you under the stress of live speaking, then do not bring it before the audience at all—they will see that you make no use of it, and they will thus consider it merely a distraction. The ideal outline is a brief, tightly worded, economically thought-out skeleton of your speech. When you look at the outline, each line in turn should provoke a short conversation on a limited topic between you and your audience. You might think of each outline entry as a complete short speech, if that helps you. The entry is a trigger for information you know and have thought about. When you run dry, look at the next entry and let it evoke another thought pattern, and so on. Used this way an outline can be a genuine aid, and not a meaningless crutch which fails when you need it most.

THE FINAL OUTLINE

The preliminary outline is useful to you for planning and then rehearsing your speech. You might even take it to the lectern with you if your teacher allows notes. In any case, you will probably be required to present a formal outline along with your talk on the day of your performance. The final outline may have a few more details added if a rehearsal reveals that you need more development.

A final outline should, of course, be typed or neatly written in legible form with complete sentences. Follow the exact instructions of your teacher, who may want you to label not only each point of the content presented but also the purpose or intended use of each entry. For example, you might be asked to put in the left margin some notes such as: Make transition here, or Use visual aid here. It might also include a bibliography or a list of sources used for your talk. In the preceding example, for instance, you might add simply the following information:

Sources

RICHARD CORSON, *Stage Makeup*, 5th ed. (Englewood Cliffs, N.J.: Prentice-Hall, 1975), Chapter 17.

Interview with Professor Thomas, University of Illinois Speech Department, January 9, 1984.

EXERCISES

1. Assign the following topics in rotation to all the students in the class and have each student list three to five possible main points which might embrace an informative speech on each topic. Assign for each topic a second student to analyze the

probable thesis, the suitable patterns of development, and the likely length of the speech.

a. Effects of dissolving the Bell Telephone System.
b. The future of Lebanon.
c. Income tax reform.
d. The future of Social Security.
e. Improving Amtrak service.
f. How to finance college costs.
g. Future prison policies.
h. Building telescopes.
i. Making wine legally.
j. Practical solar home heating.
k. Founding your own rock band.
l. Small investor's guide.

2. Each of the following topics contains an inherently complex chain of steps or divisions. State how the temptation to create numerous main points can be overcome. Show how several points can be grouped together into fewer points which are parallel in form, coherent, and complete. Discuss several ways to limit or narrow each topic.

a. The nine planets of our solar system.
b. Making a fortune in horse racing.
c. How to beat Las Vegas games.
d. The decline of the family farm.
e. Build your own boat/cabin/airplane/glider.

SELECTED READINGS

BERT E. BRADLEY, *Fundamentals of Speech Communication*, 3rd ed. (Dubuque, Iowa: Wm. C. Brown, 1981), Chapters 10, 11, and 12.

DOUGLAS EHNINGER, BRUCE GRONBECK, RAY McKERROW, AND ALAN MONROE, *Principles and Types of Speech Communication*, 9th ed. (Glenview, Ill.: Scott, Foresman, 1982).

RUDOLPH F. VERDERBER, *The Challenge of Effective Speaking*, 5th ed. (Belmont Calif.: Wadsworth, 1982), Part 3.

RICHARD L. WEAVER, II, *Understanding Public Communication* (Englewood Cliffs, N.J.: Prentice-Hall, 1983).

EUGENE E. WHITE, *Practical Public Speaking*, 4th ed. (New York: Macmillan, 1982).

chapter 5

Development:
Supporting
the Main Points

Once you have chosen the few main points for an outline of your speech, your attention should turn to filling in the facts, opinions, quotations, illustrations, and so on, which will make the main points come to life and be remembered. This activity is called development. You cannot very well just state the main points and say, "If you accept these four main points, you will reach the same conclusion I did in my thesis—namely, that UFOs come from the satellite Titan." Few listeners will accept unsupported claims. You must fill in information which makes each main point believable. You must link each one of your main points to the listeners' experiences with concrete support.

TYPES OF SUPPORT

Support takes many forms. For some types of speech the support may be drawn mainly from historical facts. For another type of speech, such support may be valueless, and illustrations and examples may be called for. Yet another speech may depend heavily on quotations on the topic from authorities whom you believe the audience will accept. Following is a discussion of some of the types of support you might choose to develop for a speech. Often you can combine several kinds of support to achieve the best results.

Details

Using details is a common form of development. As you speak, you reveal finer and more specific details to the listeners so that they get a progressively more accurate and full understanding of an idea they could not be expected to grasp at the outset. For example, you might begin a technical description of a flower with the classification of the parts as stem, leaves, and blossom. Later, you could describe more details, such as the pistil, stamen, and anther.

Examples

Sometimes introducing a striking or typical example of behavior or material can help define a difficult or new term. Suppose you are talking about ethnocentrism. You might explain that it is the notion among nearly all groups that their group is really the best one. You could cite and translate as an example any one of several Indian tribes' names for themselves. Many tribal names mean "the best people" or "the real men" or some such revealing phrase. Examples tend to give life and color to dry and abstract ideas or terms. A supreme compliment is to be called a master of the example in speech, for it not only implies mastery of a wide variety of facts, but it also reveals a sensitivity to the audience needs, which in itself is good.

Quotations

This familiar strategic device—the use of quotations—is valuable in nearly all types of speeches, because listeners may not be entirely willing to take your word for all claims. How are the listeners to know whether you are trustworthy if you are unknown? One way to help them decide about you and the subject is to quote someone you believe they will trust. Psychologically, the burden of proof is shifted from you to someone else who has presumably studied the same issues with which you are dealing and has reached a conclusion with which you agree. You are no longer alone in persuading, but you have invoked the help of famous and trustworthy authorities.

You might even go a step further and cite an opinion of someone who is known to be unacceptable, perhaps even hostile, to your audience when that person's opinion *differs* from the one you hold and offer to the audience. For example, if you are addressing an audience of union workers and you quote the opinion of a strong antiunion politician, the contrast of that person's stand with yours may be an excellent emotional appeal for your position. This strategy involves quoting a negative source. Incidentally, the value is still present whether the source happens to be right or wrong or irrelevant.

Illustrations

Somewhat like an example in its impact on listeners, an illustration of some complex term may enlighten listeners more than continued description. For instance, suppose you wish to explain how governments tend to ignore signs of impending war and to see only what their wishful thinking portrays. You might illustrate by citing the cases of the French generals in World War II who accused observers of incompetence when the latter reported accurately the overwhelming masses of German troops moving toward France.

An illustration may also be thought of as an extended example. For instance, a description of an underdog's victory over an overwhelming favorite might well illustrate the term *overconfidence*.

Analogies

Drawing a parallel between two unlike objects, ideas, or situations by implying numerous similarities is logically a weak form of support. However, such a comparison, called an analogy, is often a very powerful device in its influence on listeners. It ought not to work, but it does. Writers on persuasion have often noted that audiences feel rather than know what a speaker is driving at when he or she uses an analogy. Nevertheless, an analogy is often useful when other kinds of support do not make a point clear. It can be especially effective if it is not too far fetched. It may create an illusion of support that in fact cannot be logically defended. Nevertheless, its effects on an audience are strong.

There are two kinds of analogy. One type, called *literal analogy*, compares two things which are in fact very much alike in several respects. An example would be chess and checkers: Both are games, both use a similar board, both have the objective of taking the opponent's pieces, and so on. If you were explaining chess to a novice, you might use numerous comparisons between the two games. (This tactic assumes that the novice knows how to play checkers.) An analogy depends on assuming that two things alike in several respects will be alike in others. In this analogy, securing a new queen in chess is somewhat like being "crowned" in checkers; both games allow a piece moving entirely across the board to achieve extra powerful new pieces.

The other kind of analogy, called a *figurative analogy*, calls attention to some similarities in two things which really are not comparable in many respects. For example, an airplane might be figuratively compared with a bird. This figurative analogy compares a living creature (a bird) with a lifeless machine (an airplane). Now consider a literal comparison between impressionism in music, such as that of Debussy, and impressionism in painting, such as that of Van Gogh. In both cases imagery is deliberately nonrealistic, fuzzy, emotionalized, unorthodox, and idiosyncratic. This literal analogy compares two human artistic crafts. Logically, two human crafts have more in common than a natural creature (a bird) and a manufactured vehicle (a plane). However, listeners to a speaker are not likely to make fine distinctions. Sometimes they respond to quite strained comparisons, either literal or figurative, and sometimes even to quite irrational ones. When asked to compare his career with that of his son, the famous baseball player Yogi Berra explained that their similarities were totally different. Affection for Berra is so great that the logic of his statement was set aside by fans and his assertion was understood well enough. This writer holds that the distinction between what is logical and what is understood is rarely important as long as the analogy chosen is credible to the audience.

Comparison and Contrast

Although these methods of development involve simply the simultaneous use of earlier-named forms, they are strategically useful. For instance, a contrast between two forms of bank insurance such as the FDIC and FSLIC might use examples, details, and quotations within the overall strategy of contrasting the two corporations.

Restatement

This is another strategic form of support which has good probative force on audiences although it introduces nothing new to give greater credibility. Because listeners need reinforcement and reiteration to remember, this pattern is useful to secure the speaker's aim. Moreover, when listeners perceive that a speaker regards a detail as worth repeating, they usually assume it is important.

Statistics

For some people, the patterns of reality reflected by tables, formulas, lists, and collections of numbers have great appeal. For most people they carry a certain air of authority. However, you must handle this apparent boon to development with extreme care lest you so bedazzle and confuse your listeners that they reject the evidence. A delightful little book published by Darrell Huff in 1954, *How to Lie with Statistics*,[1] proposed that numbers are not the final and incontrovertible evidence naive consumers of rhetoric once took them to be. Twisted and transformed by skillful charlatans, statistics can prove nearly anything one wishes them to. If Little America, Wyoming (population 60) adds 20 people to its town, it has grown by 33 percent. If 20 people move to Los Angeles, however, the data would show no increase in size because, compared with millions of souls, the 20 would be a tiny fraction of 1 percent. You would be technically correct to make such silly claims as "The rate of growth of Little America, Wyoming, America's greatest crossroads, is higher than that of Los

Angeles. Here's clear proof of Wyoming's population explosion." These facts present no inaccuracy; loose claims based on the facts, however, would be fraudulent in trying to show serious intent.

Following is another illustration of how statistics can be juggled. Imagine that you get a 10 percent raise, and you were already making $50 thousand a year. Suppose that you learn a month later that there was a mistake and times are hard. The boss expresses deep regret, but your salary must be cut by 10 percent. You are right back where you were before the raise, right? Wrong.

USING STRUCTURAL DEVICES
AS CONTENT AND FORM

Development of an idea can rely not only on material directly related to content but also on a variety of structural forms which can ease the way for understanding. Sometimes material can be both full of information and functional at the same time. This section describes several forms of development which double as structural devices to guide the audience's thinking. They may give the speech an aesthetically pleasing form and serve some purpose of the speaker other than simply adding to the information.

The Question: Directed and Rhetorical Forms

Sometimes there is little difficulty in identifying the major ideas of a speech, for they may seem almost self-evident. If you give a presentation on new services a savings and loan company plans to offer, the main points are likely to be answers to the most common questions in the minds of the audience. In this case, if the staff is to be the audience, the questions are likely to be: What is the nature of the new service? Whom will it affect? How will procedures in the office be affected? Detailed answers to these questions will rather fully constitute the framework of the whole speech.

It is evident that the audience's questions also help to shape the talk. At the same time, however, you, as the speaker, must maintain control of the speech while answering questions. A means of retaining this control is to use the *directed question*: a question you turn onto the audience to gently impose direction of the presentation toward material you have chosen. From your standpoint as the speaker, your problem is to tie details, descriptions, and other developmental information together in such a way that you fully answer each question at about the same time the audience has its curiosity aroused on a particular topic. This pattern of creating an imbalance in the listener and then resolving the imbalance to create a sense of satisfaction is a standard, well-known speaking strategy. When you do it properly, the procedure keeps the audience's attention focused, its sense of involvement high, and the feeling of development in the talk quite brisk. When you do not do it quite so expertly the strategy is less satisfactory because listeners may start interrupting you with questions a moment before you expect them. This is most annoying. You may feel the listeners are impatient, when in fact they are simply having the right questions dawn on them just a moment out of step. Usually all that is necessary for you to get back in synchronization with your audience is to comment pleasantly that "You anticipate exactly my next point. I'll deal with that immediately." Occasionally the audience's jumping ahead of you can mean that your rate of developing your speech is unnecessarily slow. In this case a bit quicker delivery or cutting out some marginally interesting or useful data might be desirable to pick up the tempo.

The usual link, then, between a point and its development is the probable question in the minds of the audience members. Of course, not all of the members are in the same state of mind, and you can help to lead them into silently asking just the right questions for whatever stage your speech is in at a given moment.

Some developmental material does not concern the *content* of the speech at all, but instead relates to the receptivity of the listeners. A very common device for this purpose is the *rhetorical question*. To use it, you ask a question, but you do not expect anyone to answer it. You can use this device to bring all your listeners to the same state of expectation so that your sequence of information will achieve its maximum force. The rhetorical question can also help to achieve apparent coherence when the main points in a talk are not naturally so related that transition from one to the next is easy. You would thus use a question as a group control device and a structural tool.

The Internal Summary

One of the most useful tools when a speech is complex and difficult for the audience to follow is the *internal summary*. This device signals listeners that the speaker is going to stop, back up, and get a fresh start. The internal summary is, as the name suggests, a summary of what has been said so far, often with some indication of what is major and what is minor. It differs from the usual conclusion in several ways. First, it is not near the end of the talk, but somewhere in the middle. Second, it does not call for an action or restate the thesis. Third, it does not create in the audience a feeling of closure as the conclusion of a speech does. Fourth, it is not external to the body of content as a true conclusion is, but rather it is a reminder of where participants in the talk have been led thus far. Hence, it is more like a transitional device than a terminal one. When overused, the internal summary makes the speaker look like a mindless simpleton who thinks a summary is necessary every few minutes. However, when the subject matter is difficult or emotion laden, or when there is necessarily a tremendous amount of detail given to an audience, the form is a blessing for both the audience, who can catch its breath and recall what it has heard so far, and for the speaker, who has another chance to explain difficult material.

Transitional Devices

One of the most frequently abused and ignored components of a good speech is the transition, or changeover phrase, which links one idea with another. The transition, a signal to the listener that the speaker has finished the development of one point and now intends to talk about another, can take many forms. It can be a word, a phrase, a clause, a full sentence, or several sentences. Good transitions not only effect the changeover described, they also show relationship between the point the speaker has just left and the one to be dealt with next. Thus, accurate choice of the most appropriate transitional device for a given situation becomes a special skill that speakers should study with care. A sensitive ear, a knack for choosing precise and impelling language, and a sense of what is enough and what is too much are all important aspects of choosing appropriate transitions.

SOME USEFUL TRANSITIONS

Words: meanwhile, nevertheless, however, elsewhere, moreover.

Phrases: At the same time, in spite of, apart from, in another part of, even though, in contrast to, back at the ranch.

Clauses: While this process continued, Even though we were warned, Although the task was extremely dangerous, My purpose now is to reveal.

Sentences: So far I have described the symptoms of ____ and now direct your attention to the causes of it. Having dwelled on the history of the problem, I now propose a workable but expensive solution. Thus art began. All this background material reveals the complexity of ____.

Sometimes—for example to create the proper atmosphere for continuing the development of a long and complex talk—a paragraph or more is necessary as the transition. In general, the more complex and lengthy your speech, the more deliberate should be your transitions.

So important is the skill of transition writing that you can regard it as among the ten most potent steps to take to improve your speech presentations. So unusual is the skill that anyone who masters it stands out as an expert, even if he or she has other deficiencies.

TYING SUPPORTING MATERIAL
TO THE MAIN POINTS

So far in this chapter we have described the kinds of supporting material you might use to develop the content of a speech and the structural devices which can advance understanding as well as the content. Now we consider how to fashion all the gathered materials into a finished, plausible package of language. We began by assuming a need to address an audience and tell it something important. A purpose was assumed. From this purpose and the choice of a topic with rather few main points, we turned to support for those points. We have, by analogy, begun to build a house by looking at the architect, the blueprints, the supporting members of the structure, and finally the construction materials.

The first step in using supporting material is *classification*. The central act of classification is choosing from a great assembly of facts and details those which best shore up the claims we wish to make, and which we wish to call main points. What is a main point in one speech might well be a supporting detail in another. Do not be intimidated by such inconsistencies in others' use of data while doing research for a speech. A profound truth in one context may be a "mere detail" in another. Decisions about the importance of a given bit of information, then, may resolve to a question of how that information is most useful. For example, the discovery that the great red spot on Jupiter was actually a violent storm permanently locked in place was considered by some experts to be a major triumph, a vindication of their long-standing claims about the spot. Other scientists were more taken by the numerous high-speed winds on the planet, the new information about the moons, and the verification of the composition of the planet and its atmosphere. Thus, what to one scientist was ego-involved, personal verification was to others quite subsidiary to what they regarded as more significant knowledge. None of the cited persons was wrong; the point is that what was extremely important to some authorities was evidently of quite peripheral interest to others.

The implications for speechwriting are clear. Information is given importance by the way we choose to use it. The details of what the great red spot is can be inserted into one speech as a major division of the entire talk and into a different speech as supporting material for some other main point. While you are composing a speech and making choices about how to link the various ideas of the talk together, the conventional device to help you show classification and relationships is the outline.

If you choose major points first, the question then becomes how other points support the major ones. Let us return to the Jupiter spot for a moment. If you chose as a main point for a talk the idea that "Recent evidence indicates that life on any other planet in our solar system is unlikely," then the violent whirling winds on Jupiter could be a subpoint parallel to other data. You could state that life on Venus is unlikely because of the heat and caustic atmosphere. Life on Mars is also improbable because of the extreme cold and because of the sterility of soil samples gathered from Mars in recent experiments. In outline form, the relationships in abbreviated skeletal form would look like this:

I. Life on other planets in our solar system is unlikely.
   A. Jupiter's stormy red spot would destroy any stable means for life to get started.
   B. Venus' caustic, torrid atmosphere cannot support life.
   C. Mars' frigid, dry, airless surface has shown no life.

Now imagine the outline form rearranged so that the Jupiter storm is the main focus of attention, a main point. It might look like this:

I. The red spot of Jupiter poses some interesting technical problems.
   A. Because of its violent whirling, spacecraft will have to be very strong, highly powered, and protected from corrosion.
   B. Because it is fixed in one place, the visiting craft can expect to encounter vortex and stability problems.
   C. Because of its color and the contrast with surrounding winds, the ship can expect chemical differences from area to area.

It should be clear that here information about the spot is being used to draw some conclusions about possible visits to the planet in the future. The spot probably enjoys proportionately more attention in the talk than it did in the first outline. Stated another way, more details which represent more subdivision and more classification are explained in the second outline than would be the case in a speech about the likelihood of life on other planets.

STYLE AND VOCABULARY

Having outlined your main points, you are ready for the next step in the speechmaking process: composing your speech. Time-honored customs apply to the relationships between the ideas and the words you choose to develop a speech, as they do to the other aspects of this process we have been studying.

The actual words you choose to express your ideas convey an enormous amount of information beyond the content of the message you intend. For instance, if you use the word "pestilence" to describe your encounter with a seasonal cold instead of the more common word "flu," the listeners will credit you with some sense of humor. Deliberate overstatement of the medical nuisance is a mark of a chosen style. Some people strive to speak the literal truth all the time and avoid departures from simple, direct speech. We may say about them that "that is their style." They are laconic, parsimonious with words, candid, tight-lipped, close-mouthed, circumspect—we could go on with adjectives to describe the types of personality revealed through simple language choices. This section is about the problems associated with style. Some observations over time have revealed a good deal of surprising data.

Style

There is much misunderstanding about style. For example, although we associate personality and style, they are not really synonyms. Style is a systematic choice of language, including both vocabulary and figures of speech, which reveals personality. Language is a tool; personality is a set of expressed attitudes and emotions, and a particular mentality. It is the personality which induces someone to choose the language to communicate with the outside world—namely, everybody beyond the self. Because of the frequent need for great accuracy in mutual understanding, mastery of style is important. Occasionally situations do work out perfectly well when both "sides" of a communication totally misunderstand what the other wants and expects. Unhappily, there are many more examples of disaster resulting from what should have been the simplest of message exchanges. Personal choices in language, intended one way but perceived in quite another way, can ruin communication. In any case style, the choice of language itself, is not personality, but only evidence of it.

Another widely held misconception about style is that it is an overlaid or superimposed polish on a message. The message is viewed as a fundamental entity and the language chosen to express it as perhaps a flowery, ceremonial dressing to "civilize" or soften it if it happens to be a trifle crude. Although language is used in this way, this is not the essence of style. Another misunderstanding is to consider style to be mere embellishment. Your style begins to emerge the minute you choose ideas to present. It is the product of all the decisions you make in preparing a speech; even your consciously attempting to avoid creating a style will result in a definite style. A stark, bare style, for example, would result from deliberate effort to avoid all figures of speech and emotive language. Sometimes such a style is just what a situation requires. In other words, you can take a message and embellish it for a secondary purpose, such as to charm or con the hearers, but such a use of style is incidental rather than essential. The fact is that since all ideas depend on some kind of language for their expression, it is not possible to separate style from meaning.

The preceding idea may be hard to accept at first. To test the claim that style is inseparable from a message, consider some alternative ways of saying almost the same thing. Note that the various ways of wording an idea slightly change its meaning, often comment on the speaker's apparent intent, and sometimes reveal attitudes by accident.

A third misconception about style is that some people have one and others do not. The common expressions "She has style" or "He has no style," are not literally true. No one can avoid having a style; indeed, any one person may command several discernible levels of style. The crudest boor and the most illiterate churl both have a style, such as it is.

A fourth mistake about style is that it is necessarily a qualitative judgment about a person's presentation of self and messages. Although to say a person is "stylish" or "has style" is a compliment, and no argument here is going to change usage, the alert speaker should realize that the word is subject to as much misinterpretation as a word like *art* or *love*. The author once heard an excellent speech defining love. The talk presented eight totally different, often conflicting definitions, and warned of the danger of loosely using the word. If, during a speech, some listener thinks of love of parents, someone else thinks of love of food, another of patriotism, yet another of lust, and one more of fraternalism, then the word is not serving its user well. It is just so with the word *style*. To focus more directly upon what its use is for you as a speaker, we now define and describe it in detail.

What Is Style?

Style, as used in this book, means simply the choice of words and language patterns to convey a message most precisely in a given situation. The word *situation* is a sneaky way of including audience, topic, and occasion as determiners of word choice. Of course, you should not use two-bit words on naive listeners except to amuse them. You should not lightly banter words with a supervisor intent on rectifying a dangerous or costly production-line problem. It is possible to try, but society punishes people whose style departs sharply from the norms of speech in various situations. There is, then, a tacit code of oral style just as there are norms of dress and behavior for various groups and situations. It should be evident that style is ultimately the individual's choice of ways to adapt to people and situations and to communicate in the optimum manner for ever-changing circumstances.

Style is usually broken into two parts: the choice of individual words and the choice of combinations of them (called figures of speech). A speaker choosing words, might have an internal dialogue like this:

> I don't want to sound too formal in my speech. I want dignity in it but not arrogance or amusement. Thus, when I compare social ranks in the United States with those in England, I have to be careful not to sound either sarcastic or flippant. I'll say "middle" social class rather than "inferior" when I talk about commoners in England. I have to watch out for the word, "commoners," which sounds belittling to us, and my audience may not understand the British use of "lower class." I'll refer to them as "laboring class," which sounds neutral. And I'd better avoid the word "ordinary" applied to people, because some Americans take that word as a slur. Maybe "plain" people would be best.

We weigh and balance shades of meaning whenever we choose words, whether for conversation or for formal speeches. If you have ever blurted out the wrong word with a negative shade of meaning, you will undoubtedly recall your embarrassment.

An important point about word choice is that it must not be viewed as a static concern capable of analysis in isolation. Rather, it must be treated as a technique of finally making an overt response to others in language. The term *style* is quite contaminated with other uses. "You have a nice style in tennis." "She swims with real style." "What style of wrestling do you prefer?" "He's smart but not my style." It is little wonder that with so many meanings the term is fuzzy and ill-defined in the minds of most people. Perhaps it would be a service to language if we avoided such universal words as "art," "love," and "style," except when we are absolutely sure that our listeners know the contexts and shades of meaning intended.

We have thus established that words (vocabulary) make up the working tools of style. The decision to choose "muck about" instead of "explore ramifications" establishes several concerns immediately. The first choice implies a degree of ignorant groping on a topic to be investigated, whereas the second indicates a guarded and dignified admission that much is unknown and needs exploration. Clearly, then, not simply word choice but something else makes up the tone we convey. "Muck" brings to mind dirty, unpleasant, and uncomfortable sensations. "Explore," by contrast is a positive, constructive word. Astronauts explore, and sandhogs muck about. If the full context were something like this, we could immediately discern at least two strikingly different *levels* of style:

> Our committee met to muck about in the topic of new tax sources.
> Our committee met to explore the ramifications of new tax sources.

Which style would be best to report the proceedings to a local newspaper? Which level seems more appropriate to sit down in a local bar with a friend and have a beer after a particularly tedious session?

Levels of Style

We now examine three quite distinct styles of speaking in public. None of them is wrong, bad, or inferior. Each is appropriate for some situations, and each is inappropriate for other situations. Remember that the so-called plain style is in no way less in quality than a more elaborate one.

The plain style: Marked by direct, simple vocabulary everyone can understand, this style contains a few figures of speech or florid metaphors and depends on everyday, but still correct, language. It can be very forceful and tasteful in spite of its apparently simple level. Talks about the workaday world, instructions, descriptions, and technical information can be best presented in this style. It is not simple-minded or watered-down, but rather utilitarian and explicit.

The medium or inbetween style: Perhaps less often used, but of great force during more formal and elevated occasions, this style is characterized by more figures of speech and imaginative language than the plain style *embraces*, but not nearly as many as the highest style. This level is best limited to sermons, graduation exercises, formal recognitions and dedications, or landmark meetings. In the business world, an annual report might use this form or the plain style.

The grand or high-level style: Marked by great formality and august language, a high-level style is very rarely appropriate. Eulogies for great states people, dedications of new universities, Nobel-prize speeches, and landmark orations (almost extinct) require this ornate style. Frequent figures of speech and elevated diction, imaginative wording, references to the famous people of antiquity, and imposing presentation characterize it. Even if very carefully prepared, speeches in this mode are appropriate only when a distinguished audience and occasion confront the speaker.

What Happens When You Miss?

Your judgment of what level of style is appropriate on a given occasion can sometimes go awry. If you are retiring after 30 years at a small manufacturing firm and are given a gold watch, you might be so overwhelmed that your speech of acknowledgment becomes too florid. Or, trying to be "cool" at a distinguished meeting, you might gear the level of your remarks too low for the occasion.

If you aim for the plain style and miss, you will be considered a crashing bore. Dull and inexact, you will have little appeal for anyone. If you have heard a routine speech delivered with no spark or enthusiasm on a topic that everyone understood better than the speaker did and that any listener could have articulated faster and more clearly, then you have the picture of someone who tried for the plain style and missed. Hearing such speeches is somewhat like having your teeth pulled.

Suppose you tried for the middle style when it was appropriate, but missed. The effect on your listeners would probably be an artificiality and imprecision that would generate some contempt. Listeners dislike pretension more than any other faults a speaker might reveal. They have little better regard for ineptness. Whenever a metaphor, simile, or some other common figure of speech is attempted and fails, it calls undue attention to itself. Some listeners might perceive such a figure as unnecessarily obscure, and might fail to get the figure's significance. Others might understand what was intended but feel embarrassment for you. But what if you strove for the middle style when the elevated one was most appropriate? You probably appeared vapid, perhaps not very intelligent, and dull.

Yet a worse fate lies in wait if you try for the elevated style and miss. The effect on an audience is striking when you try for a grand level of style and fall short of it. The result might even be ludicrous. Your attempts at graceful figures, for example, could be missed or taken as pomposity. Your constant striving for effect could be seen as insincerity, arrant pretentiousness, or even charlatanism. If these dire outcomes did not occur, another equally distressing one might: you might be considered bombastic, theatrical, and melodramatic. If the occasion permitted, laughter and ridicule might result. The purpose of enumerating these horrors is not to intimidate you but to establish that style, so loosely dismissed by some people as the icing on the cake of speaking, is capable of making or breaking your entire speech. One duty you always have as a speaker is to choose the proper level of style for each and every audience and occasion.

Vocabulary

Many people think that having a gigantic vocabulary is the key to immediate mastery of speaking in public. There are supposedly about 200,000 words in the English language, depending on how you count them. Most well-educated people know only a small fraction of these words unless they play Scrabble or do crossword puzzles and need to know about such words as "pyx," "stichomythia," or "naumachias." Luncheon conversations and contract negotiations rarely require these words. Now arises the question about the optimum size of vocabulary. You could know so many words that you could mystify everyone else. Clearly, that will not do. Obviously no one brags of a tiny vocabulary. What, then, can we conclude about the role vocabulary plays in a person's communication skills?

First, a startling fact is that you can get by in daily life quite adequately with not 5000 or 10,000 words, but with 100 or 200 words! Certainly this statement is not intended to be an argument for holding anyone's vocabulary down, but it reveals a surprising fact about how few words people use. The best reason for having a gigantic vocabulary, then, is not to spring something new on listeners but to be able to choose among synonyms. You should choose the most precise and lucid possible words for your inner images. State exactly what you mean, if possible. To do so, you need to know a variety of words to show nuances. You should be familiar with a wide range of ways to state your ideas. These may be expressed only through fine shades of meaning carried in the words' connotations. Take, for example, one simple term which is familiar to all of us: "Fire." If we add synonyms, more and more subtle variations of meaning are available to all who share the term. "Conflagration." "Inferno." "Combustion." Note the degrees of emotional charge that the synonyms convey. A neutral term such as "combustion" stands in contrast to the intense word, "inferno." Knowing all these synonyms is an advantage after all, in spite of the word-count experiments which reveal that people habitually use small vocabularies. That they do so is not to say that they *should* do so. In summary, you should strive to cultivate your vocabulary to make available to you a variety of precise words to refine the quality of your thoughts. If you understand "fire" but not "inferno," then your thought process is less sophisticated than that of people who understand both, simply because we think in words. Some authorities go so far as to say that without language, we could not think at all. Without a word for some concept, they say, there is no way to perceive it or think about it. On the other hand, when a stimulus is perceived and considered, we immediately assign it a label or word. The issue is moot, but in a practical sense, words are powerful currency. Just recall how you made a judgment about someone on the basis of what he or she chose to talk about, and the only way you knew was the *words* that person used.

Some Figures of Speech

In the nineteenth century and earlier, when august occasions for public speaking were frequent and an elevated style of presentation was fashionable, a common method of giving an air of formality and depth to speeches was to use figures of speech, which are more or less standardized and stylistic patterns of language. A *metaphor*, for example, was a common stylistic figure chosen for variety, force, and grace. Rather than refer to a lady's beauty directly, the speaker might call her a flower or a vision. These implied comparisons were very common in formal speeches and crept easily into the language of courting, education, and preaching. The metaphor was so popular in literature, in fact, that is has gained a permanent place in our thought and speech and remains to this day one of rather few stylistic tropes and figures still in use. Our ancestors looked fondly back to the golden age of oratory for inspiration and found, or perhaps imagined, that the Greeks and Romans wrote the most magnificent speeches. For a time students were carefully tutored in the eloquence of Demosthenes and Cicero, among others. The elaborate and complex plays on language were examined in past famous speeches, then catalogued and taught to aspiring orators, who were expected to incorporate many of them into Fourth of July speeches, sermons, and formal dedications, graduations, ordinations, and other impressive speaking occasions. With the decline of such customs, the more difficult and subtle figures of speech fell into disuse, or at least their conscious use declined. Incidentally, many figures of speech recur in street talk, slang, ethnic usage, and jargon. Usually a person thinking up colorful terms and idioms is not even aware that nearly any stylistic device he or she can think of was already catalogued, defined, and illustrated in the speeches of great senators or leaders 2000 years ago. Departures from ordinary language are nearly always classifiable as figures of speech or thought.

Another frequently used figure of speech is the *simile*, which is an explicit comparison: "The chairman's anger rose and he stood poised like a cat as the stockholder aired his complaint." An explicit comparison uses the words "like" or "as" whereas a metaphor avoids them. A metaphor can be produced from a simile merely by dropping the "like" or "as." "The chairman was a great cat poised to spring while the stockholder aired his complaint." These two figures of speech are probably the most common ones still worked into speeches for effect. Because they, too, are relatively rare they may have an excellent impact on an audience, which considers them as fresh, lively, and imaginative approaches to commonplace material. Of course, if you use too many of figures of speech, or if the ones you choose are too farfetched and extravagant for the job to be done, the audience will perceive them as pretentious. As an exercise in flexibility of thought try to work one or two into a speech just to get the feel of them. Said with a twinkle in your eye, a figure of speech may add color and humor to an otherwise drab presentation.

A somewhat more rare but still useful figure of speech is the *metonomy*, which is simply a shift in something's name. For example, you might shift the name of the city Rome so that is stands for something else, such as the Pope: "Rome has always opposed marriage for priests." Other examples follow: "The crown owns that yacht." "Moscow is sure to protest our policy." In each case, the usual meaning of the word is not intended; the meaning is stretched beyond the definition to refer to something else. "Washington D.C. is a zoo." Here, the city's name is used to mean governmental personnel, and the word zoo is a metaphor.

Yet another useful figure of speech which can bring life and variety to your talks is the *synecdoche*, an imposing word which means simply the use of a part of something to stand for the whole thing, or vice versa: The figure may have the whole thing stand for a part. Here are contrasting examples: "All hands to the pumps!" (Hands stand for sailors.) "England will be offended and declare war." (England stands for the king or the government.) Shakespeare referred to "Old France" when he meant the king, not the nation. Because the king had all the power, king and nation were one. Nowadays, we might talk in the lofty terms of corporate reality: "The Dow will fall if we adopt your plan." "IBM won't like it if we compete in the office machine business." "Wall Street reacted angrily to the Senate's action."

Dozens of stylistic devices exist that can support a speech, but our purpose here is merely to indicate a few of the most common and useful ones. Most of the figures of speech have forbidding names and rather convoluted structures to achieve their effects. Without struggling to commit a long list to memory, sensitive, alert speakers can just say directly what they mean without recourse to formal, ritualistic figures of speech. Nevertheless, an occasional imaginative use of words will not hurt a speech.

Figures of Thought

Occasionally an extended or more elaborate stylistic treatment might be called for. In such cases, you can use devices called figures of thought, which are more complex and extensive than plays on words. For example, you might use a myth or allegory for extensive comparison with human behavior without offending listeners as much as you might using a literal depiction. Figures of thought are not recommended for frequent use, mainly because people in the world at large may not have the patience to draw the necessary parallels nor the sense of humor to appreciate the extended metaphorical language. They are mentioned here only to whet the appetites of those of you interested in pursuing more detailed studies of classical style. Occasional figures of thought might be effective in your speeches because of the rarity with which they are used in the workaday world. As an advanced exercise, you might want to commit to memory some of the figures of speech and thought.

EXERCISES

1. Recall a speech given in class in which the speaker failed to use sufficient examples, illustrations, or other forms of development. Can you remember the context or main point of the speech in which the gap occurred? Try as specifically as possible to write down a point that was left undeveloped. Then try to fit in an example of your own that would help to clarify the point.

2. As a review exercise to help you internalize the various forms of development in an expository speech, pair up with a classmate and see which one of you can recall more forms. Are there other kinds of speech development than those mentioned in the text? If so, what are they.

3. One of the best ways to repair a speech which is too abstract is to find one or two very clear examples or illustrations of each term the audience might find difficult. Select a passage from a technical magazine, a news magazine such as *Time* or *Newsweek*, or even a speech given in class, and show how vagueness and abstraction could be corrected by adding some development.

4. A frequent shortcoming of student speeches, especially near the beginning of a course, is that they run short of information. The real fault is lack of development. If a speech has three main ideas, adequate development of these could easily fill the assigned time. Select one speech given so far in the course and show how its development could be improved. Make a short report to the class.

5. Sometimes a speaker has a choice of many kinds of support. Discuss how you might know when to use quotations, examples, and anecdotes.

6. Discuss the usefulness and limitations of personal experience as a form of development for a speech. Do listeners resent a speaker's using personal experience or appreciate it? Does using it seem to be bragging? Does it have any unique strengths?

SELECTED READINGS

CHARLES R. GRUNER, *Plain Public Speaking* (New York: Macmillan, 1983), Chapter 8.

GARY T. HUNT, *Public Speaking* (Englewood Cliffs, N.J.: Prentice-Hall, 1982), Chapter 4.

STEPHEN LUCAS, *The Art of Public Speaking* (New York: Random House, 1983), Chapter 13.

LARRY A. SAMOVAR AND JACK MILLS, *Oral Communication*, 5th ed. (Dubuque, Iowa: Wm. C. Brown, 1983), Chapter 7.

EUGENE E. WHITE, *Practical Public Speaking*, 4th ed. (New York: Macmillan, 1982), Chapter 6.

chapter 6

Composing Introductions and Conclusions

People are sometimes startled at advice to compose the bulk of their speeches before they turn their attention to the introductions and conclusions. These two structural divisions of every presentation are crucially important and can establish excellent conditions for success or, conversely, can ruin an otherwise good talk.

Because an introduction may be considered as only the first sentence or two of a speech, students, and indeed speakers in the commercial circuit, tend to think about it very little. Similarly, a conclusion is often viewed as nothing more than a perfunctory summary of what has been said followed by some lame, ineffectual sentence such as, "Well, that's about it. Are there any questions?" Such a careless ending to a talk may do more to damage a presentation than lack of evidence on some point, objections from someone listening, or even an outright error. Most speakers know from the time they are asked to make a presentation until the actual occasion that they had better have some good information. However, these same people may not realize the impact that a careful conclusion has. The audience's final image of the speaker, for example, tends to be a more lasting one than that established throughout the body of a talk. Because a slovenly, ill-considered, hasty, or careless conclusion may constitute that last image, speakers might well devote much more energy to forming and rehearsing that portion of their speeches.

CONSTRUCTING EFFECTIVE INTRODUCTIONS

This section describes in detail some of the functions that good introductions can have and suggests some ways to construct effective ones. The overall point is that introductions should command attention. If they fail in that requirement, most of what follows will be ineffectual, too. Commanding attention is not the same as assuming that an audience will pay attention. When you first stand before the listeners, they will naturally show some curiosity and they will pay attention until events give them reason to turn aside or to become engrossed in what is going on. Thus, "command" is a deliberately chosen word. As a speaker, you do not just request or hope for or beg for attention. To be effective, you must create a new situation wherein listeners must attend, so compelling is the the presentation and the message. At first, it may seem like a tall order to expect a student speaker to "command" a classroom, or for an employee to "command" a conference of workers and managers. However, an excellent speaker does just that. How can *you* use an introduction to direct and control an audience? The following discussion suggests some ways.

Gaining Attention

The first way to attract an audience's commitment to listen is to arouse its interest in your topic. As a speaker, ask yourself why anyone would want to listen to you talk on the subject assigned or chosen. For some people this question is devastating, and may trigger their deepest anxieties of inadequacy and a desire to run away from a trying situation. However, once the shock is past, these speakers may realize that reasons can be found why others would want to hear them talk on exploring the solar system, making maple syrup at home, losing weight safely, the peerage system of England, or any number of other topics. To repeat, the first step is somehow to arouse interest in the topic. How could you lead the members of a general audience to see themselves involved in space travel, for example? You might call their attention to the National Aeronautics and Space Administration's offer to sell seats for interplanetary travel and exploration. You could directly challenge them by questioning their mental, physical, and emotional readiness for such a trip. Certainly you would not expect a definite commitment from anyone to actually take a space flight, but rather you would stir up the listeners' imaginations so that they consider the possibility of their own personal trips to the moon. Even those who reject the possibility and express dread of such a visit may have become aroused and involved in your topic.

Most of us can identify with anything as exciting as space travel, but you might legitimately ask how you can make the usual classroom and business subjects interesting enough to "command" an audience's attention. The answer lies in linking the subject with some kind of experience the listeners have probably already had and/or thought about. The section on audience analysis in Chapter 3 referred to human needs such as safety, food, water, companionship, approval, and so on. In your introductions, you should try to find and relate some link to these human needs. For example, if you have chosen to talk about making maple syrup, your introduction might refer to people's deeply seated need for assurance about the purity and safety of anything they eat. The beginning point of your talk on maple syrup could thus be an appeal to that need: "Do you know how many chemical additives, preservatives, and clarifiers you eat on your pancakes? I want to talk to you today about a way you can know there are none. I want to show you how you can have the best of a bygone era (notice the appeal to nostalgia also worked in here) without the expense and threat to health we now have. I want to show you how you can get useful amounts of pure, uncontaminated, genuine maple syrup from a nearby woods or even from your own back yard. A few afternoons of work and a bit of careful planning can give you a quality product that is almost unobtainable today at any reasonable price (notice the appeal to a sense of conservation)."

Nearly any topic can be made interesting and appealing if you merely strive to find the appeals within it. An audience coming to hear a speech is seeking interesting, challenging, stimulating ideas and facts. The introduction should give them a good motivation to listen. Of course, once their attention is aroused, you have to maintain the advantage and deliver a worthwhile talk. Other ways to arouse interest include asking pertinent questions, the answers to which focus on your purpose. If you can create suspense, perhaps by a series of questions or by relating carefully chosen events organized into a climactic order, you can also generate interest. Sometimes a startling statement will capture an audience. An anecdote or humorous story can be effective. For more serious topics, when humor is not appropriate or might backfire, a quotation might be an effective tool. The quotation should be related to your topic in some direct way. If your speech discusses simplifying the rigors of modern living, for example, you might quote Thoreau, who urged us to "Simplify. Simplify. Keep your accounts on your thumbnail."

Establishing Your Credibility

Another function of your introduction is to show the audience why you have an interest and some expertise in the chosen topic. Your interest need not be an issue, however, for anyone can express interest in any topic. A school teacher can express interest in brain surgery without objections from anyone. However, he or she cannot practice medicine without a license, nor can he or she create the same effect that the surgeon would when speaking on the same topic. The point here is that speakers need only reasonable care to maintain their credibility before an audience. Fortunately, you do not have to be a physician to say interesting things about medicine and be believable. The thoroughness of your preparation and thoughtfulness in anticipating the questions of your audience are reasons enough for people to pay attention and believe you.

In fact, you can go too far in striving to establish your credibility on a topic. It would be presumptuous to give too much highly technical detail when talking about something you really know very little about. For example, if you were giving a classroom speech on neural surgery to correct Parkinson's disease, you would be wise to talk in terms of general principles. The moment you make a statement such as, "We then close the surgical opening in the soft tissue with three nought soluble sutures," you may lose credibility among your listeners. The usual problem is building enough credibility on the topic to make your classmates and your teacher respect the organizational skills, good judgment, and careful planning that went into your speech. By making a statement such as the preceding example, you would have gone too far and you would probably have damaged your credibility by suddenly presenting the audience with the realization that they were hearing an impersonation, not an exposition by an interested party. Although dramatized examples and presentations are not necessarily ineffective or undesirable, audiences expecting one kind of message (objective) may be unimpressed and reject a different kind (dramatized). Your credentials to speak authoritatively on the topic are suddenly and sharply called into question by excessive measures to build credibility. A better strategy would be to state simply and directly what your own interest in the topic is. Did a member of the family have the procedure? Is your parent a surgeon? Are you a premedical student? Is your interest simply casual or a long-term one?

Establishing Good Will

In addition to arousing interest and showing your involvement with the topic, an introduction might show your good will and interest in the welfare of the audience. Simply referring to the occasion or to the audience itself in a warm, interested way may be all that you need to do to fill this function: "The other day when Jan gave her speech on raising bees on the dorm roof, I thought about how students in this class have always shown interest in nature and conservation. It seemed to me that you would enjoy a speech on _____." The mere act of thinking about what the class might enjoy, the courtesy of remembering how they had seemed to like certain subjects, flatters the listeners. They may feel lucky that you remember their talks and recall their tastes and needs.

Bidding for a Fair Hearing

Sometimes an audience may not be particularly warm and friendly, either because it is unhappy with the occasion or perhaps a previous speaker left it surly. You can often use your introduction to ask for a fair hearing if there is reason for you to believe the audience will reject your message. Of course, you shouldn't assume the audience's hostility, but when it is likely to arise you should be ready. For example, if your audience is a typical college class, listeners are probably interested in rock music. If your thesis is that "Rock music is a corrupting influence in America," you might assume some skepticism. The introduction might make such a thesis acceptable for a speech, but paying no particular attention to the audience's attitudes may lead you to an icy reception. "All of us here were probably brought up on rock music and, if you're like me you've probably enjoyed The Police, Led Zepplin, Devo, or Styx. Like me, you probably never questioned the values that these groups subconsciously represent. Now don't get me wrong; I'm not going to attack the groups. I want to lay out for your consideration three ideas you may never have thought about. After you hear these three points, then you can make up your own mind whether you agree with me that rock music can do our country some harm." This fragment of an introduction asks the audience only to consider the arguments, and seems not to impose the thesis on the listeners. Of course, in a sense it does impose one, but at least the speaker admits that the audience may not accept it. A bid for a fair hearing asks others just to consider your speech, warns that the thesis may not be agreeable, and sets as neutral a tone as possible.

Orienting Listeners

Introductions have still other functions. An extremely important one is to orient the listeners on the topic. Many a speaker suddenly launches into a topic without any cues about what listeners are supposed to remember, which ideas are important and which ones are less so, or why the audience should care at all about the topic. You might define unfamiliar terms, key concepts for understanding the speech, and assumptions you make. You may give a brief historical background as a context for your remarks. You might present an operational definition of critical terms you use in a specialized way. For example, if you are speaking on the effects of mass media on television viewers, you might want to define the term "tragic hero" as any victimized central character in a TV drama. The usual definition as a noble, extraordinary person with a character flaw or a fatal weakness may not be suitable for your purposes. Thus, your operational definition is one you would wish to share with the audience for this one presentation.

A common device is to start with some historical origin of the topic or question. If you are going to speak on Tax Bracket Creep, for instance, the natural origin is the adoption of income taxes in the country. Briefly tracing the rise in tax rates and inflation will lead naturally to the topic. Sometimes the introduction can contain a brief history or evolution of a topic which sets up the main speech. Be careful not to overdevelop the history to the point that the audience thinks the main speech has begun when in fact you are just sketching in preliminary material.

Recall the classical one-word questions posed by all editors, journalists, and reporters as guidelines for explaining events: Who? What? When? Where? Why? How? Whenever some newsworthy incident occurs, especially if it is highly emotional and far reaching, the public is hungry for answers to those simple, one-word questions. For example, the attempt on the life of Pope John Paul illustrates how the list comes to mind. Who did such a terrible thing? What occurred at what place and time? Why did the conspirators act as they did, and how did they proceed? The answers to these inquiries can furnish a relatively complete response to public curiosity about the event. You can often use the same questions as a format for a speech.

Previewing Topics

One way to help orient your listeners is to state what you will cover in your talk. This is sometimes called *previewing* your main points. Do not tell too much. State just enough to show the broad map of ground you will cover: "The topic of federal aid is so broad that I will limit my talk just to aid to black colleges. Specifically, I will deal with qualifications for aid, procedure for getting a scholarship, and financial limitations." This preview can help to motivate listeners at the same time it orients them. Concerned students will know not only the points to be covered but approximately where in the speech to expect their development. The rudiments of an outline are already visible, and especially if you are planning to use numerous facts and numbers, a simple preview of your main points helps listeners keep perspective.

Excluding Topics

Just as the introductory comments can specify what you will cover in your speech, so they can state what you will exclude: "I will not talk about the philosophical aspect of prisons. I will talk only about the costs per prisoner in this country. My speech is about the excessive cost of jails, not whether imprisonment is right, not whether it is effective, not whether there is a better way to deal with criminals." This tactic may help focus attention on just those aspects of the topic you wish to address without confusing your listeners with other complicated views on the topic. Sometimes the exclusion of matter is a ploy to avoid giving offense: "Regardless of your own personal religious beliefs, I will ask you today to consider cremation solely on practical bases. I will not address the philosophical, religious, and emotional issues this topic always raises. I want to limit my remarks to the legally acceptable, financially sound, and ecologically responsible reasons to consider cremation." This introduction not only previews the limits of the talk but evades the emotionally explosive religious and philosophical objections someone might raise. Of course, nothing prevents audiences from raising such objections in their own minds and perhaps rejecting the speaker, but at least there is little opportunity for reaction to the topics chosen.

In most talks several sentences are placed early in the speech to help listeners get their bearings and understand what the talk is all about. This preliminary material is not content about the topic itself but is rather the information someone needs to know in order to listen to the particular speech and make the best use of it. Such material helps the listeners get into the right mental and emotional framework to hear the talk. A good way for you to think about introductory material is to pose for yourself several questions whose answers will assist you in making your introduction. Not every one of the questions in the following list is appropriate for all topics and all situations. Answer those which seem important for a particular speech situation and ignore those which do not apply. However, do not ignore them just because the answer is difficult or unknown as you begin preparation.

A CHECKLIST

1. Is this topic familiar to the audience? If it is not, how can I show some reasons they should want to hear about it.

2. How much does the audience, or a part of the audience, probably know about this subject? Will it be too elementary for some and too hard for others? How far into the subject should I go?

3. Is this topic inherently important or trivial? If it seems to be trivial, can my treatment of it make it seem useful and worthwhile to my listeners? For example, I might say, "You may think it silly for me to devote six minutes to this topic, 'Dandelions,' but I hope to show you that this ever-present little pest has numerous important, even life-saving uses. From it we can make food, drink, and medicines."

4. What must the audience know about the topic before it can understand and enjoy my thesis? Is there any preliminary technical fact or viewpoint the listeners need to appreciate the topic? "Because some of you here have no technical background, I need to explain a few terms which will help you understand my talk. First, think of a super-sophisticated typewriter when I say 'word processor' and think of printed pages when I say "hard copy."

5. Is any part of the topic so much more striking or appealing than other parts that I can use it to command attention?

6. If the topic is mainly about a place, such as a city, a mountain, a lake, and so on, what other nearby places can help the audience to feel comfortably aware of its location? Is there any key phrase that shows why the place is important or significant? Examples: "Sarajevo, where many believe World War I started, is located ____" "Brenner Pass, which separates Italy and Austria ____" "Golden, 12 miles west of Denver, known for Coors beer ____."

7. If the talk is about an event in time, what preceded or caused it? What must the audence know to understand the time frame? For example, I should not just start talking about the contributions of Marcus Aurelius, but I should explain to the audience that he was a Roman emperor, a philosopher, and a writer of enduring ideas. His lifetime should be stated, perhaps as a span of dates (121–180 A.D.) or maybe only in relation to Julius Caesar (100–44 B.C.). His lifetime could be placed as "just before the middle of the 500 years of the Roman Empire." The choice depends on how much stress I want to place on the time span, knowledge within the audience, and the point of my speech. If comparing Caesar and Aurelius, I may make more of the time relationship. If my thesis concerns only philosophical ideas, a brief phrase identifying Aurelius as a Stoic philosopher and Roman emperor may be enough.

AVOIDING BAD HABITS
IN INTRODUCTORY MATERIAL

Although you have probably heard the advice not to apologize in an introduction, it must be repeated here. People seem to be driven to apologize for their lack of preparation, for their lack of skill in speaking, for their appearance, or for their lack of time to do justice to the topic. Listeners seem tolerant, for the most part, because they hear apologies so often. However, a speaker bent on improvement ought to once and for all consider the probable effects of the largely ritual and supposedly modest apologies that riddle public speaking. First, an apology starts a presentation very poorly. It says to listeners that something slipshod and half-thought-through is to be aired. If you did not have time to prepare, and you reveal that fact, then listeners have to conclude that they are to hear a hasty, incomplete version of what they wanted to hear. Of course, you usually just mean to offer a blanket excuse for any and all kinds of shortcomings, and the lack of time is supposed to inform the audience how busy and well-intentioned you are. An apology does not come off that way. It tells the audience to prepare for a disappointment.

In an effort to seem modest, speakers often say something to the effect that, "I'm not any kind of expert on this topic, but I'd like to share a few of my thoughts about it." Your making such a statement says to the audience that you may not know enough to justify their listening to your speech. Why should an audience listen to you if you know no more than they do on a topic? Further, if you are confessing to poor preparation, the audience is more likely to be resentful than forgiving and understanding. If you are just being modest and then give an excellent talk, as sometimes happens, the audience still resents the pose and insincerity of needless apology. If you apologize for your lack of knowledge on a topic, it is not hard to imagine an audience's saying mentally, "If you don't know much about the subject, sit down." Audiences wish to share information, not ignorance. On the other hand, do not be intimidated by your inability to discover everything about a topic. Nobody knows everything. Find out everything you can gather in a reasonable time, but do not burden your listeners with your inability to locate the ideal data. Do the best job you can with what you have after honest, dutiful effort.

In summary, even if you are guilty, do not confess to shabby preparation, lack of speaking skill, or lack of preparation time. If you really are inept, everyone will know soon enough without your emphasizing the point. If, as is more likely, you feel insecure and do not wish to appear overbearing, you still do not need to apologize or try to seem modest. People like a confident, competent, well-prepared speaker. Omitting the apology just might help to create that image of you before your listeners. Why destroy that advantage and injure your audience's pleasure? Even if you are pressed for time and could not do the thorough job you imagine as ideal, listeners may still perceive the merits of the job you were able to accomplish. Do not, in effect, instruct them to notice all your deficiencies.

DELIVERING THE INTRODUCTION

Although Chapter 7 contains suggestions for delivering a speech, a special caution is necessary here. Because your first impression is created in the introduction, you need to pay careful attention to the first few sentences of every presentation. Many people tend to speak rapidly, especially when they are nervous and insecure. The beginning of a speech is precisely the point at which you are likely to be most tense. On the other hand, an audience hearing you for the first time is unfamiliar with your voice, your personality, your characteristic vocal inflections, and even your pronunciations. They require a little time to get used to the voice of anyone unfamiliar to them. One of the most effective changes you can make in your speech habits, therefore, is to consciously slow down your rate of delivery and to carefully articulate any unfamiliar words or expressions in the early part of your speech. The somewhat old-fashioned notion that every speech should begin with a joke or anecdote has some merit, after all. The audience can use the inconsequential, amusing portion of the speech to get used to an unfamiliar voice, and by the time you present the meat of the talk, the audience will have adjusted to your voice and manner. In any case, sensitive speakers strive to slow down and speak with very deliberate clarity in the introduction to give listeners some time to become accustomed to their voices.

Just as tense speakers tend to speed up their rates of delivery, so do they also tend to soften their volumes. This lowering of the voice further complicates the audience's job of hearing and interpreting the talk. Unfortunately, if you do this, the audience may miss most of your crucial introductory material. Listeners are forced to struggle to reconstruct what you must have said, and to so burden them is unnecessary and risky: They may not take the trouble to pay attention to difficult ideas, in which case some portion of the speech is lost to them.

MAKING EFFECTIVE CONCLUSIONS

This part of the chapter discusses the purposes and strategies of concluding remarks. For some people the conclusion is the most troublesome and difficult part of a speech. Like the introduction, the conclusion is often one of the last parts of a whole speech to be developed. Imagine that you have assembled the bulk of data, information, opinions, and arguments you need for a speech. After you choose all the necessary material and arrange it, there remains the question of how to lead into the topic interestingly and how to exit from the presentation gracefully.

In general, the tasks of the conclusion are to remind listeners of the importance and specifics of the thesis, to summarize the points made, and to establish a feeling of finality or satisfaction. Note that satisfaction is used in a specific way here, as a feeling within the audience about the wholeness of a speech, not necessarily a feeling of positive emotions about the topic or even the conclusions reached by the speaker. For example, a listener could feel satisfied that a speech about the refusal of some people to accept the truth of the Holocaust was clear, complete, and accurate. However, that same listener might remain appalled at the conclusion of the speech—namely, that a sizable part of the population does not believe that the persecution of Jews by Hitler ever took place at all. Thus, satisfaction here refers to assessment of the speaker's effort, and is not with the facts explained in the speech.

Other tasks of conclusions are to inspire some action called for in the speech, to restate arguments or viewpoints expressed, and to create a sense of finality, completeness, or thoroughness. You need not exhaust a topic to create aesthetic satisfaction with a speech, but you should have enough data, enough supporting material, and enough development to create a sense of adequacy. Consider an analogy: A wonderful meal should not leave diners uncomfortably stuffed, ill, nauseous, or jaded. It should create a sense of fullness and contentment. Nothing needed was left out. Nothing desired was missing. Nothing excessive was included. So, too, with a speech.

Following are some specific ways of creating these feelings in a speech:

> You can appeal directly for action, if the speech is to convince or persuade. "My presentation today has been directed toward reassuring you that giving blood is safe, altruistic, and needed. I once more urge you to visit your local blood bank and give of yourself that others might live."

> Often a speech that is awkward or embarrassing to conclude will benefit from an apt quotation. "I must conclude my report on our finances by noting the lack of growth in our treasury. You may recall that the last Board of Directors' meeting

prohibited both of the fund-raising projects we had proposed. I feel that Will Rogers' comment about Calvin Coolidge applies to me. Rogers said that 'the country wanted nothing done, and he done it.'"

Persuasive or expository speeches on problems often end with a proposed solution. Such an ending gives food for thought to the audience, ends the speech strongly, and may invite questions if these are desired at the end of a talk. "The simplest solution I can think of to this taxing inequity is to simply raise the personal exemption from $1000 to $2000. I believe that if you think about this proposal after you leave here tonight, you will find, as I do, far more merits than problems in our future taxation."

A common concluding remark is to call for further research or study of a problem or issue when no resolution is yet possible. Such controversial topics as nuclear generators, human genetic engineering, or good-samaritan laws may not be easily resolved in a local situation, even when a majority has made its views known. A relatively safe exit from a speech on such an issue is to frankly admit that no solution or satisfactory resolution is possible yet. Then you can call for continued study and investigation of the topic. When overworked, this device seems to be an evasion of an issue, but it frequently is the only honest outcome of discussion and speeches.

A time-tested device of conclusions is to appeal to the human needs, attitudes, and motivations known to prevail in the audience. Such fundamental motivations as interest in pleasure, social approval, ownership, safety, and so on, often work well. "If you follow the few simple steps I have just outlined, you can impress your neighbors as you build your own wine press, save money on cider and wine, and get valuable outdoor exercise."

Some Common Mistakes

Probably the most annoying habit of speakers is to indicate to listeners that the speech is just about over and then launch back into a new main point. If you have this habit, you might create a sense of finality at the wrong place, which is probably worse than not creating it at all. Sometimes you are unsure whether you have made all the intended points. As an afterthought, you might tack on a new idea not even included in your original plan for the speech.

Another kind of weak conclusion is nervous repetition of several of the main points. If you do this, the audience will consider you as indecisive and as unsure of what you have covered and what you have left out. Credibility can be damaged by this kind of ending. To avoid it, plan specifically for the conclusion. Have a sentence or two that definitely end the talk and then, under the pressure of emotion, which is almost inevitable during the speech, say the planned conclusion.

Making a conclusion too long is still another flaw in a good talk. There is no absolute formula for determining the length of a conclusion, but, in general, the shorter it is the better. You can combine in one sentence several purposes and, for example, call for action and restate the thesis. One sentence could appeal to basic human needs and at the same time reestablish the goals you share with the audience. "If this senseless waste of tax money through cost overruns and price gouging on military contracts is to be prevented, you should join me in sending a letter to our congressional representatives."

When you give a very long speech, such as an hour-long commencement address, an after-dinner speech at a business meeting, or a major speech for a religious or civic club, the conclusion can be somewhat longer than the usual few sentences. You can summarize the main points, indicate what they all add up to (restate the thesis), and call for action or conviction. Give an appropriate quotation or anecdote which crystallizes the thought of the talk. Such a conclusion might occupy several minutes.

Because audiences resent a speaker's going overtime more than they do a speaker's talking too briefly, it is better to err on the side of brevity. Religious clergy are well aware of the irritation their congregations show when their sermons go on too long. The rustling, coughing, and fidgeting can be observed by all. In addition, many congregations are quite vocal in objecting if the sermons go on too long too often.

We might find an insight in this example. The problem here is not a question of anyone's objecting to the absolute length of a speech; it is more a matter of having one's expectations thwarted. If a clergy member announced that he or she would speak for 1 hour and 15 minutes, and that to accommodate everyone's plans he or she would start the sermon earlier, then probably everyone who normally attended the services would arrive a few minutes early. In the earlier days of this country, sermons went on for hours, but everyone knew the conventions of length and accepted them. If you are to speak for 4 hours, and you quit 10 minutes early, no one will object that you short changed them. However, if you speak for 4 hours and 10 minutes, you may be assaulted!

Ethics of Appeals to Motives

Many students feel embarrassed, guilty, or hesitant to use all the tools of rhetorical strategy, such as appealing to motives. They may doubt the ethical validity of direct appeals to deeply seated human needs and motives. However, nearly any assertion in support of a speech can be traced to such needs. First, to appeal deliberately to someone's needs and wants is not unethical, assuming that the overall intent of the speech is honest. Specifically, suppose you want to inform listeners on the sport of hang gliding; appeals to pride, social acceptance, or self-image are perfectly appropriate. However, if you use those appeals to sell the audience a line of commercial gliders, then you have a little more complicated issue. Sales of all goods and services now freely exploit every known human need and desire. It does not seem reasonable to hold the individual speaker to standards no corporation or commercial concern can meet—namely, absolute candor and concern solely for the welfare of the target audience. Still, every speaker is expected to be truthful, fair-minded, and honorable in addresses of all kinds. Also, if you appealed to all your listeners' emotions in order to sell defective or inoperable gliders, then clearly there is no question about the immorality of your ethics. The point of this discussion is to remind you that ethical questions must be confronted and resolved. Even when you are presenting informative, not persuasive, speeches you are asking others to believe assertions and you should thus be aware of your ethical responsibilities. Where does orthodox skill in strategy and organization end and contrived exploitation begin? What appeals in a conclusion are legitimate and what appeals are unfair, exploitative, deceptive, or fraudulent? Your answers to these questions eventually determine how listeners will evaluate your ethics and credibility.

EXERCISES

1. Assume that a 6- or 7-minute speech on the following topics has been assigned for classroom delivery. The topics are straightforward in their development. Make a very brief conclusion for each topic, imagining what has been said in the speech.
   a. Anorexia nervosa.
   b. Dangers of cigarette smoking.
   c. Amnesty for illegal aliens.
   d. Firearms control.
   e. Abortion.
   f. Food additives.
   g. Nuclear power plants, or nuclear waste.
   h. Saving the whales (or seals or condors).
   i. The 55 mph speed limit.
   j. Campus policy on alcohol rules.
2. For each topic just listed, state three main points that must have been made in the imaginary speech. If students actually said aloud the conclusions they deemed appropriate for each topic, then other students should be able to reason what the main ideas of the speech were. Similarly, they ought to be able to determine the thesis for each conclusion stated aloud.
3. Discuss in class the relative merits of the following devices as used in introductions and conclusions:
   poetry   quotations   anecdotes   jokes   quips
4. During a scheduled speech presentation, assign a class member as a "specialist" or "technician" in introductions and another as the same for conclusions. In addition to any general critiques offered in the class, have these specialists comment on the respective divisions of the day's presentations.

SELECTED READINGS

BERT E. BRADLEY, *Fundamentals of Speech Communication*, 3rd ed. (Dubuque, Iowa: Wm. C. Brown, 1981), Chapter 7.

EUGENE E. WHITE, *Practical Public Speaking* (New York: Macmillan, 1982), Chapters 10 and 11.

chapter 7

Delivering a Speech Effectively

This chapter is about matters you can control and use to maximize your impact on your audience during an actual presentation. The topics for study are posture, gesture and movement, and eye contact. Other concerns are subjective ones, such as appropriate dress, intensity, and dynamics of voice arising out of particular situations such as unexpected noise, interruptions, or danger.

Improving your performance depends on your being aware both of the effects you can create by good and bad use of all these actions and of the interaction of these actions with your voice. For example, if you adopt a slouching, slumped posture your breathing can be shallow and weak, which in turn can lead to a weak vocal tone. The total effect is that a listener might perceive you to be a vacillating, ineffectual person: "He doesn't seem very vigorous, his voice is weak and hard to hear, and he doesn't seem to care very much about his subject." Similarly, evasive eye contact may suggest duplicity, or excessive loudness may create an illusion of an overbearing manner, poor audience adaptation, or even overcompensation for weaknesses in conviction or evidence. The impressions may be totally wrong and unfair, but those attending to a speech have to make judgments on whatever cues are given them. No rehearsal can tell you exactly what it is like to address a live audience, for even if you practice in the very room where your speech is to be given, the absence of a full audience completely changes the effect, both on you and on an observer. The differences are comparable to playing with a toy gun and a real one. The most ingenious and accurate reproduction of a firearm does not create the same emotions in us as a real weapon would—we know the toy is not loaded and is not like the real firearm.

Neither is an empty auditorium. The acoustics of the place change the moment human bodies fill the seats, and the sound of your voice (as you hear it) will change slightly as the absorption or reflection of sound in the auditorium varies. Nevertheless, it is wise to visit the place of presentation if possible to discover any adjustments you may have to make later. Among these are the possibility of using a louder or slower delivery than is usual, if the room is "boomy" or has dead spots. For example, some rooms have peculiar focusing and absorbing qualities with the result that a speaker may be more clearly audible to listeners in distant seats than to those seated considerably closer. It often happens that listeners in the rear seats can hear clearly whereas those closer perceive muffled, inarticulate sounds. Concert-goers learn to find good seats and avoid dead spots where music, like the voice, is so distorted.

Because different speaking situations require different loudness levels, rates of speaking, and degrees of effort in enunciation, you should strive to develop maximum flexibility in your voice. This vocal range is not for showing off, but for adapting to realistic situations. For maximum utility, you should stretch and exercise your voice just as you do the muscles of your body. Although the analogy breaks down because of physical differences, still, the emotional security and pride that you may develop seem to be adequate justification for thus developing your voice. Flexibility also permits ready adjustment to unexpected and unusual speaking situations. With adequate control and range, nearly anyone can speak without strain to groups from a handful to 1000 or more auditors.

Most people would feel slightly insulted when told that they do not have complete control of their voices. However, few people have trained their voices near their potential for force and expressiveness in ordinary conversation, much less for public presentations. No one is born a good speaker. Everyone starts out with a bawl and by good models, effective practice, alert and constructive criticism, people achieve markedly different levels of expertise. Of course, individual temperamental differences and abilities predispose some persons to easier, quicker success. But we live in a talking society with adequate opportunity for finding good models and competent criticism. It remains for interested people to plan, practice, and monitor their improvement in systematic ways. The effort required to achieve excellence may vary among people, but competence can be achieved by all through intelligent practice and criticism.

The effort needed to transform yourself from a merely adequate speaker into a really competent, forceful one is really quite considerable because no one comes to a program of improvement like an inexperienced child with no preconceptions, practices, or prejudices. Young adults have built strong vocal habits which are hard to overcome, even if they are very bad practices. Just try to stop saying "Uh" repeatedly, if that is one of your habits. It requires determination, open-mindedness, practice, and emotional toughness to progress. Several quite different processes must be studied, reformed, and maintained to avoid loss of progress.

The voice itself is a good beginning point for self-improvement, whether in preparation for a single speech or as a long-term overall self-development project. Many people find that attention to the voice helps them progress strikingly in general. Because vocalization is a physical act, and not an entirely mental process, the effect of changes in its use are quite noticeable. The following section analyzes and discusses the voice, its qualities, its range, and the variables which can be controlled to secure improved vocal control for speaking. Later in the chapter, the mental and emotional concerns of public speaking are discussed, and suggestions for exercises to replace bad habits with good ones are made.

THE NATURE OF A GOOD VOICE

Because your voice is the chief instrument linking your inner self of mind and emotions with the outside world of other people and objects, it seems obvious that you should want to have the best vocal instrument possible for expressing yourself efficiently and accurately. By speaking efficiently, you run the least risk of leaving unsaid that which you ought to say or of saying more than you should in a situation. By speaking accurately, you avoid creating false impressions. You can achieve the maximum degree of control due you in a social situation. How can you discover what kind of voice is best for securing these desired ends? Centuries of critical observation and reporting have shown repeatedly that several particular qualities of voice produce what is considered maximum effectiveness. These qualities are discussed next. But remember as you read that merely practicing them until you produce a beautiful sound does not guarantee you automatic control of your listeners. Your message and your mind set are best revealed by a cultivated voice, but that skillful use of voice which works to charm your audience can also reveal your faults as certainly as it does your strengths.

Adequate Vocal Power

Nearly anyone in good health can improve the power or strength of his or her voice through directed practice. A matter of weeks is often enough to make a noticeable difference. The trick is not to seek greater loudness just to blast listeners into submission, but to cultivate an adequate range of loudness so that you are comfortable in a great variety of speaking situations. What should you do in a speech if the microphone goes bad and quits? If you are addressing a few hundred people, you should be able to step aside and, without hurting your voice, without screaming, and without losing a sense of natural inflection, continue your presentation and ensure that everyone can hear comfortably. Many people simply do not believe that they have the capability to thus develop their voices, bound as they are by habit. However, consider for a moment the generations of high school actors and singers, the performers in college and little theatre presentations, and the lecturers who addressed perhaps a thousand people for an hour or more without apparent strain or difficulty in projection. How did they manage? The answer is simple: Rehearsal, vocal practice, criticism by an attentive director. The constant monitoring of your own voice can produce a strikingly more interesting and powerful voice which may lead to great satisfaction and confidence. The chief risk to avoid is vocal strain. It is probably better not to try to progress too fast, for gradual stretching of the limits of loudness is much better than attempting a sudden improvement. Avoid shouting and raising the pitch of your voice in an attempt to project further. The best advice is to work with a sympathetic speech or drama teacher rather than to rely on practice by yourself to increase your vocal power rapidly or to markedly higher levels. The risk of straining your voice by eagerness to progress is too high, and vocal strain can not only set you back in your program of self-improvement but also physically damage your vocal mechanism. If you get a sore throat after practice, you are straining too hard (or maybe smoking too much). If your voice is hoarse after practice, you are straining some muscles. Practice for short periods and rest your voice frequently. Long practice at high volume levels may create irritation of the throat tissues and delicate surfaces of the vocal mechanism. Hoarseness, temporary loss of voice, and soreness can result.

Adequate Inflection

Inflection means the rise and fall of pitch in the voice. If you say the word "no" twice—first as if you are angry and will not permit someone to borrow your new car, and then as if you are asking the question, "Isn't that true?"—you will notice that your voice slides up or down in pitch. English is a language in which a great deal of meaning is determined by the way we use our voices as well as by the way we pronounce the words; it is thus said to be a highly inflected language. People who show very little emotion when they talk may be missing a great deal of communicative potential and risking misunderstanding. Recall for a moment the dead-pan comedians, such as Buster Keaton, whose whole comic routines depend on withholding the normal vocal cues and the normal expected responses to situations. A lack of response, then, is just as much a communicative response as giving one. When people refuse to laugh at our jokes, we wonder "What's eating them?" Similarly, when a speaker understresses everything, often from the fear of seeming too demonstrative or "hammy," the result may be unintentionally funny, or perhaps boring. Some experiments have shown that restricting the pitch range of voices causes a loss of attention and may cause a severe loss of intelligibility of even clearly articulated speech. If people are turned off by your manner of delivery, they may conclude that you yourself are not very interested in what you are saying, and therefore they have little reason to attend either.

Inflection can verify or contradict your words. It can reveal some nuances in meaning that the language alone is not capable of showing. It can add interest, emotion, and qualifications to what you are saying. Although some authorities deny that inflection carries meaning, all of them agree that it certainly conveys contextual clues and colors the meaning of our utterances. Therefore, control of adequate range of inflection is just as important as control of power in building and maintaining an adequate voice.[1]

Just as it is possible to abuse the voice's power, so can you go too far in using inflection. Unusually large pitch excursions can create the impression of insincerity or pretentiousness if those tone slides are not appropriate to the situation. Imagine the sound of the following sketch: A self-important society matron is speaking to a garden party guest whose social class is clearly beneath her own, yet she has to seem to welcome him to the party. "Oh, how do you do. I'm so-o-o glad you could come."

The attempt to get too much inflection, as mentioned, can create a very artificial, posed effect. However, in the United States, the opposite abuse is far more widespread. Our culture is relatively dour, restrained, even inhibited compared with some others. We tend to shut off access to much linguistic coding by our relatively static, overcontrolled speech habits. No one appreciates excessive affectation and theatrical airs in everyday discourse, conversation, or speeches. But one of the most persistent American habits is failure to use adequate pitch range in situations in which more range is called for. Failure to use adequate vocal change is just as much a defect as poor word choice or pronunciation. Certainly one of the most annoying and damaging speech habits is inflectional inhibition, or in blunter words, lackluster voices. Your aim should be to create precisely the desired mood, setting, or context for your words. Although listeners will not punish you for substandard language, dysfluency, or colorless presentations, neither will they grant you the rewards that interesting, vibrant speakers get. With equal intelligence and experience, people with the knack of revealing their interest and enthusiasm often gain the edge in social and professional life.

Fluency

Nothing is so annoying as lack of fluency in a speaker. How often do we hear a highly competent person stumble and grope through a presentation which with just a little practice could have been far better? What was intended as helpful, informative, or ceremonial enjoyment turned into an ordeal. Of course, inflection and adequate loudness are a part of the enjoyment of a presentation, but among the qualities of appealing speakers, fluency certainly ranks high. Fluent speakers do not omit all pauses, they just put the pauses in the right places. Read aloud these two sentences, putting pauses in the blank areas. You will see the effects of one kind of dysfluency:

1. It gives me great pleasure   to be here today.
2. It gives   me great   pleasure to be   here   today.
3. It . . . uh . . . gives me great . . . uh . . . pleasure . . . to . . . uh . . . be here today.

A moment's study should indicate that the pause after the word pleasure in sentence 1, while unnecessary, still does not unduly disrupt the flow of the idea. In sentence 2, the same words are so ill-marked with the pauses that the sentence hardly makes sense. Anyone pausing as the example shows would be perceived as forgetful, tired, or emotionally so upset as to be out of control of delivery. Yet many speakers reveal poor rhythm by pausing in the wrong places. Sentence 3 is unhappily a more common rendition of the same words. Grueling to listeners when repeated for any length of time, the "uhs" are hardly noticed by the speaker. Some people use vocalized pauses such as "er," "ah," and "uh" to fill time, for they fear that momentary silence will make the listeners think that they have forgotten what to say. Other words are used similarly—as unconscious fillers of imaginary gaps in thought. "The best advice, you know, for someone like this, you know, is to tell them, well, you know, like to listen more closely, you know, to what they actually say."

One kind of broken rhythm in speech is caused by insufficient air intake to supply both the body's needs and the air pressure necessary to generate and sustain vocal sounds. Speech requires more air than normal life-supporting breathing, both because more energy is being consumed in speaking and because the rate of outgoing air is artificially regulated by the speaking. (Normally an automatic adjustment by the brain helps us breathe at just the right tempo and depth to supply our needs.) When we speak with some force, the needs of the body and the needs of the performance may happen to coincide, or they may be at odds with each other. In fact, a vigorous speech may make the speaker light-headed from excessive oxygen because the amount of air for delivering the speech may be too much for just living! Practice and experience can help you discover the proper balance so that you must neither gasp for air in midsentence nor sigh at odd junctures in the speech to expend surplus air. Some speakers start talking late in the "outbound" part of the breathing cycle and find themselves with insufficient air to support a phrase near the end of a sentence. The result is that they start out "behind themselves" and their breathing cannot catch up with their talking. Take a good deep breath before saying anything. Use nearly all the outbound air to speak. Plan the pauses so that you breathe *in* on the pauses and *out* on the vocalizations. Although proper breathing sounds simple, many a good speech has been filled with awkward gasps for air at strange places in a sentence or paragraph. The whole problem of rhythmic breathing for speaking may be compared with that faced by singers. A singer has to plan his or her breathing so that at no time does a word "run out of air" or sound strained. The phrasing of a song must also make sense both musically and linguistically. Finally, the end of a musical phrase must not be weaker than the beginning just because the singer's breath is running low. Note, however, that even if you are an accomplished singer, you may not discover much carryover into your speech from your conditioning for music. Although much of the training for singing is similar to that for professionally acting or speaking, there are some crucial differences in the conditioning and skills required for the two arts.

The role of memorization in fluency. Singers memorize words, breathing patterns, and melodies to repeat again and again, and they monitor their performance until just the right tones and inflections result. In most speaking, such as everyday conversation at work and in social situations, we do not rehearse at all, but say whatever the immediate conversation requires. We also have no opportunity to choose among various inflections. The usual result is dependence upon a stock of more or less stereotyped, overworked patterns of speech which we call up. These reveal, possibly, adequate information about our feelings but may not give the very best, most accurate impressions we intend. In contrast to singing or acting, in which the same thing is said over and over in rehearsal until it is both aesthetically appropriate and clearly articulated, everyday speech is relatively haphazard. We often speak eloquently by accident. But speakers who seek a greater probability of being understood clearly need a greater degree of assurance that their voices will perform predictably and will respond well to precise pitch control. Thus, a means of calling into use the benefits of memory enjoyed by singers and actors should be available to public speakers. The casual speech habits of day-to-day talking do not develop speaking skills very much because little or no deliberate rehearsal occurs, and therefore no opportunity to select the best of several utterances is available. In other words, habit dominates us, and unfortunately, what is habitual is so easy that it persists even when something different is needed.

You may now begin to feel uneasy. If memory is used to improve speaking and habit is to be controlled, are we to become mechanical and insincere-sounding speakers? Are we to rehearse and master 100 prepackaged, contrived patterns of speech and plug in the best one in each of our utterances in real life? No. The advice that follows is based upon selecting and expanding beyond present limits the best among habitual patterns of speech. Thus, reinforcing your range of expression will allow you fuller, more accurate speech. Memory will serve in a secondary role, somewhat as it does in music and drama warm-up exercises. These exercises stretch the limits of musical and emotional expression, sometimes beyond any practical uses, just to illustrate to the performer some choices that might have been made, but which were rejected in favor of the most appropriate of the many possible choices.

Vocal Distractions

A significant step in improving your presentations is to delete distracting mannerisms, vocal sounds, and gestures. Although gestures and movements are not voice actions, bodily action is so closely tied to voice that they interact. Attempts to control your body's motion may generate stress for the voice mechanism, and control of your voice may lead you to unusual, nervous mannerisms. For example, you may shake your hand impatiently, as if symbolically brushing away some annoying constraint. Similarly, your voice may take on a shrill or impatient note if you realize that you are fidgeting, slouching, shifting weight, repeating a meaningless gesture, or putting your hands in your pockets. The variety of nervous actions that can accompany a speech is large. Controlling them does not mean totally excluding spontaneous action, but rather it means putting the nervous energy to constructive, meaningful, and pleasing uses.

The following steps can help you control annoying vocal mannerisms: First, isolate the distraction by listening carefully to a tape-recorded speech or have someone who can objectively describe the effect help you discover what the distraction is. Then carefully and deliberately practice a sentence or two without the distraction. For example, if you repeatedly tack on "OK?" at the end of every sentence, either slowly and deliberately talk to the friend who called the mannerism to your attention, or record a speech of several minutes' duration on a recorder or cassette. Do not worry about any other problems with the speech; just concentrate on the one annoying habit. The task, thus, is to discover and then reject or replace the bad behavior with a good one. The most common vocal distractions are vocalized pauses, the "Ahs" and "Uhs" we put into our speech as if to demand that listeners stay attentive while we think of the next phrase.

Some people actually cultivate the habit of saying a long-drawn-out "Ahh-h-h" to keep voice-actuated radio transmitters or electronic equipment in operation. The sound of the voice is used to automatically turn on and keep on the equipment, and to stop speaking for more than a second or 2 causes the radio to turn itself off, or in some cases, to key some other equipment. Airline pilots, tower operators, amateur radio people, and other personnel using such equipment should learn to turn off their "professional" voices in everyday speech, because the habit can be most annoying to those who do not realize why it is so pronounced.

The source of some of our speech habits is, simply, other people. We tend to imitate those we admire, and often we unconsciously assume mannerisms, pitch slides, and characteristic inflections of those people. When your peers observe such imitative behavior, they may not realize the unconscious nature of the copying. In fact, they may resent it and attribute to you insincerity and flattery if you so emulate others. What is charming and distinctive in one person may be ugly and unbecoming in another.

Avoiding vocal distractions can be a frustrating and painful task. First, asking a friend to point out your flaws is akin to inquiring whether you have offensive breath or body odors. Any answer is embarrassing and intrudes upon the ego. Next, speech is so powerfully habit-bound that any change is hard to make. A habit may tend to come back even after you think you have overcome it. Because other people around you also share the habit, there is ample opportunity for modeling your speech on what you hear. Bad models are as easy to copy as good ones. However, persistence, high standards, and practice will eventually produce fluent, purposeful speech free of the bad habits you wish to avoid. Finally, do not let yourself be discouraged by the "backsliding" and attendant frustration of slow progress. You may well discover that the first real improvement you make is the hardest-won victory in your campaign at overall growth. The confidence so earned makes the next steps easier.

Optimum Rate of Speaking

Recent investigations into the effects of extremely fast and unusually slow rates of speaking have produced some interesting and unexpected results. Teachers of speech have long sought to have their fast-talking students slow their rates of speech in order to improve intelligibility and understanding, assuming that listeners find fast speech much harder to attend than "normal" rates of delivery. Surprisingly, as long as pronunciation is clear and precise, most people can understand speech at double the normal range of 125 to 180 words per minute.[2] Nevertheless, for aesthetic reasons, if you habitually speak so fast that your listeners judge you to be tense, anxious, or excited, it might be advisable to try to slow down your rate of delivery. Furthermore, some information is harder to receive and interpret than other data. If you are describing Einstein's special theory of relativity, for example, your speed should certainly be slower than if you are relating conversational patter. In general, the more technical and unfamiliar your content is to the audience, the slower should be your rate of delivery. Finally, you should be alert to the audience feedback. When, in your judgment, the feedback indicates a high degree of comprehension and approval, you may maintain the tempo to hold interest. On the other hand, when feedback suggests that the audience is having trouble following the data you are presenting or that the audience seems troubled or doubtful, you should probably retard the tempo of your delivery. Remember, pause is a powerful device to emphasize a point. Pausing just after stating a profound idea is a good way of underscoring its importance.

Slowing down your speech rate is not very easy. Experiments have shown that speakers who attempt to slow their rates at first succeed, but shortly thereafter they tend to revert to their habitual rates.[3] These habitual rates resist attempts to change them. Perhaps personality so dominates our speech habits that changes in mood, level of anxiety, degree of interest, and so on, are expressed with no conscious control just as they always have been. The conditioning of a lifetime cannot be abandoned easily.

It might be more appropriate, then, for you to direct attention to clarity of articulation of speech sounds at whatever rate you have established as your normal rate for speaking. If under stress, in all kinds of moods, and in nearly all social situations you can ensure precise clarity of your speech sounds, there is very probably not much reason to try to change your rate. Sometimes people will ask you to slow down, reiterate, or speak up. In such cases your rate of speech may or may not be the problem at all, even though listeners think it is. Any lack of precision in enunciation creates an illusion of excessive speed.

Some people have the opposite problem. A very slow rate of speaking tends to put listeners to sleep or to create several unfortunate effects. Audiences tend to grow impatient with slow talkers, imputing to them dull personalities, lack of sharp intelligence, or other substandard qualities ("squareness," old-time mentality, etc.). A most amusing and instructive illustration of the effect of societal expectations of speech is "Slow Talkers of America," a Bob and Ray comic sketch. Supposedly an interview of a man attending a convention of slow talkers, the sketch is maddeningly tedious to the interviewer, who reveals his own impatient personality through his speech rate, which contrasts with that of the man he interviews.

Exercises for Vocal Development

Following is a list of some exercises that can help you develop your voice.

1. Count from one to ten on one breath. Be sure that you say the last number just as forcefully as the first one. Gradually increase the number of words until you cannot go any higher.

2. Count on one breath so that each larger number is slightly louder than the one preceding it.

3. Say clearly and rapidly your favorite tongue twisters. Following are some examples:
    a. Rubber baby buggy bumpers.
    b. Around the rugged rocks the ragged rascal ran.
    c. Theophilus thrust three thousand thistles through the thick of his thumb.
    d. The skunk sat on the stump. The stump thunk the skunk stunk and the skunk thunk the stump stunk. It was the skunk that stunk, we thunk.
    e. She sells sea shells down by the seashore.

4. Take a deep breath and gently say a prolonged "Ah-h-h." Sustain the sound as long as possible without changing its quality or force. Have a contest with a friend, who decides when your voice control loses its firm, sustained tone. Then you, in turn, become the judge of your friend's control. The one maintaining the pure "Ah" sound the longest wins.

5. Express emotions using only numbers. For example, say one as if angry, two as if happy, three as if bored, and so on. Have a contest in which a friend tries to detect the expressed emotion. After six tries, reverse roles, so that you try to guess the emotion attached to numbers spoken by your friend. Quit as soon as tempers flare.

6. Make a list of tongue twisters heard on radio or TV. A surprising number of almost impossible combinations appear on news broadcasts and lead to embarrassing blunders by newscasters.

7. Conduct a discussion on the aesthetic differences among letters of the alphabet and combinations of them. Are some sounds more pleasing than others? Are some combinations of sound offensive, regardless of their meaning ("barf," "krud," "scum")? Make up new words that sound either attractive or repulsive just because of their sounds. See if you can get agreement about whether combinations are universally appealing or not. (For example, *L* and *R* have been called "soft" and "beautiful" sounds, as in such words as Lili Marlene, Lorelei, Arlington, etc., whereas *K* and *Z* are thought to be "hard," "coarse," or "rough.")

8. Some words are onomatopoetic, or suggestive of the act or sound they represent. Such words as "sizzle," "sneeze," "plop," "buzz," and "snap" copy the sounds they signify. Other words do not. For example "rain" and "walk" do not suggest the actions they mean. By contrast, "thunder" and "slurp" do. Invent a descriptive new word.

POSTURE

Nothing is so obviously linked to a favorable personal impression as your stance before an audience. Nonetheless, countless speakers ruin their effects by slumping, hiding behind lecterns, clamping onto tables, staring down at their notes with heads bowed, or shifting their arms nervously in front of themselves. Thrusting your hands into your pockets because you do not know what else to do with them or standing at parade rest with your hands clenched behind you are both stances that most viewers find distracting or at least revealing of uneasiness. A full-length mirror is a valuable tool to help you understand the importance of your posture when you are in a speaking situation.

Stand in front of a mirror and look at yourself in various postures. At this stage, you may giggle a bit at yourself. Slump. Stand up straight with your hands at your sides. Spread your feet slightly and grab your hands behind your pelvis. Shift your weight more onto one foot than the other. Stand up straight again. Repeat these trials until you are free of embarrassment and can be objective in assessing the effects of various moves.

Which stance looks best? You will probably agree that standing up straight looks best, but you may also protest that it looks too stiff or that you cannot maintain that stance all during a speech. We discuss movement later, but for the moment, consider the alternatives: Do you really think it would be better to use any of the other stances you tried? Are there any attractive alternatives? If you sit down while speaking you may be relatively invisible, inaudible, and unimpressive. Though perhaps hard to accept, the simple, straight stance is usually easiest on the viewer. It also helps to keep you alert, balanced, and in optimum form for breathing, preparing for bodily action, and vocalizing while you are speaking. Gestures and movement are based on this stance.

The stance to cultivate, then, is best described as alert but not stiff, much like a military posture of attention but a bit more relaxed, and free of fidgeting arm motions. A major reason for assuming such a position is that from it you can respond quickly to the ideas in the speech. Because it is a relatively neutral position, it allows you the maximum variety of choices. By contrast, if you are slouched, have weight shifted onto one foot, or assume the parade rest stance, then any accommodation to ideas in the speech requires you to go from the unbalanced position first to a balanced one and then into the desired gesture or posture. Thus the timing of gestures is necessarily slower than it would be from a balanced stance. In short, gestures originating from a neutral stance may be quicker, more accurately timed, and less distracting than those originating from substandard postures.

GESTURE AND MOVEMENT

The range of gestures and the variety of meanings that can be conveyed by them are great. When you establish rapport with an audience, your gestures can become very subtle cues indicating precise nuances in meaning, emotional climate, and relative importance of each idea you present. When ill-timed, repeated too often, and improperly chosen, gestures may annoy and alienate an audience because listeners simply do not know how to interpret the chaotic and meaningless signals given them. If you are hesitant, inhibited, or explosive with gestures you give your auditors contradictory or at least inconsistent messages. Some research indicates that when audiences are confronted with verbal messages which are inconsistent with nonverbal cues, they tend to believe the nonverbal communications. "What you do speaks louder than what you say," goes the old critique.

Gestures should ideally come from your natural impulse to show direction, dimensions, shape, motions, changes of size, and so on. Your gestures should be decisive, not half-executed. The entry into the gesture should be quick, but not jerky. You should hold it long enough so that it registers clearly with the audience. Then, you should return your arms to their normal, so-called neutral position at the sides of your body. Again, no effort to hurry the gesture should be evident. The important point is that you should time the gesture just with the word or words with which it naturally fits. It is better for the gesture to be a split second too early than too late. A comical, over-

Figure 7-1

rehearsed, and very contrived or insincere effect may result from even slightly mistimed gestures.

Try this exercise: Stand at a lectern or table and say a very decisive sentence with the word "not" in it. As you say "not" use a gesture such as a clenched fist tapped on the lectern to emphasize your words: "I will certainly *not* raise your salary this month!" Try to discern the difference in meaning and effect that can be created by putting the gesture at different points in the sentence. You might accidentally reveal indecision, dissimulation, or anger, depending on precisely when the gesture occurs.

Students often wonder how many gestures to use. Practice varies so widely that no hard and fast rule is possible. What is too much for one person may seem not enough for another. Some quite effective speakers use practically no gestures, and their variety and spice comes from lively ideas, responsive voices, and appealing personal qualities. Most people, however, will appear static, dull, and unresponsive if they use no gestures at all. At the other extreme, a few people tend to be overanimated; they move about the platform freely and gesture almost constantly. Sometimes these performers are amusing and entertaining because of their free and uninhibited manners. Sometimes a speaker is appealing precisely because he or she seems to violate the usual norms. To help decide how many gestures to use, you must answer several questions about your own personal style: Are you naturally tense, reserved, inhibited, uncomfortable when you have to speak? If so, then perhaps you need to practice exercises which will free you somewhat from a tight, overcontrolled delivery style. However, a sudden change in style will probably backfire. People who know you have come to expect a characteristic behavior. Adding a few gestures to your next speech would seem to your colleagues a noticeable, perhaps striking change. To add many large, sweeping gestures and great animation might startle them and make them question your intentions or even your sincerity. Moderation is in order. Gradually add a few telling gestures, if you have used few or none in the past. As you become more secure and confident, add a few more until you find the optimum for you. That optimum is defined as the number and kind that are most comfortable for you, that produce the best feedback while you are speaking, and that result in the best comments from your listeners when you finish. It may be that the more you add, the more you will want to add later. A natural limit is more or less built into your mind, however, because of the years of conditioning in your society and social groups. If your family was taciturn and rewarded silence, then you may be rather less demonstrative than others. By contrast, if you are naturally an effusive, highly energetic person, outgoing and gregarious by nature, you might tend toward excessive hand and bodily motion. Some very active people make others extremely tense and upset by their seemingly frantic activity. Between these extremes, the task is not one of wholesale reform but simply of polishing whatever style you already feel most comfortable with. If you feel you need more gestures and liveliness, you probably do. In our culture, lack of animation is very common. Because it is almost a norm, those who show more spirited behavior seem superior to the drab, everyday speakers who drone on methodically with little verve.

At some point you may wish to solicit the opinions of others regarding the optimum level of animation for you. A professional speech teacher or consultant might help. A workshop at your college or university, a local speaker's club, or a private seminar for business personnel wherein television recordings of your performance can be made and viewed could help you decide if the issue becomes pressing. Even casual listeners with no particular expertise can assist you, as long as you have several opinions and respect for the quality of those opinions. Ultimately you will have to decide upon what is comfortable and aesthetically pleasing for you, because the tastes and opinions of your listeners will inevitably vary widely.

Practicing on Your Own

Again, the mirror is your best friend in the early stages of improving your gestures. Select a passage of reading or a portion of a speech with which you are familiar (to minimize having to concentrate on what comes next in the speech) and present it to the mirror. Try saying key phrases with and without gestures. Repeat at different tempos and with different gestures. The idea is to discover what looks right and feels comfortable to you at the same time. Do not be surprised if you feel embarrassed even with no one else present. We do not normally have to look at ourselves while we speak, and we have an unconscious image which tends to flatter us a bit. Therefore the literal truth which the mirror cannot help but present may not measure up to our wishful thinking about our bodies as seen by others. Remember, too, that we tend to be hard on ourselves. We would prefer an ideal figure, face, and voice. Most of us do not possess them—movie agents would have grabbed us long ago if we did have ideal configurations! However, just as we are tolerant of and indeed love and esteem those around us who are less than ideal specimens, so too are we accepted as we are. It is wise just to want to be a little better and to merit their esteem, not to remold our lives into fantasies. A few students envision a whole new self which will overwhelm others, deliver them from a hum-drum existence, or lead to visionary success. Although such results have occasionally been achieved, a more modest outcome is likely. Renewed respect among associates, some degree of professional advancement, and personal maturation are more probable achievements. Aside from social and professional motivations to improve, you may discover a pleasing sense of self-mastery and confidence arising from exact control of your gestures.

Bodily Action

Sometimes, as listeners, we are tempted to yell out, advising the speaker to stand still. At other times, the speaker's degree of control is so great and his or her motions so few, that we get stiff necks just from watching the motionless figure. The optimum amount of acceptable movement depends partly on the length of the talk. If you must talk at length, then you may build into the speech certain changes of position just for the sake of visual variety and emphasis. Very brief speeches may require no actual movement at all. You simply stand for a few minutes and depend on vocal variety and gesture to carry your ideas. However, when you think of movement, you need to consider not simply obvious motion such as walking around in front of listeners, but subtler motions such as shifting weight, clamping onto a lectern, or hiding behind it as an emotional fortress into which you can retreat for protection from the hostile eyes of the imagined enemy, the audience. To come out from behind the lectern, then, might be considered a declaration that you regard the audience as all friends, from whom there is nothing to fear, to whom you wish to speak intimately, and before whom there is nothing to hide or be ashamed about. The mere act of emerging from the formal confines of an ornate lectern and podium can thus shatter the stiff, cool atmosphere of a speech and create an open, warmer, and informal setting. Some situations do not warrant such informality. Imagine the breach of taste and expectations if a junior partner at an august, formal board meeting were to so presume on the other members as to violate the norms established by the senior members and chairperson. A flip or informal presentation would be as jarring as inappropriate dress or vulgarity. Decisions about how much and what kind of movement, accordingly, must be based on the degree of formality, the length of the talk, and the perception of yourself you wish to convey. Following are some suggestions for deciding on matters of bodily action during a speech:

Do not wander aimlessly around the room. If in doubt, keep still or move occasionally to a nearby spot if you feel that such movement would create a sense of variety or emphasis.

Time your motion, if possible, so that it occurs during a natural transition in the talk. "What are the implications of these facts I have discussed for future growth in the company?" Such a transitional question is a natural place in the speech for some movement to fit.

Avoid repetitive movement from point A to point B and then back to A. Such a movement might seem refreshing the first time it occurs, but then listeners will begin to wonder what the repetitive act means. The conclusion is likely to be that such action means nothing except that you are nervous.

Do not clamp onto a table or lectern. Keep as free as possible. You should not look down at your notes as if reading, nor should you actually read them. A possible exception would occur when extreme caution is necessary to precisely word some momentous policy decision. Then the controlled, measured, and meticulous wording may justify a severely controlled action. Among the relatively few occasions that might call for us to be so studied would be announcing the appointment of a new executive officer or explaining the necessity for a major employee cutback.

Avoid distracting motion. Going over to a window, adjusting the shades, cleaning dust off the lectern, examining your fingernails, or hunting through papers for something while talking are all behaviors calculated to distract the audience. The listeners may interpret these acts as merely ways to avoid eye contact at any cost. Your credibility may be damaged by such evasion.

If in doubt, especially if you are tense, keep still.

EYE CONTACT

One of the most powerful controls you can have over an audience is eye contact with it. The eye is the most expressive part of the body—the window to the soul, in ancient idiom. From your eyes listeners can apparently detect the strength of your conviction about what you are saying, any insincerity you might betray, and any fears or other emotions you might feel. Of course, observers make many mistakes, but the point is that they believe that they can accurately detect much about you and your message from your eyes.[4]

Another extremely important matter is your own perception of the audience. Watching people as you speak to them allows you to determine whether they understand, how well they can hear, how agreeable they are with your message, what their assessment of you is, and in what state of alertness and interest they are. Obviously, to avoid eye contact is to shut yourself off from all the information so useful, and sometimes essential, to your success. Mastering your emotions to the point that you always watch audience response is a very important key to improving your overall speech skills. Because none of us hold absolute power over other people, we cannot afford the arrogance and luxury of not caring what their responses are. Evasion of eye contact may seem to your listeners as a rejection of them and their opinions.

DRESS AND GROOMING

For maximum effectiveness in the presentation of a speech, you should control every possible element that contributes to the total impact. Because listeners see you as well as hear you, and because the total impression you create includes a visual component, your appearance should be controlled just as your voice is. Adapting to your expected audience should thus include attention to your clothing and grooming.

Of course, you should not overdress. We have all seen plays and movies concerning misunderstandings about costume. A couple's coming to a formal dance in clown suits or pirate garb, thinking the dance to be a costume ball, or attending a sock dance dressed in a tuxedo and gown illustrate comic, although painful, failures to adapt to social norms. Even though obvious attempts to curry favor with a group by emulating their dress seem to be insincere, still some degree of quiet conformity will gain you favor. The familiar example of politicians' attempting to secure identification by donning at least one piece of dress characteristic of the group being addressed illustrates this point: Wearing a miner's hat, a construction worker's hard hat, or some badge emblematic of the workers is a typical bid for approval.

On a smaller scale, the individual speaking to a board meeting, testifying in a hearing, or giving expert opinion during a company's briefing on some problem should not overlook the expectations of the situation. Obviously, a supervisor called in from the floor in a dirty, greasy environment cannot be expected to change on very short notice for a staff meeting. If he or she has enough advance notice, however, and if the meeting is to be held in a formal setting with higher management, visiting dignitaries, or the like, then the situation might call for taking the trouble to change into street clothes. Many employees overlook the unspoken demands of taste and propriety that an announced meeting requires. If you do not know what the expectations are for a given situation, then you should make discreet inquiries.

Sometimes the tone of a company's policy is studiedly informal, and to be neat can provoke amusement; on the other hand, other companies have rather merciless policies on employees' appearances. In addition, some jobs require work both indoors and out in all kinds of weather. For example, in years past, before jobs and appropriate apparel for them were specialized, airline agents commonly worked on the ticket counters and also on the ramps loading the planes with freight, baggage, and express mail. The same agent might have scurried about in and under the aircraft in rain and snow after loading it. Then he or she might have started the engines with dirty, oily battery chargers and safety equipment. Once the plane departed, the wet and begrimed agent might have returned to the office or counter where he or she might have had to face the public immediately and maintain a good image for the company. On such days, it was necessary to have several changes of uniform available. Company expectations thus cost agents a great deal of expense in laundry and cleaning bills.

In applying the just-noted observations to a public-speaking situation, you should strive neither to call attention to dress by extravagance nor to create negative images by insufficient attention to dress and grooming. Crumpled suits, unshined shoes, gravy-stained ties, clashing or badly mismatched clothes, or other inappropriate choices of dress can tell an audience that you care little for their values, and by extension, for them. Particularly when your desired outcome is some degree of persuasion and personal acceptance you should plan carefully for the visual effect you want to create.

In recent years the trend toward personal freedom and dispensing with societal constraints has led to a general attitude among young people that matters of dress are not the business of others, including employers, and that concern with such trivial matters is "phoniness" and intrusion into personal matters. But some employees and speakers have learned painfully that the world is intolerant of slovenly dress and manner on the grounds that outward disarray reveals inner carelessness, which is an employers' concern. Attention to details of personal appearance, conversely, are thought to suggest a characteristic concern with detail and a sense of thoroughness and pride in mental and physical activity, again concerns of an employer. Affectations such as cowboy hats and boots in New York City, Greek sailor caps in small towns, and scraggly beards and hair trimmed into peculiar configurations are all frowned on in some circles. If you pay attention to the mores of the group you are to address and then present a neat, clean-cut image, the rules of appearance are tolerant of some individuality. It is not individuality or even eccentricity that others find displeasing, but if you blatantly flout custom and propriety you are almost sure to breed resentment among and rejection by those who adhere to the group norms.

A public speaker is to some extent a public guide and representative of a group's customary style, taste, and mores. Listeners want to identify with and be proud of their guides. To generate suspicion by ignoring the public norms during the presentation of a speech seems to be an unnecessary risk, especially when to do otherwise requires so little extra effort and involves so little surrender of personal freedom.

Figure 7-2 ". . . As you see on line 8 of the chart, . . ."

AUDIO-VISUAL AIDS

Using Visual Aids Effectively

Properly used visual aids can be an enormous help to the public speaker. Conversely, poorly used aids can create problems so severe that the speaker might be much better off without using any visual aids at all. Not only can the visual aids fail to help the speech, they may also damage the credibility of the speaker and confuse the audience so that later speeches to it may fail. The advice which follows, therefore, is built on the assumptions that any device you use in a speech must be capable of aiding you in the first place and must be, in your best judgment, necessary to the presentation. The following general considerations are applicable to all visual aids.

The visual aid must be visible to all members of the audience. If the audience is seated in a semicircle or on three sides of you, or if the room is very wide compared with its depth, you must exercise particular care to use only aids whose details are truly clear enough for everyone in the room to see them.

You must show the aid to each part of the audience long enough for everyone to see and digest the information. Do not keep the aid in continual sweeping motion from side to side; in such a case no one will have a chance to take in the content.

Make key symbols on aids bold, unambiguous, and unique. Test them. If the audience is so far away that you have to read the content of a transparency to them, the aid probably was not worth the time and cost to make it.

Time the use of the visual aid properly. Do not leave aids within view of the audience when they are not in use, for they may distract from your presentation. Show each aid only when its content is being presented orally. Do not let the audience see the details of the aids except when they are displayed. Store the aids flat on a desk or stack them unobtrusively facing away from the audience until you need them, and replace them with as little fuss as possible. Do not simply read the content of any projected slide or transparency to the audience. Although it is common, this practice is insulting, suggests that the aid is gratuitous, and makes your self-presentation subsidiary to the aid itself. Moreover, nothing will make you seem more naive and artless than just reading aloud visual aids which the audience can read for itself.

Do not pass around objects for examination during your talk. You lose the attention of a constantly changing segment of the audience as each person in turn gets to examine the objects. If the objects are particularly interesting, their capacity for distraction is also high.

Remember that any visual aid is at its best when it shows some relationship or insight that is too complicated for listeners to grasp through language alone. Do not use a visual aid to escape your responsibility to choose clear and accurate language.

Beware of creating sensory overload in the audience. This is caused by presenting too much information through a well-intended but misguided effort to achieve perfect clarity. Not every idea in a speech is equally difficult to understand. Most ideas need no visual aids to support them. Reserve aids for those ideas which are difficult to grasp, those insights which emerge from displaying related data, and those trends you want the audience to observe as they emerge from portrayed data. Particularly when you are presenting highly technical information in slide after slide, listeners may become saturated and may simply ignore additional data beyond some point. Prune your aids carefully. It is better to have an aid evoke questions within the audience than to bore listeners with the obvious. However, aids should generally be designed to answer questions, not pose them.

Examples of Visual Aids

Fortunately for speakers, there are many kinds of visual aids from which to choose. Each kind has certain virtues and pitfalls. In this section we consider some forms of visual aids that can serve you uniquely, and some cautions applicable to each one.

Photographs and/or 35-mm slides. Actual photographs or slides of described objects or places can be valuable supplements to the content of a speech. Although excellent descriptions of places or objects are often sufficient to illustrate your points, detailed photographs and/or slides can also be revealing. However, if you plan to show slides, you are inevitably at the mercy of fallible equipment. You should always have an extra bulb available in case of sudden failure of the projector, a heavy extension cord to permit desired placement

Figure 7-3 A typical SLR camera.

and distance from the screen, and a three-prong adapter so that you will be able to adapt to unexpected circumstances in a strange locale.

When showing slides, make sure the room is dark enough to permit good contrasting images. Avoid using too many slides to make a point; it is easy to belabor a point or image. Also prune out mercilessly any defective, dark, or unsatisfactory slides. Do not apologize for poor pictures. If they were made under adverse conditions, either do not use them, or, if you must show them, briefly explain the circumstances: "The UFOs were visible only for a moment." "I meant to photograph the beautiful tree just as lightning struck it, over-exposing the film."

Overhead projector. Because of its flexibility, the overhead projector is one of the most frequently used—and, unhappily, misused—visual aids. If you are not careful you can become a slave of the device by being too dependent on it, by using it unnecessarily, or by using it carelessly. Some people regard their presentations as being entirely composed of their transparencies, and their roles as speakers as being merely to present the transparencies. Such an approach suggests that a handout of printed material would be as good as an oral presentation, or perhaps even better. If you are to give a speech, then *you* should be the central focus of the session, not just a tool.

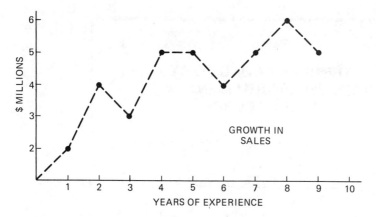

Figure 7-4   One common form of data presentation.

Following are some suggestions to help you use an overhead projector as a tool:

1. Keep each transparency uncluttered and free of distracting symbols. An audience can only concentrate on a limited amount of information at any one time.

2. Anticipate questions or misunderstandings that might arise from each transparency and prepare clarifications (or revise the transparency). Explain what the illustration is about or why it is important. State the implications of the content.

3. Try to work in some variety or aesthetically pleasing visual symbols (as long as they are pertinent to the point you are making). Avoid showing a succession of transparencies all cast in the same visual format. If a black marker pen and clear plastic sheets are all that you have, there may be little advantage in using an overhead projector at all. At least place symbols in varying ways on successive transparencies for aesthetic reasons.

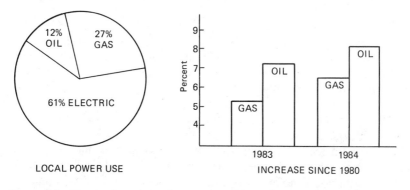

Figure 7-5   Pie charts and graphs are adaptable to illustrate certain kinds of information.

HYPOTHETICAL RATINGS OF THREE EMPLOYEES WITH IDENTICAL TOTAL SCORES

TRAIT	POINT RATINGS		
EMPLOYEE	A	B	C
SKILL	10	5	5
COOPERATIVENESS	5	10	5
POTENTIAL FOR DEVELOPMENT	0	0	5
TOTAL	15	15	15

Question: Who is best?

Figure 7-6   An appropriate and useful transparency for use with an overhead projector.

4. Make sure everyone has time to observe and consider the film.

5. Using an occasional cartoon may create variety and humor, or a change of pace and mood. Particularly if the humor is in good taste, your using cartoons is likely to reveal you as a balanced, alert person who sees things in a healthy perspective. However, do not carry the humor too far. Above all, do not poke fun at people, institutions, or events your listeners hold dear. They may not share your notions of what is clever and amusing.

6. Do not attempt to project a transparency containing a densely typed page. Most people will not even pretend to read it, but instead will resent your showing it. Try to develop a sense of how much symbolic data people can comprehend comfortably and do not overload your aids. Concentrate attention on a reasonably small unit of information.

Blackboard and chalk. A blackboard, though a familiar visual device, has several pitfalls. If you write as you speak, your back will be turned to the audience for an awkward length of time and you will not be able to see your listeners' responses. On the other hand, however, if you put all your information on the board before your speech, observers will read ahead of you, get out of step with the points you are making, and possibly misunderstand them.

To avoid this problem, you might be able to write the information out fully before your speech and then cover it with strips of paper or otherwise block its visibility until you are ready to use it. If this much trouble is necessary, probably a different visual aid would have been preferable.

If you do decide to use a blackboard, note that it must also meet the various tests described earlier for photographs, slides, and transparencies.

Flip charts. If they are large enough to be readily visible, flip charts are superior to blackboards in that you can control the rate and time of revelation of the facts. Note that flip charts work best in small meetings or seminars.

Models. Attractive and not as overused as some kinds of visual aids, static or operating models can furnish graphic illustrations of how some things work. If you are using a model take care that it does not dominate your presentation. Simply using a cloth covering for it or controlled illumination of it may suffice.

If you are using scale architectural models, vehicles, cutaway engines, or other complex devices, allow plenty of time for viewers to satisfy themselves that they understand the models. Offer to allow more examination time after the speech if you must control the time for scrutiny and move along in your talk. Be aware that in some ways models may mislead observers. Scale distortion, resulting from the fact that full-size objects may exhibit quite different qualities from those of the models, may create a false sense of understanding. For example, most conveniently sized models of the atom are quite misleading.

Handouts. The handout is a common aid but you should be aware to use it very carefully to avoid subverting your whole speech. Giving your auditors a list of subjects about which you will talk merely invites the impatient ones to read ahead, size up what you might say, and then to "turn you off." Even worse, they may begin formulating questions and objections which could be answered if they merely listened to the presentation carefully. It is generally best, then, to save handouts until the end of the speech, when they may be given out as memory aids of what you said.

Occasionally charts, maps, graphs, or tables must be handed out in advance, but if you do so, you can have a hard time controlling the rate of information flow. Keeping a group's attention focused on the matter at hand is surprisingly difficult when listeners have several pages to study. Typical situations requiring handing out information in advance of a speech involve very complex data such as operating budgets, demographic tables, or statistical figures. Such materials may be too densely packed for practical use as transparencies or flip charts, and line-by-line scrutiny might be possible only by giving everyone an individual packet of detailed data. However, explanation and careful study of such minute details is likely to be an ordeal for both the speaker and the listeners. Therefore, advance distribution of data is recommended only when the most careful and deliberate evaluation of particulars is appropriate, as, for example, in a policy hearing, an audit, or a board meeting.

Using Audio Aids Effectively

Much that has been said about visual aids applies equally to audible information. Everyone must be able to hear the presented sounds just as they must be able to see visual information supporting a talk. No one should have to strain to hear. Listeners who have to struggle to hear you or your machines will inwardly rebel and soon ignore you, as well as the aid. You must also avoid distractions.

Always explain the point or purpose of an audio aid, unless it is obvious. Do not burden your listeners with useless audio materials or with superfluous data, such as a recording of your voice saying something you can say just as well in person. You could make an exception to this general rule if you have a tape of some distinguished or captivating person, and the effect of the recording might be far superior to your merely quoting the person. For example, a recording of Churchill saying his "Blood, Sweat, and Tears" speech is likely to be much more moving than your reading it aloud.

Examples of Audio Aids

Following is a discussion of some audio aids that might be helpful to you when preparing a speech.

Tape recorders. If you plan to use a tape recorder, you should set it up and adjust it to the proper level of sound and tone for the location before your audience arrives. If the desired portion of the tape is not at the beginning, position it ahead of time so that you can begin at exactly the right point. There is no excuse for forcing your audience to wait several seconds while irrelevant material is played or embarrassing silence occurs. Use the volume control carefully so that no sudden blasting or awkward silence occurs. Set the tone controls, if any are provided, so that a crisp but not piercing or strident sound results. Speech is muffled if the tone is too bassy. Usually a mid range setting of the controls is best.

Cassette recorders. Cassette recorders are very convenient to use, but they lack the power and fidelity of reel-to-reel tape recorders. If you are playing only speech to the audience, the quality may be adequate, but if you are playing music, the sound will usually be less satisfactory. Its pitch may vary and the result could be very unpleasant and unrealistic. At least pretest the cassette on the machine to be used to determine whether the player can be set for adequate loudness and fidelity. Remember or jot down the best setting of the controls so that you can reset the machine quickly and with little fuss.

Next, rewind the cassette to just the cue you want, so that as the need for the sound arises in your talk all you have to do is press the start button. Many machines have counters to help you do this. At the beginning of a tape, set the counter to zero. Then jot down the number showing when you reach the desired portion of the tape. Rewind the tape. When you are ready to use the tape again, reset the counter to zero. To find the desired cue, run the cassette at fast forward speed until you reach the number noted. Press stop. You will now be quite close to the desired cue.

Phonograph records and record players. Phonograph records and record players are capable of producing an excellent quality sound, but they may be difficult to use because the record-player's needle must be set accurately and silently at just the right place to avoid blasting and possible needle damage. Practice with the actual machine and records in the location you will use if possible.

Records are also relatively fragile and easily scratched or warped by heat and pressure. If you have access to tape and phonograph equipment, you may find it more convenient to record the phonograph record onto a tape or cassette and use the tape during your presentation. This procedure is particularly effective when you need several isolated passages of a record for your talk but do not wish to hunt for them or hear intervening passages during the speech. It may be nearly impossible to find brief segments quickly and accurately on a record, but a leisurely session of recording the desired passages onto tape permits you to present precisely edited sounds.

Specialized audio equipment. If you plan to use any type of highly specialized audio equipment, such as code practice machines, computers, musical instruments, electronic games, and so on, you should position them for quick availability, minimal distraction when not in use, and predictable behavior when in use. As we have stressed so far, practice with the actual device in the location you will use for the presentation is virtually essential to ensure confidence.

Acoustics. The acoustics of the room in which you are to give a speech can be considered an audio aid. Really thorough preparation for a speech would include some attention to this "device." If you have heard someone clapping his or her hands or saying a word or two the first time he or she entered an auditorium, that person may have been merely testing the room for echoes and its peculiar acoustics. Some rooms seem to swallow up sounds and make speakers difficult to hear. Other rooms are quite live, and they may create echoes which require speakers to slow down their rates of delivery and use very careful articulation in order to be understood. Still other "live" rooms may carry voices quite well with little distortion. Some rooms may have one or two "dead spots" where audibility is poor. In any case, knowing the acoustics of the room in which you are to speak can certainly aid the successful presentation of your speech.

Discussion of Audio-Visual Aids

The most effective use of audio-visual materials requires practice with mechanical and electronic equipment, which sometimes intimidates public speakers. Your first decision is whether to use such aids. Once you have made the decision to use an aid, you are obligated to master the technical demands of the particular equipment and the psychological forces inherent in the chosen device. Once you have learned the quirks of the chosen movie projector or available tape recorder, your next step is to rehearse your whole speech using all the aids and equipment, preferably in the location where you are to deliver the speech. Do not neglect details, such as the exact location of projection screens and connecting cords, the condition of bulbs, and the manner of packing equipment in storage cases. Note how much time is required to set up, use, and take down the equipment. Do not assume that minor problems will work themselves out during the actual presentation. Make explicit plans to avoid awkward timing of aids, fumbling, or embarrassingly long pauses. When you use an assistant, ideally that person should rehearse with you. If practice is not possible, at least make sure the person is very clear on what duties are required. If, for example, the helper is to operate a slide projector on cue, make sure the cue word or signal is understood and, in actual delivery, is given to the helper clearly. The one word "next" may be adequate for a signal, although some people like an impersonal cue such as a beep from an electronic signaler.

The essentials in using audio and visual aids, then, are: judicious choice of aids, careful preparation of materials and their use through rehearsal, self-assessment after a run-through, and planning for all contingencies you can foresee. Watch other people who give particularly good and particularly bad programs to see the effects they achieve. Determine why you like or dislike some effect. Keep the best ideas and incorporate them into your next speech.

EXERCISES

1. Recall and describe an occasion on which you were much impressed with someone's presentation using visual or audio aids, or both. Try to recall what accounted for the impact of that presentation.

2. Recall and describe an experience you had when someone failed to use audio-visual aids effectively or when you were struck by someone's poor use of them. Try to account for the failure in terms of specific suggestions in this chapter. If there were other reasons, mention them.

3. Imagine that you are to give a major speech in your classroom or some familiar auditorium. Further, assume that you have to use two aids, one visual and one audible (e.g., slides and a cassette). *Write down* the following information, using simple sketches to prove the feasibility of your plan: the location of all electrical outlets, the placement of any needed machines, the person who will control them, the handling of the cues, and the placement of speakers and screens or any other display devices (tables, charts, etc.).

4. Give the information stated in the preceding problem to a classmate and in return take the information he or she wrote down. Now try to demonstrate that your classmate's plan will fail and show how it is inadequate. Meanwhile, have the classmate try to do the same to your plan. If both plans fail, start over! If only one plan is defensible as foolproof, work together to improve the other.

5. Sketch a commonly used, familiar auditorium with which your classmates are familiar. By showing the relationships of seating to stage or platform, describe the good and bad features of the place for public presentations. Do not forget to comment on the acoustics.

6. If your instructor or class interests permit, visit a familiar lecture hall, auditorium, theatre, or large classroom when it is not in use and compare its acoustics then with those evident when an audience is present. Describe the difference in effect.

SELECTED READINGS

LARRY BARKER, *Communication*, 2nd ed. (Englewood Cliffs, N.J.: Prentice-Hall, 1981), Chapter 12.

ERNEST G. BORMANN AND NANCY C. BORMANN, *Speech Communication*, 3rd ed. (New York: Harper & Row, 1981), Chapter 15.

D. GUNDERSON AND R. HOPPER, "Relationships between Speech Delivery and Speech Effectiveness," *Communication Monographs*, 43 (1976) 158–165.

STEPHEN E. LUCAS, *The Art of Public Speaking* (New York: Random House, 1983), Chapter 11.

RICHARD E. WHITMAN AND PAUL H. BOASE, *Speech Communication* (New York: Macmillan, 1983), Chapter 12.

chapter 8

Fundamentals of Persuasive Speaking

In the entire field of speech communication, no topic is so misunderstood and surrounded by misinformation as that branch called *persuasion*. Some people view it as the expression of purposeful influence by one person over another. Others see it as some mysterious skill with carefully guarded secrets handed down from one generation to another and shared grudgingly with a few outsiders who somehow earn the respect of the mighty ones. Once accepted into the privileged circle of those sharing the secrets, it is believed, a person can sway others magically, sell anything, rise professionally in any job, and get others to do whatever the persuader wishes.

It is perhaps fortunate that no such magic power exists. No one can learn a package of secrets which will produce masters of persuasion. However, anyone can, by study and practice, develop his or her speech skills to a high level. Such a hard worker and careful organizer will seem to others to be the wizard who can influence other people and succeed in a chosen field. The secret of success in persuasion is the same as that in violin playing: Careful, persistent study of a few principles and many hours of directed, thoughtful practice will lead one to success in either art. Because most people do not wish to study and practice laboriously, most people never become very good at playing the violin or at persuading other people.

A common error about persuasion is that some individuals know something—a knack or skill—which forces other people to do whatever the persuader wants. How often have you heard someone say, "He can sell anything to anybody!" Supposedly legendary used-car agents have a gift of gab so powerful that no one can resist their pitches. Although clever and expert salespeople can seemingly "do wonders," the truth is that most wonderful feats of persuasion are not at all what they seem. Let us examine a case study to reveal why persuasion seems to be so powerful, or even magical in the hands of some people.

A CASE STUDY: FREDDIE

A large car dealer in Chicago hired a salesperson we call Freddie. Although the name is invented here, there was such a man and he did have an amazing sales record. Freddie was thought to be so skillful at persuasion that he could sell people any kind of car and still make the buyers like their choices. In fact, his sales record was higher than anyone else's in the company for the time he was employed. He seemed to have such success that other employees watched his techniques to try to learn how to increase their own sales. That was the trouble: As a customer came into the sales room and looked at the new models, the other salespeople *watched Freddie to see what he would do and say.* They did not go to the customer, the only person present who was likely to buy a car. They watched. It does not take great insight to realize that by sitting back and watching, the other salespeople gave Freddie the most *opportunity.* It is easy to forget, too, that the opportunity to sell is better than chance in this situation merely because the potential customer is already motivated upon arriving in the sales room. People who take the trouble to go to a car lot have at least a wish to buy a new car. Lots of people do wish for things they cannot afford and they do "shop around" a bit before they make a decision. On high-cost items, such as houses, airplanes, yachts, and automobiles, people naturally take longer to decide and they may make repeated visits without purchasing. Some prospects are really interested and able to buy and some are out for a leisurely stroll and "drop by" to see and feel the new model vehicles. In a sense, then, people are persuading themselves. Freddie had to be available and alert for just the right moment when the customer had almost decided and *wanted* to be persuaded to buy.

Next, the observers noticed, Freddie would walk up to the customer with a friendly, relaxed smile and would talk quietly for a moment with him or her. They noted that soon Freddie would do one of two things: Either he would walk away apparently unconcerned and leave the customer to window shop leisurely or else he would hover closely over the shopper, answering questions or explaining features of the cars. In the long run, he seemed to know who would buy and who was having a brief fantasy by shopping around. Yet, there was Freddie's record of sales—higher than anyone else's. From the standpoint of persuasion, what was actually happening was this: Freddie decided whether or not persuasion was possible. When Freddie realized an immediate sale was not possible, he left the shopper to browse with a friendly comment, "If you have any questions, call me." Freddie then walked away, saving time and energy. No amount of persuasion could make an unemployed shopper decide to buy immediately. Freddie built good will for *a later shopping trip* by leaving the shopper alone, while still offering to help when needed. Sensing that there was no opportunity to sell at *this* time, Freddie was sensitive to the situation's *timing.* He was also content with building good will.

But sometimes Freddie did not walk away. He followed the shopper with great interest and attention. Without being overbearing or pushy, he demonstrated every good feature he could, sensing from the customer's questions and reactions what would probably be most appealing to him or her. Freddie did not know that he could sell this or that individual a car, but he could tell from the questions and responses only when he *might* have a chance. This realization kept him going, pursuing the possibility that some one thing or a combination of features of a car might appeal to the customer. In many cases the customers really had already made up their minds to buy a car and had one picked out, but they worried about spending so much money and wanted someone—an expert—to reassure them that their decision was right. Freddie would discuss what he knew the customer wanted to hear more about and he would stress the advantages of a model the customer seemed to prefer. Sometimes, people simply want someone else to verify the wisdom of a choice they have already made, rather than to initiate a selection. Persuasion, then, is often a matter of emphasizing what people are already committed to.

Dishonest? If Freddie knew that the person was making a bad mistake, he might direct the customer toward another model. However, Freddie had committed himself to selling a brand of car because he liked or at least respected it. His conscience told him that brand *A* he was selling was as good as brand *B, C,* and *D* which competed with it. If he thought the car was junk, he would soon move elsewhere and use his "magic" selling something he felt was an honest value. The use of sales strategies is dishonest only when the salesperson tries to mislead, cheat, oversell, or hide something. The customer announces a need for advice by appearing in the showroom and describing some need. To answer all questions and guide the customer is perfectly ethical and honest. To sell someone expensive and unneeded add-ons when it is clear they are not wanted is unethical. To urge one to buy whatever is in stock or whatever brings the highest commission when it is known the customer wants a minimally equipped vehicle is shady practice. Even so, if the customer wants something *today* and is unwilling to wait for the exact model and equipment desired, the salesperson can hardly be blamed for the sale of whatever is in stock and pleases the buyer.

One definition of persuasion is "to make sweet" or to please. The bad name that rhetoric has often suffered throughout its long history is the product of overly aggressive urging to a course of action, or a sale, when the persuader knew that the message was false, misleading, harmful, or exploiting. The shady uses of rhetoric have been compared to the misuse of a knife. Like a sharp knife which is useful for eating, carving, building, and shaping, rhetoric is useful for informing, teaching, inspiring, and leading. Either tool can be perverted to evil uses. Normally we praise the skillful, expert manipulation of all useful tools, as long as they are used constructively, honestly, fairly.

Freddie has done nothing wrong or unethical. To sell effectively he has learned how to know when a customer is interested and when the timing is right. He then alertly engages each customer with prompt, courteous attention. Even when he abandons a prospect, he is nearby and has left an invitation to ask more questions.

One day, George, another salesperson at the same dealership, grumbled that a customer to whom George had tried to sell a car on several visits came back and bought a station wagon from Freddie. Alert readers will notice another "secret" of persuasion being revealed here: When the customer bought the car, did he become persuaded at that moment? The answer is critical to a definition. If the behavior of buying represents persuasion working, then persuasion is defined as *successfully* leading someone to change his or her behavior. On the other hand, are we willing to throw aside all that effort by George during those preceding weeks? Who is to say whether some comment by George was the decisive one that led the customer to buy the station wagon? After all, the man did come back repeatedly to shop, to weigh and balance, to ponder, and finally to buy. Suppose for a moment that the purchaser came to the decision to buy the car at 6 o'clock in the morning and went to the sales room at 10 o'clock. Suppose that Freddie comes up and asks if he can be of assistance, and the man says, "I've decided to buy the wagon." Did Freddie persuade him? Did George's repeated efforts persuade him? Was the attempt to sell the car persuasion, or was there no persuasion until the customer bought the car?

A WORKING DEFINITION OF PERSUASION

The insight here is that persuasion includes all efforts, whether immediately successful or not, to influence others. Even if those efforts never succeed, as is often the case, the intended and repeated attempts qualify as persuasion. In a sense, most efforts to persuade fail. Think of the *unsold* goods in commerce. Think of the number of times that preachers cannot guide their flocks to righteous lives. Good teachers fail to convince their students to learn what they need, and honest prosecuters fail to persuade juries of the guilt of criminals, who then go free. Lots of efforts fail. It is likely that more persuasion fails than succeeds.

Looking at Freddie again, for a moment, we can see something else about his supposedly marvelous powers. Freddie took advantage of previous exposure

Figure 8-1 A rundown railway station. Local conditions are often a source of good topics for persuasive speeches.

even though his question, "Can I help you?" seemed to be his only persuasive effort leading to the sale. In fact, as in much successful persuasion, the outcome is not the result of just one effort but rather the end product of a long line of pressures put on someone being persuaded.

In short, the combination of energy and circumstances which seem to reveal Freddie as a magician of the car lot in fact show him to be a sensible, alert, efficient salesperson. He does not waste time on hopeless causes—trying to sell penniless people cars. He lays the groundwork of good will for future possibilities. He alertly takes his cues from customers and neither pesters them nor ignores them. He uses timing, exploits previous efforts without being too pushy, and tries to sense what the customer wants and needs. His reputation as a wizard holds no mystery when his actions are thoughtfully studied, but if you look only at results (sales) and ignore the hard work, clear thought, and good will Freddie practices, then his sales performance will seem miraculous. Much persuasion is quite similar to sales. One person envisions a desired outcome or behavior and then seeks all of the useful ways available to bring about that outcome. Whether the aim is to sell a car or to elect someone to office or to lead others to donate blood, all of the following elements apply to successful persuasion:

There must be an opportunity—a time and place where persuader and those to be persuaded get together.

There is usually a clear intent to cause a change in attitude or behavior. This intent is supported with information, arguments, and reasons why the persuader's proposals should be accepted. (We can assume in the car-sales example that both salespeople called attention to their make's attractive style, economy, durability, roominess, and so on. Each of these features can be considered an argument for buying the car.)

There must be free choice on the part of the person or people being persuaded. Forcing someone to hand over a wallet at gunpoint is not persuasion. Threats, blackmail, and coercion are not usually thought of as persuasion, although they are sometimes combined with true persuasion.

Persuasion usually takes a definite form or pattern, which consists of two essential parts: a proposition and its support. The proposition is one or more statements which, if accepted and believed by those being persuaded, will lead them ever closer to the desired outcome. Each of these propositions has to be proven or backed up by evidence. When listeners accept and believe all of the persuader's propositions, they are supposedly persuaded. If they believe everything that has been claimed but still will not behave as the persuader intended, several reasons may account for the failure to act. The persuader may have chosen some propositions badly, or the people being addressed may not have the power to do as they are asked. For example, a prisoner of war trying to get fellow inmates to overpower their guards and escape may give eloquent reasons and convince the prisoners, but if they are injured, chained down, ill and malnourished, and locked securely in a cell compound, they cannot act on the suggestion, no matter how persuaded they may be.

THE VOCABULARY OF PERSUASION

We should consider the working vocabulary and concepts that persuaders use because the implications of the terms and some contrasting terms are far-reaching. A thorough understanding of these terms is important for every person who tries to influence others and is the object of persuasion by others. These terms are presented in pairs because each key term is closely associated with a companion one, and is sometimes confused with it. The contrast between the items in these pairs of terms is thus pointed up by treating two concepts together.

Evidence and Proof

The first and crucially important concept to grasp is the distinction between *evidence* and *proof,* two terms often confused with each other. Many people respond during speeches as if evidence presented were proof. It is not. Evidence can be thought of as the raw material used to produce the final product, proof. Just as iron ore, coke, and chemical additives are eventually combined to produce steel, various arguments and strategies are combined to produce final acceptance by an audience of a line of reasoning and a case. The term *case* is the word applied to the whole package of arguments we want someone to believe. Lawyers refer to a case as that whole complex of issues and principles surrounding some court proceeding. Was a bus company negligent when a driver had an accident with 24 passengers aboard? If so, were the injuries sustained by a particular client mild or severe? If they were severe, would they probably affect the client's future professional career and income? These and numerous other issues constitute a case whose ultimate outcome depends on the answers to each question.

Evidence is never proof. It is merely the bits and pieces which produce *proof,* the ideal outcome of a persuasive speech or debate. Proof itself is an elusive term. It is not quite as absolute a concept as some people believe. When we say we have proved that oxygen and hydrogen make water, we can demonstrate over and over that the two elements properly mixed will make water every time, along with an occasional explosion. But even the explosion produces water. Now consider another example. We say that we have proved that honesty is the best policy. But have we demonstrated it in the same way we proved oxygen and hydrogen make water? Most people would agree that a few cases could be found in which honesty is not necessarily the best policy. We tell white lies to protect the feelings of our friends and loved ones. We do not bluntly inform the dying of their conditions, but evade the truth. Hence, we cannot be said to have finally established once and for all that honesty is the best policy in the same way that we have established that the earth circles the sun, or that gravity pulls everything downward toward the center of the Earth. Proof, then, in persuasion is not absolute demonstration.

Proof is acceptance by a given audience of a position. In a particular sermon on a particular occasion a minister might once again prove that divine love exists, or that honesty is best after all, but those conclusions may have to be established all over again for another audience on another occasion if they are not absolutely taken for granted. When your audience believes, you have proven a case. If it does not believe a case, even if some superhuman power knew the case to be absolutely true, for that audience proof has not occurred. Hence, proof is a relative term, not an absolute one.

Probability and Truth

Another very important distinction to make is that between *probability* and *truth.* In the fourth century B.C. the Greeks confronted the problem of discovering absolute truth. They realized that even if we could somehow know it, we might be unable to communicate it to someone else. Consequently, the best we can do is to establish what is *probably* true, that which is plausible, credible, likely. We say that something is true or false as if we could know, but much of the time what we claim to be true is only *probably* true. Courts of law accept the concept of probability routinely, because centuries of legal practice have demonstrated the difficulties of determining the truth about events and intentions. The persuader's task is profoundly influenced by the distinction between probability as a basis of proof rather than truth as the only basis.

A persuader has a much better chance of proving an assertion is likely than proving it is absolutely true. An eminent geologist used to startle her classes by taking them to the top of a mountain ridge and showing them thousands of clam shells. She insisted that students account for all the shells, which extended for miles. They might have been explained as decades of clam shells discarded by picnickers, but it seems unlikely that so many people would flock to the remote and otherwise rather unimpressive ridge. There were no shells nearby at lower levels. It became more and more evident that the professor was leading the students to discover that the shells were deposited on an ancient sea bed eons ago and that the mountain ridge had once been below sea level. Written evidence and observation and reasoning all led the students to the *probable* conclusion that the shells were ancient sea-bed detritus thrust upward millions of years ago. No one can ever know, for we have short lives. Most people seeing and reading the evidence would say it is true, but they are really saying only that they are convinced of the explanation. Those who deny geologic "truth" might claim that Indians transported millions of clams from lakes 550 miles away and ceremonially ate them on the mountain ridge for many centuries, but that explanation seems unlikely, farfetched, improbable, and untrue.

Probability is the best compromise we can make when we cannot know the truth. We would prefer the truth, but it is often not attainable. A persuader, fortunately, does not have the responsibility to demonstrate truth, but only to make a believable, likely case.

Claims, Propositions, and Cases

A few other terms need exploration and definition. A *claim* is an assertion a persuader wants us to accept. Once we accept it, the claim may become the basis for further claims: "These clam shells are powdery, crumbling, and smaller than the nearest shells," said the professor. Students examined them, agreed, and then were ready for the next step. "These shells are ancient and are unlike any modern clam shells found anywhere in the world," said the professor. "They were furthermore deposited here and not transported in here by people." Since no body of water was nearby, it was not evident to students from where the shells could have come. No one brought them in for a clambake in such numbers, they were ancient, and there were many of them. Then the professor built on these facts and made a new claim—namely, that the mountain ridge was once below sea level, a much harder claim to accept. But if everything else already accepted was true, then this last claim would also be likely.

A *proposition* is an explanation or a claim, which if true, leads the audience closer to accepting the speaker's case. A *case*, then, can be viewed as a large number of related propositions: "I put it to you that the murderer entered the room, locked its door, shot the victim, and then left by the window," says an investigator. "But all the windows were locked," says the defense attorney. My client could not have left by the window and then locked it." The defense rests here on rejecting the proposition or explanation offered by the prosecution. A claim is just an assertion, whereas a proposition is a technical term in argumentation. A claim is a general statement which is the basis for belief, whereas a proposition is a specific link in a formal case. For example, if someone says "It's so hot and humid that we're sure to have a thunderstorm tonight," that person has made a claim. It is not a proposition in the technical sense because it is not a link in a larger case. The person's reputation and career do not rest on whether or not a thunderstorm occurs, and no further action or belief depends on whether it rains as predicted. However, in a court case or a hotly contested persuasive campaign, if a speaker's propositions do not stand up, then reputation and credibility might suffer. A client's case can be overturned or an election may be lost.

Propositions are often classified into three or more formal types with clear distinctions between them:

1. Propositions of fact are statements about whether something is or is not true. They can be verified by investigation, statistics, testimony, demonstration, and so on. "Eighty percent of alcoholics are malnourished" is a proposition which is either true or not. "Illinois has the largest death toll from tornadoes, even though Oklahoma and Kansas have more storms" is a statement which can be verified or rejected simply by discovering the recorded data.

2. Propositions of value are assertions about the general desirability of some behavior or condition. "Drunkenness is shameful" is not an established fact, but an expression of a general value or opinion of drunken behavior. Sometimes the words "ought" or "should" are indicative of value statements, but unfortunately they can also occur in the third type of proposition. "We ought to exercise regularly" or "We should support medical research" are primarily assertions about the general appreciation of good health and the moral good of encouraging medical research in general.

3. Propositions of policy, which also contain the words "should" and "ought," are specific advocacy of a plan of action. "We should build fifty more nuclear submarines" and "We should abolish the sales tax on medicine and food" are both assertions about very specific plans of future behavior. It is important to note the shades of meaning in propositions of policy which distinguish them from propositions of value. "We should vote for Wilson next Tuesday" is a specific advocated policy statement. "Good citizens should vote" is a general assertion of value, which might be made less confusing by ridding it of the "should"; "Good citizens vote" is a bit better, but it could still be confused with a proposition of fact.

The choice and ordering of propositions and claims is not random or haphazard. A persuader puts them together by logical patterns which listeners can follow and agree with. If you say that the city should issue no more liquor licenses, it will not do to merely state assorted facts and opinions. The listeners will demand that you first state how many licenses now exist, what abuses of them take place or what conditions suggest limiting new issuance, and why the city administration should consider limiting the permits. It will not do to state that "there are too many drunks wandering our streets now and too many bars for the police to monitor effectively." You could bring in those details later, but until you show some strong reason to change the present policy, no action is likely, and the city will continue to issue new permits. To have some effect, a pleader must use systematic, logical means of building a case.

A skeletal example follows. You might show that the city has more bars per capita than any other comparable city in the state. You might then cite accident statistics which show that more motor-vehicle fatalities in the area are attributable to alcohol consumption than anywhere else in the state. You might proceed to depict the dangers to children and others from the high incidence of drunken driving in the town. If each claim or proposition is convincing, then the main proposition to limit new licenses will seem logical, moderate, and sensible. Now contrast the rational pattern just described with the disjointed, random set of previously described claims, which, by the way, were in fact just as true as the ordered claims.

Some years ago, agitated citizens in a western state made just such a proposal to the city council, but had utterly no success. They were considered to be zealots, do-gooders, kooks, and unstable people. Their fault was disorganization, not untruth. They wrote letters to the paper and radio stations with such claims as these: "There are more bars here than churches," "There is a bar in this town for every nine inhabitants," and "Our children have a poor civic model with so many taverns here." The claims were ineffective because, though true, they were isolated, emotionalized statements which were hard to structure into a credible case. Everyone knew the town was only a few miles from a much larger city which had no bars at all. Drinkers were thus forced to leave the big town and seek their pleasures in the smaller one. The claim about a bar for every nine residents thus became irrelevant, for the customers were not the local citizens but visitors from out of town. Moreover, the number of churches per capita was equally irrelevant, since no one had ever proved that a city was better than others because it had more churches per capita. In point of fact, what eventually happened was that the larger city changed its laws and opened several bars. It was no longer necessary for drinkers to leave town, and they turned their business to local bars. The suburban town not only forgot about the issue, but lost so much business that many of the existing bars closed, and few applicants for new licenses were found. The economy of the town was hard hit, because it depended heavily on out-of-town business, and its population declined markedly. In the sense that less bar traffic occurred, the pleaders won a point; but in the economic decline of the community, their arguments did no one much good and caused some economic harm to their own fellow citizens.

INDUCTION AND DEDUCTION: LOGICAL FORM

Two kinds of logical patterns in thinking have been recognized for many centuries. Recent modernizations of the patterns of thought have been attempted, notably by Stephen Toulmin, a British philosopher, and others who have developed his method. The late Douglas Ehninger elaborated Toulmin's basic model of reasoning in *Influence, Belief, and Argument* (1974).

According to this model, three related statements are the foundation of all reasoning. For example, you might make a *conclusion* that airline travel is safer than any other mode. For others to accept this claim, you must back it with *evidence,* which is a statement of facts supporting the claim. The evidence offered for your claim about airline safety might be the assertion that for two recent years there were no airline fatalities at all, and that during all the years of airline travel, the rate of annual fatalities was smaller for planes than for cars, buses, and trains. The third component of this type of reasoning is the *warrant,* a statement that shows how the evidence is related to the conclusion. In the example, the warrant would be the statement that the form of transportation with the fewest fatalities per year is the safest one. In addition to the three essential parts of the argument, speakers often add one or more *qualifications,* or limitations on the evidence. For example, you might point out that the best indicator of relative safety among various forms of transportation is the number of passenger miles traveled. This figure is simply the number of people boarding all vehicles multiplied by the number of miles traveled. A flight boarding 200 passengers and flying the approximately 3000 miles from New York to Los Angeles would build up 600,000 passenger miles. If you drove alone, your trip would yield 3000 passenger miles. It should be easy to see that if 600 people drove the same route, chances are fairly good that one or two of them might have accidents. Furthermore, the great speed of airplanes compared with that of cars would mean that automobile travel requires much more *time* in which accidents could occur. Nevertheless, passenger miles is a useful concept for comparing accidents among various forms of travel. A complete argument using the simplest structure looks like this:

Then, if people accept the evidence and the warrant, they are likely to accept the claim. Of course, much more complicated chains of argument are derived from this pattern.

However, the fundamental patterns of classical reasoning continue to dominate Western thought. These patterns are called *induction* and *deduction*. Both forms are used continually and in fact depend on each other. Their unique qualities are described next.

Induction

Induction is a pattern of intelligent association of our daily observations. We observe that days are shorter in the winter than they are in the summer. After perhaps years of observing this fact, we reach a conclusion that if today is a midwinter day, it is going to be shorter than a day in midsummer. Tomorrow the same thing will be true. We learn to extend a pattern observed over many years so that we can predict well into the future that any December day will be shorter than any July day in North America. We have made a generalization or a rule from repeated observations. Such a pattern of thought is called induction.

Although induction is valuable, it has some pitfalls. We may make our generalizations too soon. If it snows on May 1st in Denver for 3 years in a row, we would be hasty to conclude that snow is common in Denver as late as May 1st. Although it may sometimes snow much later, such occasions are so exceptional that we should not generalize that snow in Denver is common in May. Hasty generalization is a fallacy based on insufficient cases. Even ten or more observations may be insufficient to establish causation in matters as unpredictable and complex as weather. Nevertheless, induction is useful and is the source of many of our rules and laws of nature, our ability to predict the likelihood of future events, and our everyday conclusions. "Every time I go by Jason's house his dog barks and startles me. I have to go by there today, and I suppose he'll bark again." This pair of statements illustrates the inductive reasoning pattern we use all the time. However, another somewhat different pattern is also useful.

Deduction

Deduction is the pattern of thought that exists when we already have a rule or generalization as a starting point for thought about some person or act. We then apply that generalization to one particular case and draw a conclusion about that case. For example, we may say "All animals eventually die. Hardwicke, our cat, is an animal. Therefore, someday poor Hardwicke will pass on." If our rule is true, and if it indeed applies to the particular case, the conclusion is inevitable. However, sometimes the generalization is wrong, or the particular case does not properly fit under the generalization. Consider the following examples:

All mushrooms are poisonous.	(not true)
This is a mushroom.	(true)
Therefore, this is poisonous.	(may or may not be true)
All our cheerleaders are blondes.	(true observation)
Mary is a blonde.	(true observation)
Therefore, Mary is a cheerleader.	(not necessarily)

In this example, all cheerleaders fit into the larger class of blondes, but many other people are blondes without being cheerleaders. Obviously, there are many ways for deductive reasoning to go wrong.

Deductive reasoning can take several patterns. The formal device that all deduction uses is called the *syllogism,* which consists of three parts:

A major premise	the general rule
A minor premise	the particular case examined
A conclusion	the result of applying the rule to the particular case

Following is an example of a syllogism:

All mammals nurse their young.	(true generalization)
Whales are mammals.	(a particular kind of mammal)
Therefore, whales nurse their young.	(correct deduction)

For a syllogism to work properly and for deduction to be correctly used, the premises must be both true and applied correctly. When the rule or a premise is simply not true, we say the deduction is not *reliable.* Even if the reasoning itself is correct, whenever a premise is not true, we do not know whether the conclusion is true or not. It might be by chance. When the premises are properly related to each other and the conclusion is correctly drawn, the syllogism is said to be *valid.* In summary, a formal syllogism must be both reliable and valid to be correct. If either truth or premise relationship is doubtful, we cannot trust the conclusion.

Dogs are people's best friends.
Jim is my best friend.
Therefore, Jim is a dog.

Most of the time we do not go to the trouble of stating fully our claims based on reasoning. We do not talk in full syllogistic patterns but leave out a part of the formal structure. The resulting device is called an *enthymeme.* Even though many people have never heard the word they use the form frequently.

Any part of a syllogism can be left out to produce an enthymeme. Consider these examples:

Seeing the heavy traffic, I knew that the movie was over.	(major premise missing—namely, that traffic increases when the movie is over)
Whenever the score is tied at the end of the game, we play overtime. We are tied as the game is ending.	(conclusion missing)
Since all natives of North Carolina are Tarheels, you are a Tarheel.	(minor premise missing)

The syllogistic form of reasoning is widely used in debate, in argument, in persuasion, and in scientific inquiry. Even when an enthymeme is used in place of a full syllogism, all the rules of applicability, truth, and formal reasoning apply. An enthymeme always implies a syllogism, for the missing premise or conclusion is supplied by listeners. If someone says, "Take this umbrella so that you don't get wet," we assume it is raining. This enthymeme has several underlying assumptions, such as that rain will wet us, umbrellas will prevent the wetting, and it is raining.

As you might guess, the type of syllogism shown so far is not the only one. The one shown is called a *categorical syllogism* because it depends on classification into categories. The syllogism on mushrooms, for example, categorizes things as mushrooms and nonmushrooms, poisons and nonpoisons. The syllogism on cheerleaders classifies people into blondes and nonblondes, cheerleaders and noncheerleaders. The syllogism on whales talks of mammals, nursing animals, and other kinds of nonnursing animals. By placing individuals into the proper categories, the truth or falsity of a conclusion can be demonstrated.

Sometimes the syllogism takes the form of alternatives, and the name applied is the *alternative syllogism*. An example follows:

Either you are rich or you are my enemy. You are not rich. Therefore (you can supply the conclusion).

Just as the categorical form and inductive reasoning have their pitfalls, so does this form. For example, a hidden fallacy may lie in some alternative choices. "Either you study or you fail. You study. Therefore you pass." We cannot be sure of this conclusion, even though you certainly would fail if you did not study.

Study the following examples and determine whether they are valid and reliable, and what is missing in each one:

1. Either be quiet or leave. I won't be quiet. ____
2. Gambling or drinking is sinful. You are a sinner. ____

3. Learn to swim or risk drowning. I learn to swim. ___

Be careful with numbers 2 and 3, for there are other ways of sinning and other reasons for drowning. Number 1 allows you to conclude that "I leave." Number 2 implies that "you either drink or gamble," but the alternatives do not alone account for your being labeled a sinner. Similarly, in number 3, good swimmers may risk drowning from other hazards not included. Even if you accept the terms of numbers 2 and 3 as they are shown, you still cannot accept the implied conclusion as sole cause. This is a particular risk of this kind of structure in an enthymeme or syllogism.

There are many more subtle details to consider if you want to master logic, but a full discussion of logic is beyond the scope of this book. Two excellent sources for further study are Monroe Beardsley's *Thinking Straight* and, for the Toulmin form, Douglas Ehninger's *Influence, Belief, and Argument.* For a guide to logic in debate, see Abne Eisenberg and Joseph Ilardo's *Argument.*

WHY PERSUASION OFTEN FAILS

Unfortunately for persuaders, sometimes failure occurs when it ought not to, simply because the world is often unjust. Good speakers fail and bad ones succeed, both using the same principles of logic, evidence, strategies, and devices to influence other people.

Beside failure attributable to a speaker's shortcomings, sometimes listeners being asked to respond in a certain way simply cannot do what is asked of them, even if they want to do so. A young couple may not be able to afford the house that some salesperson has convinced them is a great bargain. You might still have to pass by the dream stereo you find and can afford because you know your landlord will evict you if you were to play music at the level you prefer.

Some of the reasons that persuasion fails are not well known. For example, audiences may reject speeches if the topics are too frightening for them to think about,[1] or they may have been previously conditioned on the topics before the speakers even address them.[2] If you are unaware of how much your audience already knows, you can alienate it by covering old ground.[3] Similarly, you could fail to understand some local prejudice, custom, belief, or attitude. More is said about audience analysis later in this chapter. For the present, suffice it to say that several causes of failure involve the audience, but there are other reasons for failure that lie within the speaker or possibly in the topic itself.

As a persuasive speaker, you might fail for any one or combination of the following reasons. If you are interested in developing skill as an influential speaker, you should pay careful attention to all of these matters:

You may seem untrustworthy to the listeners. It does not matter how honest and sincere you really are, if people think you are acting selfishly, dishonestly, or irresponsibly. If you are caught lying, faking evidence, or distorting facts, people will not trust you in the particular case and, even worse, they will distrust you later.

You may seem to lack enough facts, evidence, and sound reasoning to arrive at the claims made. People often fail to be persuaded by someone even though they already believe what is claimed. They seem to demand not only truth but a good case to prove what they already know. Many politicians have found to their sorrow that when they took for granted that their audiences agreed with their speeches, it was easy to skim carelessly over their evidence. Later, the listeners who formerly supported them turned against them because of the poor jobs they did in stating positions with which everyone agreed!

You might present a powerful case which contains good, sound, and thorough evidence, yet the audience might still reject it because of something you left out that the listeners considered important. Sometimes this effect comes from lack of enthusiasm or commitment, as perceived by the listeners. Sometimes it comes from the audience's belief that there might be other alternatives to whatever you are arguing for. For example, if you argue that schools are in desperate need for more funds and that a tax increase is necessary, listeners might agree with everything you say except the specific way you propose for increasing funds. If they believe that a grant could produce the funds or that dropping extracurricula events would save a large amount of money, they might still defeat a tax bill. In this case, you succeeded in convincing the listeners of the need for funds but even your best arguments failed to persuade them to follow through and accept the specific solution offered. Even if your logic and presentation are perfectly sound, audiences may still fail to be persuaded if they suspect that there is something better, as yet unsaid.

Studies of speakers' organization skills indicate that listeners much prefer to attend to someone who is well organized and that they are likely to reject messages from those who are not organized. Although they will tolerate some errors and are forgiving of minor mistakes, when they perceive too many organizational weaknesses they react negatively.[4] If the listeners feel that they themselves could have done a better job of the presentation, they may reject the persuasion. Apparently they do not reject the logic and the evidence, but they seem to resent the speaker's bumbling and prefer to wait for the same message from a more credible source before acting.

Although most people claim to judge arguments on the basis of facts, evidence, organization, and personal credibility, much of the time they still act on the basis of emotion. If you can stir the audience to active involvement with your message or your personality, you are likely to succeed more than a cold, detached speaker, no matter how competent. We like to be persuaded by those we find compassionate, attractive, and warm.[5] We are thereby susceptible to personal charm; sometimes we even are taken in by charlatans with that charm. If, however, an audience does not like a speaker, it tends to resist his or her messages, no matter how believable and carefully presented.[6]

HOW TO IMPROVE YOUR CHANCES
OF SUCCESSFUL PERSUASION

Now that we have dispelled some myths about persuasion and have discussed some of the reasons that persuasion fails, we can see more clearly how to set up conditions which will permit us to succeed at it. As was stated earlier, understanding audiences in general and the specific audience you wish to persuade is an important part of studying persuasive speaking. A major aspect of speech preparation is making a detailed analysis of everything it is possible to know about an audience. The research effort you make to discover facts and proof for a speech is essential, but it may all go for nothing if you do not consider the audience for whom you are tailoring the speech. Before discussing specific strategies to use for persuasion, we need to consider one more topic in some detail: the difficult or reluctant audience. Anyone can persuade people who already believe as the speaker does, using just a minimum of effort and care. The real challenge to a persuader is an audience which for some reason seems to resist the message, dislike the speaker, or resent the occasion.

Control of the Difficult Audience

Sometimes in speaking to a group you must present bad news, argue for an unpopular action, criticize or correct persons and their pet policies, or otherwise upset smooth relations with people through your speech. We would all rather be liked, respected, and welcomed than to be disliked, mistrusted, and shunned. However, sooner or later everyone has to present a difficult speech, to feel the sting of audience rejection, and to risk the loss of good will because intelligence and conscience require him or her to present an unwelcome message. In personal encounters with others no amount of tact can rescue anyone from the pain of having to convey the news to people that they are fired, that a raise or promotion has been denied, that some tragedy has befallen a family member, or that someone has made a stupid, inexcusable blunder. Similarly, having to tell a group of workers that a sizable work reduction, fewer benefits in an employment situation, and new unpopular work rules must occur are unusually stressful and challenging tasks. Anyone who must report bad news in status conferences or trouble-shooting meetings shares the pressure to which every speaker is heir. Speakers are thus sometimes practically guaranteed hostile listeners. This section helps you deal with such listeners and situations.

Definition. Consider the resistant audience to be a group opposing your opinions on one or more issues and unwilling to change on the issues for which you are arguing. Note that such an audience is not necessarily opposed to your stance on some other issue or to you personally, although reactions in the group may make you feel that you are disliked, resented, and unwelcome. It is of the utmost importance that you prevent or delay the audience's opposition to an issue from turning into animosity toward you. When the hostility of a group changes from dislike of a topic to personal distrust, a speaker is unlikely to have much impact on the opinions of the group.

Discovering the source of resistance. The first possibility to consider is that the audience may feel that its self-interests are somehow threatened by the position you take in a speech. Listeners may also be virtually powerless to support you. Peer-group pressures from sources such as families, religious affiliations, social groups, political parties, or local traditions may cause previous commitments to some position which are hard to abandon, even if members of the listening audience were fully open-minded and responsive to your message. They might privately agree with you and even wish to change their attitudes or behavior, but group pressures influence them to maintain their previously held positions.

The message you bring, too, might be unpalatable or fearful. Your listeners might prefer to avoid facing the issues or stirring up dissonance within an organization, club, or family. An example of failure to persuade people was the campaign to get Americans to build backyard atomic-bomb shelters. When people thought about all the terrifying implications of building, stocking, and defending themselves in bomb shelters, as well as just surviving under the necessarily primitive living conditions, they reacted by refusing to do anything or even to think about the problem. Some rationalized bitterly, saying that if war comes they hope to be right at the center of a missile's impact.[7] Needless to say, when strong emotions are inherent in a message you must present, extraordinary care and tact are necessary to prevent total rejection of the topic.

Sometimes people who have no strong opinions on a topic you present will appear hostile to you, when in fact their feelings are not their own but reflect those they know to be held by opinion leaders in the community. Your listeners may resist change solely on the grounds that they would prefer not to court the disfavor of those leaders.

Sometimes audience members mistrust you personally because of some cue or "vibrations" you give them accidentally—for example, if you tell a joke that happens to backfire. The author recalls with embarrassment an occasion when he was asked to give an entertaining speech to a "social group seeking some contrasting amusement, a relief from their usually serious club work," as it was explained by the contact person. A W. C. Fields routine on the evils of water and the virtues of gin seemed to be timely, and in fact was approved by the entertainment chairperson. Noting that the presentation was not going well, and that some people were suppressing their laughter when it was appropriate, the speaker felt acutely uncomfortable. Afterwards it became evident that the group was a church affiliated, socially dedicated club for whom the material was utterly inappropriate and probably offensive. Failure to inquire fully into the nature of the group and the poor judgment by the entertainment chairperson led to the embarrassing fiasco.

Even more subtle cues can annoy an audience. Quite mild humor might turn out to be improper for an occasion because of some event in the community, such as a bad auto accident, a fire within recent memory, or the like. Your dress or accent may annoy some people. A perceived attitude on a matter totally irrelevant to your speech could stir some listeners to be wary or disapproving of you.

Some strategies for regaining good will. Some ways to prevent accidental alienation are to study your audience, to develop your own sensitivity to or knowledge of others, or to have a friend within the group you will address. This ally can alert you to customs and even prejudices within the group, act as a testing ground for any ideas you think might possibly create ill will, and even signal you during the presentation if something you say needs softening or qualification. Beware of excessive concern, however. It is easy to become obsessed with audience approval, and the desire to please everyone can lead you into an inhibited, nervous mood unlikely to please anybody.

Fortunately, the classroom rarely presents a speaker a truly hostile audience. Of course, you can alienate listeners by heavy-handed, coarse humor or overbearing opinions. Most of the time, students are aware of their own vulnerability and cooperate. Some of them even refuse to enter into worthwhile criticism of their mates because there seems to be a tacit agreement: "I won't blast you if you'll take it easy on me." Most of the examples that follow, therefore, are drawn from the competitive real world where individuals' feelings are subordinate to the good of an organization. Criticism is neither subtle nor always concerned with the feelings of the person evaluated. When clashes of opinion occur in the classroom, egos are sometimes hurt and anger can rise. But when conflicts of opinion arise in industry, business, or the adult social world, sometimes enormous monetary costs and influential personal relationships are at stake. It behooves us to so conduct our personal and professional lives that alienating others is unlikely. William Byrd, an early Virginia settler, defined a gentleman as one who did not accidentally offend others. It is all right to offend them deliberately, of course, but someone who alienates others unconsciously may lack self-awareness, consideration for others, or self-control. It goes without saying that you would do well to reflect on how extreme or moderate your general views and opinions are. Then consider how loudly and insistently you impose these views and opinions on others. To become too agreeable is, of course, just as bad. We do not want others to see us as spineless lackeys. Like Byrd's gentlemen, we want to avoid accidental, unnecessary hostility in others.

First, and most important, do not be too hasty in assuming the worst, expecting rejection before it appears, and becoming defensive at the very beginning of a speech. If your attitudes and preconceptions about a situation are geared to deal with animosity, *you* might seem to listeners to be the source of any hostility. They may indeed pick it up from you and assume the very stance you are trying to prevent. Your prophecy of audience hostility becomes self-fulfilling and you indeed face resistance generated from your own tensions.

The best advice is to try to maintain a positive, constructive, even cheerful demeanor as long as you possibly can. Sometimes this tone is hard to generate and sustain. Go into a speech situation with the thought that most people will give you a chance, that they will be polite even if you give them some bad news, and that all that they can expect of you is that you present the message clearly and honestly. Some people find that a sense of detachment—almost to the point of not seeming to care—helps them. Of course, you do not want to convey the impression that you really do not care. The point is that you should not be so impassioned on a topic that you lose clear judgment concerning it, yet you must make clear your own position on the topic. Further, it is possible to go too far in pre-establishing your public image. If you assume a false good humor, a fake cheerfulness, or any hint of duplicity, then you can be sure of audience animosity when it discovers the real tenor of your message. Do not con your listeners. When people learn your true meaning, you may suffer a permanent loss of credibility with that audience. Similarly, gaining a reputation as a manipulator of people is undesirable. Of course, every influential person is to some degree a manager of ideas and people, but the control you exercise should be for everyone's benefit and organizational health. The issue of what is enough and what is too much "management" is one of degree. Sometimes we do not reveal all we know and we make choices about how much to say in our own self-interests, or for the good of an organization, but when exploitation of others and wholly selfish motives drive us, we will be found out and resented.

Establish your credibility on the specific topic early, and seek to build a warm, constructive relationship with your audience. Establish, if possible, a reputation over time, but also cultivate on the spot an image of being a prudent, reliable, and positive person. If you accomplish this first, then resistance to an unpleasant message you deliver is likely to be less than if your credibility is either unknown to the audience or weak. If resistance is evident early in the speech, you may have to appeal directly for a fair hearing. If the response is heated and disruptive, you may even have to abort the presentation entirely.

For example, a large manufacturer scheduled a staff meeting to confront an explosive issue that arose some weeks earlier. Opinions and feelings were growing stronger as informal discussion of the issue progressed off the record. On the day of the meeting, senior officers of the company judged that such a climax of polarization had grown that they should cancel the meeting until enough time elapsed for feelings to cool down. Even at the price of financial loss to the company while the issue remained unresolved, continuing good interpersonal relationships among the staff and managers was deemed more important than the issue. Sometimes, as in this real case, half-truths and oversimplified ideas take on a dramatic life of their own and sway people to irrational stances. It is as if a theatrical, unreal air of strife or crisis grows up around some issue or policy, and a melodramatic acting out of responses to it can occur. In such cases, it may be better to prevent the drama's unfolding, because things may be said and done that will have to be lived with for the rest of the staff's career together.

Following is a discussion of some helpful changes you can make in the structure or content of a speech. Seek whatever common ground you can find with the audience. You might refer to common goals, ideals, and points of agreement you share with them. By stating these at the outset, you may secure better identification with your audience and head off friction. Build your message from your perception of the base on which you and listeners already agree, and move toward the points on which you do not agree. We taste the sugar coating on a pill before its bitterness; consider this analogy, but do not carry it too far. The sugar coating is a disguise; the establishment of shared views is a strategic choice in the organization of a talk, and should in no sense be a disguise.

Extend your introduction beyond its usual rather brief scope. Building step by step toward the thesis rather than announcing it at the outset of a talk prevents or at least inhibits premature evaluation of your message. A very common phenomenon in presenting "bad-news" speeches is that the news is not as bad as it might seem, or that bad as it may be, there is a silver lining to the cloud—there is some good to come from an unpopular change in policy, for example. If you can just get past the unpalatable part of the message, the good part may be quite welcome in the audience. In such cases the introduction may be the place to insert some of the good news along with the caution that "there is a price to be paid for this good fortune." Again, avoid disguising the truth. We are talking here only about using the introduction to create the best possible atmosphere for your total message. Unfortunately, if that total message is entirely bad, then the preceding advice is not likely to help you much.

Be sure to select the optimum order of main ideas or points in your message. This order is unique to each individual speech task. However, do not blurt out your thesis prematurely, saying, for example, "I'm sorry, but we must all pay a 15 percent increase in tuition or the University will have to shut down next month." As you move toward revelation of your thesis, choose an order of points which creates a solid basis for any reasonable person's reaching the same conclusions you have. However, on a few occasions in which fear and expectation have built up to unrealistic levels, you might find that blurting out the thesis creates only a momentary shock. Then listeners realize that the situation is not nearly as bad as the anticipation of it. Such a strategy seems risky, but it might be better to plunge into the thesis, get the shock over, and then develop the speech as the audience settles. Anticipate likely objections against your case. The ideal order would be one which answered questions immediately as they arose in the minds of listeners. However, no speaker is likely to predict accurately in every case *what* somebody else will think, and certainly not *when* any given thought will occur in one or more listeners' minds.

The task here is thus partly a matter of having complete coverage of the topic and sufficient information to answer the most obvious questions. If, for example, the news you are delivering is about losing several scholarships, obvious questions follow: Who will be affected? When will the effects be felt? How long will the crisis last? What other provisions will be made, if any, for those losing scholarships? Your presentation, then, might address all these questions in the order shown.

The chosen order can include meticulous defense of each step in your reasoning and lay the groundwork for the next and later points. Show your listeners how you arrived at your views in step-by-step fashion. Because you want to maintain as rational a response as possible, your task is to prevent the audience from being suddenly shocked, emotional, or defensive. Emotionally upset auditors are poor listeners. They are likely to misunderstand what you say, jump to conclusions, and make the situation worse than it really is.

Another strategy that may be feasible is to lower your demands on listeners. You might be able to modify your thesis so that you have less expectation of response from listeners. A less radical or threatening message can sometimes be constructed from a given set of facts. Rather than upbraid all the staff for declining sales records during a given month, a district sales manager might give a presentation showing exactly what the figures were and offer several possible explanations for the slump: "If we take into account that two new competitors arrived on the scene, the figures indicate that we may need some change in advertising policy. If we consider that this time of year is always slow, things don't look so grim." If the speech is tailored just right, the salespeople will still get the message that business is down and that if it is to improve, they must be the key. The expectation or demand of the speaker, however, has been lowered. It has been changed from explicitly saying "Sell more goods or get out" to "You ought to know that sales are down and here's why you might need to change your sales strategies and goals." Clearly the implied message is still present.

Sometimes you can make concessions in a speech that will aid your whole objective, even though you would prefer not to concede any point. This is a fundamental assumption of arbitration, but in a speech the intellectual equivalent of a business transaction can occur. For example, to concede that a competitor produces a fine product might make you seem more fair-minded and sensible than to insist that the competitor's line is entirely inferior to yours and that your line is the only good value on the market. You still argue for your product, and indeed point out flaws or weaknesses in the competition. In speeches not centered on business, but more concerned with cultural values and opinions, you can often be more persuasive by giving a little on pet assumptions in order to seem less dogmatic. A zealot in religion, philosophy, or even gardening can be a nuisance. Some people feel a moral duty to defend and impose on others their views—or prejudices—about subjects which are largely a matter of taste, such as music, art, politics, or religion. They cannot bring themselves to concede anything even in casual conversation. Such persons find concession to be a threat to their integrity, but their listeners may see only inflexibility, egocentrism, and selfishness. It is a mark of social grace and maturity to keep a healthy sense of humor and perspective. Insistence on winning every point in phatic, unimportant speech will probably be interpreted as immaturity.

In trying to persuade others, a useful device is that called *external commitment,* or public agreement to do something. In this procedure, you get agreement first on one minor point, then on another, and so on. You try to get respondents to agree aloud—and ideally in the presence of other people—on more and more of the proposition. Once people "go on record" aloud, they tend to back away less than if they had said nothing. A well-known sales pitch among encyclopedia salespeople is to get prospective customers to agree first that they want their children to be well educated. Then the salespeople get the customers to say aloud that they do not want their children to be at a disadvantage in study, proper use of library and research facilities, and instant access to the world's ideas. Finally, the salesperson asks whether the family wants the status of owning a fine set of books. As one says "Yes" over and over, presumably it becomes easier to say "Yes" when a signature on the dotted line is requested. However crass the comparison may seem, some of this sort of effectiveness of public agreement seems to accrue for a persuader. However, research and even ancient classical opinion support the notion that when the personal interests of the persuader are obvious to the listeners, appeals of all sorts are less likely to succeed. People are not persuaded against their wills, even by the most sophisticated ploys. They may succumb, but they are not really persuaded in the sense that they fully agree, comply, and like their decision.[8]

An attractive and popular device some people use to ameliorate the embarrassment they feel in public-speaking situations is humor. If you know an audience very well, or if there is little pressure in the speaking situation, or if the occasion demands it, humor can be used with good effect. It breaks the tension at the beginning of a speech, shows the speaker to be (or seem to be) relaxed and full of good will, and makes the burden of listening easier. In some situations, everyone knows what will and must be said, and a little originality and consideration for listeners is appreciated. However, when you anticipate a hostile reception, be wary of using jokes because they may make matters worse by trivializing heartfelt sentiments in the audience. Moreover, what you find humorous may not be at all amusing to your listeners. To poke fun at someone's pet ideas is to court certain ill will. Although humor is often just the right aid to reestablish rapport with an audience, it also has a high probability of annoying those listeners who are already ambivalent or inclined to reject you and your message.

Another device speakers sometimes use when they feel it is important to make a strong impression on listeners is the appeal to fear. As mentioned earlier, fear appeals have been repeatedly shown to have little force in persuading people. A classic study on the effects of fear appeals presented subjects with weak, moderate, and powerful arguments for brushing one's teeth regularly and seeing a dentist every 6 months. Those who saw the powerful presentation with slides of advanced dental decay, jaw infections, and bone malformation were the least persuaded. Those who got the mild or moderate presentations with less shocking arguments and images were more apt to accept the message than those seeing the dreadful appeals.[9] The mechanism is not entirely clear, but experimental results at least seem to be fairly consistent in indicating that strong fear appeals are likely to produce withdrawal from the situation, not facing up to it. There are times when heavy-handed, fear-laden messages may be necessary, but it seems safest to avoid any unnecessary use of such tactics. Other strategies seem more effective.

SUMMARY

Persuasion is defined as all efforts to change attitudes, beliefs, and behavior. These efforts may or may not be successful. Opportunity, intent to persuade, free choice among respondents, and carefully structured appeals are all characteristic of persuasive discourse. Persuaders use evidence to produce proof, or when proof is impossible, they try to establish the high probability of their claims. The traditional forms of inductive and deductive logic are useful frameworks for planning and constructing believable arguments. A newer form of logic developed by Toulmin, Ehninger, and others may be easier and less involved, but either form requires rigorous testing of assumptions, classification, and awareness of fallacies. Even with optimum performance by a speaker, efforts to persuade may fail from a variety of forces outside the speaker. Among these are imperfect audience analysis, eagerness of listeners to protect good social relationships with opinion leaders, and the inability of listeners to comply with a persuader's requests.

When it is certain that you must face a difficult audience, there are several steps you must take to prepare for the experience. First, get a good grip on your emotions and resolve not to be intimidated by the listeners. Do not expect the worst and waste time in useless fretting. Try to determine the source of the obstacle. Is it inherent in the message or is it likely to be based on your own image before the group? Decide what, if anything, you can do to soften or modify the impact of bad news. If your own role or personality is a source of irritation, discover any corrective strategies you think might make you more acceptable to the group. Consider the strategic choices discussed earlier. Often so-called hostility is not directed at the speaker at all, and you only need to proceed as if the situation were normal. In some kinds of jobs high levels of stress and tension *are* normalcy. Modifications of the message, of the organization of the content, of your own attitudes, and of the image as interpreted by the listeners are all possible ways you can make the best of a tense situation.

EXERCISES

1. Which of these statements are probable and which are true? "The Earth is 4 billion years old." "Paula is a blonde." "Paula is a natural blonde." "The sun is 93 million miles away." "A meter is longer than a yard." "Ted seems smarter than John." "The moon is larger when low on the horizon than when high in the sky." For any statement you claim as true, state the basis for your claim. Can an objective reality be true for one person and false for others? If so, how is it possible? Discuss.

2. Sometimes it is hard to tell what is evidence and what is truth. For the following pairs of statements, which statement is evidence for the other one?
    a. I love Tony. Tony's future is bright.
    b. Marian is rich. Marian is famous.
    c. The lake is unpolluted. The lake water is clear.

3. When we reason with others we often omit some parts of the models of reasoning. That is, we leave unsaid some assumption or premise, assuming that our listeners will fill in the missing information. State what is missing but implied in the following statements, and recall that more than one assumption might be made:
    a. Take this umbrella so that you won't get wet.
    b. Don't forget to pack a bathing suit and suntan lotion.
    c. Take these quarters and dimes for your drive through Chicago.
    d. Jim swears he'll never eat salami again.
    e. Don't order Camembert cheese until you taste part of my order.

4. Sometimes persuasion fails because listeners mistake the intended ideas in our arguments. In the following cases, state two possible meanings that could result from listeners' choosing an unintended assumption:
    a. When the police officer arrested Joe, he pulled out a gun.
    b. We were all mistaken about the teacher's competence.
    c. During the tornado, Jane fainted in the shower but was saved by a watchful janitor.
    d. I'd be happy to introduce you to some very worthwhile friends.
    e. Your teacher says you think badly about scientific topics.
    f. We can always advise you how to make friends better.

5. The question of whether fear appeals are very effective devices for persuasion remains unanswered. In a class discussion, relate incidents in which you personally were or were not persuaded by appeals to fear. Avoid trivial cases such as parents' saying, "Eat your spinach or you'll get no ice cream." Try to decide how the class feels about the use of threatening information to guide and control them. Are class members aware of fear appeals in daily life? Are some threats necessary just to get us through the day? Does the repeated use of fear appeals weaken their effect on us?

6. State whether the following conclusions are based on inductive or deductive reasoning:
    a. The dog will pick up the paper tonight at 6 as he always does.
    b. Even though this thing looks like a twig, it is probably an insect, because it has six legs as other insects do.
    c. This applicant must be a dancer, because all of the applicants are either singers or dancers, and he refuses to sing.

d. This man is probably gentle, for he is very big, and all the big men I have known over the years were gentle.

SELECTED READINGS

MONROE BEARDSLEY, *Thinking Straight,* 4th ed. (Englewood Cliffs, N.J.: Prentice-Hall, 1975).

RICHARD CRABLE, *Argumentation as Communication: Reasoning with Receivers* (Columbus, Ohio: Charles E. Merrill, 1976).

DOUGLAS EHNINGER, *Influence, Belief, and Argument* (Glenview, Ill.: Scott, Foresman, 1974).

DOUGLAS EHNINGER AND WAYNE BROCKRIEDE, *Decision by Debate* (New York: Dodd Mead, 1963).

ABNE EISENBERG AND JOSEPH ILARDO, *Argument,* 2nd ed. (Englewood Cliffs, N.J.: Prentice-Hall, 1980).

JEANNE FAHNESTOCK AND MARIE SECOR, *A Rhetoric of Argument* (New York: Random House, 1982).

DARRELL HUFF, *How to Lie with Statistics* (New York: Norton, 1954).

HOWARD KAHANE, *Logic and Contemporary Rhetoric* (Belmont, Calif.: Wadsworth, 1971).

STEPHEN TOULMIN, *The Uses of Argument* (London: Cambridge University Press, 1958).

chapter 9

Strategies
of Persuasion

Whenever you set out to persuade others, whether by a formal speech, a conversation, or a written essay, your goal is to change the audience. Until urged to follow some new action people tend either to do nothing or to continue their present behavior in regard to some subject. As a simple example, people who take the bus to work each day have probably already considered the advantages of buying packets of tokens or annual passes to reduce transportation costs below those paid when they use cash fares each day. To bring about a change in behavior, the bus company might advertise heavily and play on the theme of how much commuters can save by buying an annual pass. In this case the company stands to gain certain ridership and a minimum profitable income from the sale of its annual passes. The riders in most cities offering bus passes can expect to save a considerable amount, assuming they ride the bus every day. Extensive sale of such passes then becomes an argument the company can use for even more sales: "Look at how many sensible people have bought our annual passes. You, too, can get in on the great savings and convenience of having a pass." The decision to announce how many hundreds or thousands of passes were sold is called a *strategy* of persuasion. If the company sold only 96 passes in a city of 400,000 population, of course the management would keep quiet and choose some other strategy.

Strategy, as used in this book, is the choice of some plan of argument or persuasion. The term carries no necessary implication of manipulation, propaganda, or exploitation. As mentioned earlier, it is, of course, possible to pervert any science or art for selfish, even illegal ends. There is no known way that strategies can be approved as ethical or condemned as dishonest in advance. For example, a decision to reveal great emotional involvement while persuading a group to give more money to a particular charity is not necessarily insincere. A speaker deciding to use such a strategy may have made a searching examination of the issues and concluded that the need for financing, the good the charity does, the past history of laggard support, and the evasion of members' responsibilities to pay their fair shares all require a showdown. The speaker's decision to "lose all patience" and become visibly emotional during the speech, even though planned or allowed to happen, might seem to some people mere "acting" and exploitation. Cardinal Maury, grappling with this issue during the French Revolution, wrote in his impressive book on rhetoric that one should envision a dear friend about to make a very unwise and far-reaching decision. It is our duty to plead, argue, exhort, and use tears and shouting to help our friend avoid the pitfalls we see. Of course, if people discover that we have some personal stake in our persuasion they may take us less seriously.

One other caution needs mention before we turn our attention to the numerous available strategies open to us, and open for use upon us. The persuader must always remember that the most well-intended strategy can backfire and not only fail to persuade others, but also positively damage an otherwise good case. Listeners can misinterpret our motives, thinking we have some personal gain to secure or some status to acquire by persuading them. Or, some recent event unknown to us or a local situation we have no means of knowing about might ruin our persuasive efforts. O. Henry's touching story about a family entering a clothing store to buy a suit for their son while the salesperson blathers on about the durability of the suit ends with a revelation that the son is dead and the suit is for his burial. Like many an unwary persuader, the sales agent is horrified at his own words once he learns of events which conditioned the parents in ways he did not realize.

CHOOSING SPECIFIC STRATEGIES OF PERSUASION

You can use any of an enormous variety of tactics to move your listeners to belief in your ideas and to change their behavior. The strategies described throughout this chapter are by no means the only ones available to speakers. Some of them refer to the message, some concern presentation, and others count on audience reactions. Speakers choose not one but a variety of strategies during preparation, and they frequently select one or more alternatives in case the original plan proves ineffective. In other words, if they judge that the audience is not responding during the speech in predictable and favorable ways, speakers often decide to change their strategies and emphasize new ones. It may seem a heavy burden on a speaker not only to prepare the speech but also to prepare several versions. But in speeches on important issues and before critical, well-informed audiences, such preparation may sometimes be necessary. Ordinarily, for class assignments, one strategic plan is chosen and adhered to.

STRATEGIC USE OF EVIDENCE

The most common persuasive tactic is to present such good quality evidence and enough of it that audiences reasonably must accept it. Ethical use of evidence requires that it be true, or if you cannot know whether it is absolutely true, the information must be at least probable and consistent with other facts. It is simply dishonest to make up statistics and pretend that they are true. It is also extremely risky for two reasons. First, faked data have a way of sounding quite unconvincing, inconsistent with other information, and improbable. Second, there is a good probability that someone in the audience will know the true facts, realize the swindle, and expose the truth. Not only will the rest of the speech be utterly ineffective and suspect, but also you will have no credibility with the audience again.

Assuming that they have chosen high-quality arguments, students often do not know how much evidence they need. Some speakers use too much evidence. You need not overwhelm your listeners with six or seven authoritative sources to secure the advantages of sound material. Usually three unbiased authorities are sufficient. If their opinions agree, or even if those opinions are not exactly alike but are merely consistent with one another, you will probably get all of the available impact without belaboring documentation. In fact, overly documented speeches may tend to arouse suspicion. Audiences might detect a concern that some point is vulnerable to attack and the excessive support for it may thus backfire.

But evidence itself is not always the source of belief among your listeners. What you do with evidence also determines its impact. Thus, you must know how to choose the best among strong pieces of data for a particular case. For instance, if seven authorities all say virtually the same thing about the dangers of cancer among smokers, then clearly you must choose from among those seven sources and present about three that seem most likely to help your speech. If one of the sources is a rabid moralist, then it might be prudent to ignore that bit of evidence. If one source is a big tobacco grower or wholesaler who let slip a remark about the dangers of using tobacco, then that evidence might have more impact than someone else's because the admission of danger would normally not be in the best economic interest of the grower. Hence, the information about the source becomes as useful as the opinion itself. Sometimes you may find that citing the stance of an authority is necessary to get maximum use of the data. For example, to say "Doctor Smith believes that minimal medical treatment should be given in cases in which abortion is suspected" does not say much other than that some physician believes in conservative obstetric practice. If, on the other hand, you tell the audience that Dr. Smith is an obstetrician in a major clinic and has been a respected authority for decades, the audience is being told not only what the physician believes but also why he or she should be believed. However, although citing the stance of the authority may give credence, it may also damage it. For instance, if some doctor had said earlier, "Save the mother at all costs, and do what you can for the child," then any subsequent testimony from that doctor concerning abortion might not be considered totally objective, in the eyes of the audience. Similarly, if the doctor had taken the opposite stance, *other* members of the audience might consider the position wrong.

As a speaker you can, to some extent, manipulate honest statistics. The old saying that "Figures don't lie, but liars figure" is accurate. The particular data you present, the order in which you present them, the context in which you mention them, and your decisions to omit some which do not strongly support a claim are all ways you can get the most out of honest figures. You can also present information with an air of scientific fact when the data may actually not be very reliable: "Three out of four doctors interviewed recommend *X*," claims an ad, but if only four doctors were asked about practically *any* product, you might well find three in agreement. Further, does the claim mean that 75 percent of many hundreds or thousands of doctors agreed, or does it mean that once the four original interviewed doctors yielded the seemingly overwhelming agreement, no more doctors were interviewed? Were the doctors employed by the advertising agency? Were the doctors all physicians, or were they perhaps other kinds of doctors? The note of scientific survey in this example can be played up to appear more decisive than the actual data indicate. Thus, both your accepting polls, investigations, or studies in an uncritical manner, or, on the other hand, your leading the audience to accept them by manipulation are both shady practices.

Tests of Evidence

Any evidence or testimony you use to persuade others and all of it presented to you when you are being persuaded should meet certain tests:

Is there enough evidence to warrant the claims you make for it? *Sufficiency* of material, then, is the first requirement for your case. Just as a snow flurry may not indicate that a blizzard is coming, so a few cases of plague do not presage an epidemic. You need to be careful not to claim too much for limited data. If several independent sources all report the same thing, there is some likelihood of a valid claim. But what is enough? Several people have claimed to enter flying saucers and communicate with visitors from outer space. Thousands of people have claimed to see such saucers, yet there is at present no firm evidence of the existence of interplanetary visitors.

In addition to sufficiency of evidence, you must always try to be sure that the origin of the evidence is beyond reproach. You must make sure that the *source is unbiased* and competent. Check it out. Does the source have anything to gain by spreading the information? Is the source credible or suspect? If someone stands to gain by having other people believe a claim or if that person will lose something if others do not believe, then the person's credibility is suspect. For example, if the Loch Ness monster is proved to be entirely imaginary, writers on the subject may sell fewer books than they would if the myth were continued. Claims for some fad diet made by someone selling a diet pill or the currently popular foods in the diet are not as trustworthy as claims made by someone with no interest in pills, food, or book sales.

Broad consistency of any piece of evidence with other evidence is a great concern. One problem with believing in flying saucers from other planets is the realization of the enormous distances and speeds required to go to any other planet. Another problem is the lack of agreement between the known conditions on Mars and Venus and the likelihood that any creatures could come from them. In other words, known scientific facts are inconsistent with the conclusion that little green people from Mars are visiting us. A piece of evidence such as a convincing photograph and several eye witness reports still cannot overcome the skepticism of scientists, primarily because the new evidence is not consistent with other evidence.

Logical consistency, or agreement with tests of reality, is a good measure of the usefulness of facts, opinions, and beliefs used. Consistency of a piece of evidence with common sense and your prior experience is an essential test. A street vendor once offered this writer a gold ring for $4. The vendor was unlikely to be fooled by his own product, to be unaware of the price of gold, to expect anyone to believe that the ring was gold, or to walk the streets with a valise full of gold jewelry. The buyer certainly knew the value of gold, had never heard of such an inexpensive gold ring, and could not justify the purchase on any logical grounds. But it was pretty and just maybe—it turned green within hours. As in this case, we often do not bring logic to bear on situations which need it, and we act or believe on the basis of wishful thought, greed, or whim. Logical consistency means that a statement is consistent with what we know of human nature, the world, and natural laws.

The evidence ought to be *current* and *timely*. Citing data from the 1940s and 1950s on the incidence and treatment of tuberculosis (TB) is of historical interest only, for both the number of cases and treatment are quite different now. To use the figures as evidence that we ought to require every school child to receive injections to detect TB would be rather futile. Listeners will want to know what is going on right now. Of course, if the old data and new figures are both used, then any trend or change might indeed be understood and thus useful in the argument. Further, when data are timely, they apply to claims which were true when the data applied. That is, it is quite correct to use 1940s data on the incidence of TB if the point of the speech is that shortly after the discovery of a new drug the incidence dropped. Comparing data from the 1940s and 1950s would then be both valid and timely. The main concern is not to use outdated and hence irrelevant statistics when newer ones are available or should be available. Sometimes facts are gathered slowly, such as census data, average income figures, and any information from very large samples. The meaning of the figures gathered may change by the time they are compiled. Figures on incomes, for example, are very hard to compare sensibly, for "average family income" of just a few years ago is now below the official poverty level. Any claims or conclusions based on comparisons of incomes a decade apart have to be made with great care.

Evidence must show *pertinence to a claim* with which you are associating it. To show statistics on the decline of highway accidents and claim them as evidence of the value of drivers'-education classes might backfire. Someone could point out that for many years the number of accidents rose in spite of the rising number of courses in drivers' education, and that the recent decline in accidents is more related to a lower speed limit than to drivers' education. Similarly, you cannot assume that simultaneous events are causally related. For example, many physicians now prefer not to remove tonsils from children, even though the procedure was once widespread. Someone compiling statistics might erroneously conclude that there are many fewer tonsil removals from children, and that therefore there is less incidence of tonsillitis among children than there was 30 years ago. New drugs to control inflammation could account for fewer operations, and the number of cases of tonsillitis itself might not have declined at all. A claim that "fewer tonsillectomies among children proves that inflamed tonsils are now infrequent" is therefore fallacious because the evidence (number of operations) is not really pertinent.

Any authority or expert cited as a source of evidence must meet certain tests for the testimony to be acceptable. For example, if we are told that a prominent doctor believes that the dangers of smoking are overestimated, we need to know what specific expertise the source has on medical practice associated with smoking. If the doctor turns out to be a doctor of philosophy or law, then however brilliant and famous he or she is in another speciality, a likely expertise in the medical implications of smoking must be suspect. Even more common examples of this dilemma are found in endorsements of all kinds of products by sports figures. Athletes, for instance, simply have no more expertise than anyone else on beers, clothing styles, cosmetics, cigarettes, and the like. The use of an expert in one field to endorse or praise something beyond the established competence of that person is merely an appeal of personality, and provides very weak evidence of very low credibility.

REDEFINING ISSUES AND CLAIMS

Most persuasive discourse concerns propositions, or claims that someone offers and expects the audience to believe. When a claim is disputed or open to dispute, then an issue is created. An issue is simply a clash of opinion. Moreover, issues are often extremely important in persuasion, for until one or more issues are resolved, the whole point of the speech may be uncertain. For instance, before you can persuade members of an audience to have smallpox vaccinations, you must convince them on at least two issues: (1) Is smallpox already extinct in the world? (2) Is the danger from infected needles and the injection greater than the risk of getting smallpox? If smallpox is extinct, then there is utterly no reason to be vaccinated. Whether or not that issue is settled, if the members of the audience believe the widely published claim that deaths from vaccination are higher than from smallpox, then they are unlikely to accept the thesis of a speech urging vaccination. If the two issues cannot be settled, the speech is still unlikely to succeed. As the listeners understand it, if they do get vaccinated, the effort may be useless and there is also some danger. If they do not get vaccinated, there may be no danger from the disease and certainly none from injection. They are, therefore, better off doing nothing in the face of the unresolved issues. Consequently, your speaking strategies often address the possibility of changing or redefining the issues. You can do this by pointing to one aspect of a question as most appropriate for examination and then arguing on your own terms. For instance, in the smallpox speech just described, you might minimize the needle issue by saying that the data on illness and death from vaccinations merely show carelessness, incompetence, and laziness in some hospitals. Failure to sterilize and protect needles and vaccine thus becomes an issue which is much easier to dispose of than the issue of number of deaths from vaccination.

Sometimes, if you are in a debate or you are confronted by questions from an audience, you can just "start over" by placing the arguments and issues on a new footing. For example, you might give the just-discussed speech a fresh start by arguing that the statistics on the dangers of vaccination are drawn heavily from a few substandard tropical hospitals and consequently are not really applicable to general medical practice in North America.

Certain ways of reshaping issues are more subtle. You might ask your audience a hypothetical question which it cannot answer without implying agreement or some concession to your stance. "Have you ever known anyone with an infected vaccination?" "Do you think that routine injections in local hospitals are less dangerous than those against smallpox?" If the respondent says "No" to either question, you have gained ground. Even if someone has known of a bad vaccination, the second question will redirect the issue. If one injection can cause inflammation, then all injections can do so, you seem to imply. Now the audience is left wondering whether there is any general danger from injections, whether smallpox injections are more threatening than, say, penicillin shots, or whether all needles are dangerous. The new questions tend to drift away from the original point, but strategically they water down the effects of opposing information. Instead of one issue, there are now several.

Other strategies concerning the use of evidence, claims, and issues exist. You might describe an issue in oversimplified ways to create an illusion of a simple, forceful stance when the issue is in fact quite complex. For example, in arguing for a gold standard for our money, you might say, "The issue is simply whether our paper money is to be guaranteed by a metal regarded as universally and eternally valuable, or whether we are to just take somebody's word that our money is good." Audiences might find the notion clear and direct, but in fact a great many subsidiary issues are hidden in such a statement. Is gold eternally valuable, or could its supposed value change? Is faith in metal somehow superior to faith in governmental agencies or officers? Does a gold standard guarantee the value of a nation's currency? What happens to our currency's value when elsewhere in the world gold prices go up or down?

You could also choose the opposite strategy. You may feel that the audience or an opponent has oversimplified terms and issues and seek to describe them in more complex terms. You can make either strategy work when you adapt it to the situation. If you can lead the audience to see that someone has muddled issues by making them seem overly complicated, you may weaken the credibility of that person. On the other hand, if you can succeed in making an audience believe that an opponent or perhaps the press has grossly over-simplified complex issues and that you have a better and more accurate, even if complicated, grasp of those issues, then you can persuade.

Speakers sometimes present a case in such a way that only one possible conclusion can be reached—namely, the one desired by the speaker. Of course, to some extent we always try to lead the listeners systematically to our desired aims, but this is not what is described here. In a *contrived discovery* all data and development are chosen to establish a presumption in the audience. To illustrate, suppose a speaker were to present a talk on the future of prisons in our state. The pattern of the talk might be the presentation of several logical questions. The answers to those questions might inevitably lead to the speaker's conclusion. "How many cell beds are now available in this state? How many prisoners are sent to jail per month? What is the present prison population? What is the trend of courts in sentencing criminals to jail? What tax assets have been allocated to prisons over the last 20 years?" Statistical data are chosen and presented to answer these questions as if there were no other important questions on the topic. The audience, hearing of overcrowding, increasing crime, tougher sentences, poor tax support, and so on, reach the "predicted" discovery that we are just going to have to increase taxes and build more prisons.

CONTROLLING THE FOCUS
ON DEVELOPMENT

You may use a variety of other strategies to keep attention centered on those ideas and issues you wish to deal with or to avoid. This group of devices concerns ways to control focus. You might, for instance, appeal to principle in order to justify (or to criticize) some practice: "It is never right to torture prisoners, no matter how heinous their crimes." "Even if a few criminals escape justice, the risk of unjustly executing an innocent person is too high." "Freedom of assembly requires that we tolerate Nazis parading in Skokie." All these statements are claims to some higher aim, a value system which takes precedence over the temptation to take drastic action. You can make a decision as to which aspects of a proposal are most appealing and you can construct your message so that those favorable points get the most stress whereas the unfavorable ones are either dismissed briefly, omitted, or explained away. Repetition can give an idea unusual emphasis. By contrast, you can minimize some point by explaining that it is an extreme, abnormal, unusual, or rare sample or example.

When you judge that an audience is disposed to agree, then you can cite ends to justify the means. For example, ridding a suburb of stray dogs by poison baits might be urged on the ground that the extermination of the animals is justified by higher goals, such as avoidance of attacks upon small children, freedom from disease, and protection of property. Mentioning the threat of rabies and depicting the horrors of that disease might succeed in selling the eradication plan, in spite of objections that poisoning is inhumane.

Sometimes you might envision and describe for the audience a set of consequences of some proposal to show how the proposal would either become a disaster (if opposed to your stance) or a great benefit (if proposed by you). The projection of a future situation is always risky, however, for someone could turn the imagery back upon you if either the whole vision or a significant part of it were suspect. Finally, you can also influence the focus of a topic by how many details you choose to bring up. In debate, one kind of persuasive effort, a common strategy is to bring up so many objections and detailed flaws that the opponents cannot possibly deal with them all in the allotted time. This "shotgun" strategy, wherein speakers assail opponents with many detailed arguments like shotgun pellets, can also be used in single speeches. You might pose such an array of objections to opposing views that the audience cannot deal with them all and accepts your position as a simpler, less problematic one.

Reversal of Content

When it is certain that some individual or strong evidence in opposition exists, you can sometimes reverse an apparent weakness and make it a strength. One way is to show that what was thought to be a criticism is actually a strength. For example, if you argued that we ought to develop our own supersonic transport plane rather than rely on the model built by the British and French, a likely objection would be the enormous cost of labor to produce such a craft. You might expect such an objection and point out the desirable generation of new jobs, the hiring of engineers and technicians now unemployed, the stimulation of the economy, and the economic growth both directly and indirectly issuing from the decision.

Sometimes you can get the upper hand in a situation by anticipating a major objection before anyone else can bring it up. To expect it and answer the objection effectively can be a powerful stroke in persuasion. However, you can be too clever. If the issue is considered to be a false or trivial one, or if the explanation is lame, you are worse off than if you had never raised the issue at all.

Another way you can profit from the "reversal" strategy is to grant the opposition a point and then show how that point works against the opposition. For instance, if your thesis is that the United States should accept Puerto Rico as a state, someone might object that such an act would be seen as encroachment and a provocation upon Cuba. "The act would indeed extend our influence in the Caribbean," you might reply, "but that extension would be a symbol to our Pan-American neighbors of our concern for the wishes of Puerto Rico, who petitioned for statehood. It would be an act of consolidating Western nations. It would give unmistakable signs to Cubans that their suspicions about the United States' concern for its southern neighbors are wrong." Sometimes you can adopt the language of an opponent, whether that person is a speaker or perhaps a columnist. Using similar or parallel language, you can often gain credibility by repeating the opponent's claims and then subtly shifting them, either to show an irony or to reveal inconsistencies in the opposing case. Adolf Hitler, commenting upon Churchill's statement that Hitler had "missed the bus" by not invading England in 1940, quoted Churchill's question about whether the Nazi leader would attack, and then added a direct reply to Churchill: "He's coming. He's coming." The propaganda effect was immense, and given the subsequent ordeal of England in the World War II, Churchill's unfortunate remark was turned against him to his great embarrassment.

A common strategy of reversal is apparently to accept an opposing proposal, and then explore it in such a way as to ridicule it or extend it to expose what you regard as fatal flaws. You might, for example, argue along these lines: "The proposal to accept all current residents now considered illegal immigrants as citizens of the United States has been made and ably defended by some sensible and thoughtful people. Let's look into the matter a bit more deeply. Assume that everyone who wants to be a citizen is welcomed and declared a citizen. Many of our new citizens could not speak English, could not hold jobs, and could not pay a dime of taxes, much less generate new tax sources. They flock to cities. The cities are precisely the worst places for unsophisticated, poorly trained, desperate newcomers with no financial assets at all. They could not afford decent housing in already overcrowded and expensive city housing; they could not afford to get essential retraining; and they could barely educate their children. Frustration would rise, understandably, and their disillusionment with their adopted country would become great." You could develop such a hypothetical line after you apparently accepted the premise of giving citizenship to aliens requesting it.

Persuaders sometimes proceed in their talks as if the audience has a choice of only two directly opposing stances. Often this polarizing of a topic is an attempt to keep the issues simple and clear for the audience. Much political oratory, for example, poses the views of candidates as if the voter can choose only progress or stagnation, fresh ideas or stale ones, honesty in government or graft, and so on. Particular issues are similarly polarized. Either we accept school busing for minorities or we perpetuate racism, a candidate might claim. We must vote for preserving the environment or destroying it by choosing a particular candidate, says another. Because this country has a two-party system, this simplification into two "sides" or "choices" has become very common. Since presidential elections nearly always go to either the Democrats or the Republicans, polarization is in some ways convenient. However, we must always remain on guard against excessive use of the device against us by others, or of irresponsibly casting complex questions into just two opposing possibilities.

A frequently used ploy is to state some issue as if one and only one conclusion is possible. So common is this pattern that it has earned a dubious name, both in strategy and logic. It is called the fallacy of *begging the question*. Suppose someone says, "I will prove that the incompetent pilot of flight 22 was negligent and overshot the runway, which led to the injuries." This speaker has undertaken to show negligent, improper piloting technique. But before he or she even gets around to proving the charges, he or she has already labeled the pilot incompetent. The point of the claim is that if negligence can be shown, we will then know the pilot is incompetent. Yet the speaker has assumed as already true just what is to be proven. If we say, "This felon is guilty of a crime," the word felon assumes guilt. Inattentive or emotionally charged audiences sometimes fall for the device. Uncritical and naive listeners who have already decided to act can often be stirred up further by someone who wants to ensure that they follow through on their plans. For example, a union leader who wants workers to strike in order to eventually secure better salaries and conditions may say, "Dishonest managers will continue to exploit you and grow fatter on your fair share of profits." One of the obligations of this speaker would be to show somehow that managers are being dishonest, yet that adjective describes them before the speaker undertakes the task. Begging the question, then, is assuming that what you wish to prove is already true. Consider one final example: If you are asked the question, "Have you stopped cheating on exams?" then either a yes or no answer assumes that you cheat on exams.

A device that resembles begging the question is offering a question whose answer concedes some point you wish to gain. For example, suppose you ask, "Would you be fair-minded enough to approve a plan for a reduced work week if you could choose which shift to work?" The attractiveness of working preferred shifts might encourage people to respond favorably or at least without hostility. However, someone's saying "yes" is equivalent to that person's granting the point that reducing work hours might be acceptable. If, on the other hand, the answer is "no" you have tricked the respondent into conceding that he or she is not fair-minded and open to reasonable proposals. This example underscores the risks of contrived word choice. Words like "fair-minded" and "reasonable" sound perfectly harmless and even suggest a friendly attitude by their user. Yet, in the example just given, either response to the question tends to put the audience in a defensive position, when that position rightfully belongs to the speaker advocating some change in policy.

STRATEGIES IN REBUTTAL

Frequently, persuasive speeches are not given in isolation but as direct responses to someone else's claims and proposals. The term *rebuttal* refers to efforts to answer and weaken someone else's claims, evidence, and reasoning. In a debate, for instance, the first speeches are called the constructive ones and, once both sides of the debate have made their cases, the later speeches attempting to refute opponents are called rebuttals. Even when no formal debate has taken place and no one has directly claimed the opposite of your stance, there may be an implied objection to yours within an audience. If you are proposing some new idea or plan, then you have a responsibility to deal with probable objections, even if no one brings them up. Hence, the strategies of rebuttal presented here assume that someone is debating your proposals. Some of these strategies are useful both in formal debates and in single persuasive speeches.

The most obvious strategy is to deny the truth of an opposing statement. "No causal link between smoking and cancer has ever been demonstrated," might claim an attorney speaking for the tobacco industry. Such a denial of repeated, general, and implied threats to health made in the press would be a direct rejection of the evidence.

Another strategy is to point to inconsistencies in the evidence presented by opponents. To continue the example of smoking, the attorney might say, "If smoking causes cancer, why is it that millions of people who smoke five packs a day never in a lifetime contract the disease?"

Yet another rebuttal strategy is challenging the logical validity of a claim. The tobacco interests' attorney might say, "The statistics on the incidence of lung cancer show that there is more correlation between where you live in this country than there is with whether you smoke. If moving to Iowa triples the incidence of cancer and smoking just doubles it in the general population, I cannot see how your claims about the dangers of smoking are valid." Note that *neither* claim is valid here, for we do not have any data on which state is being compared with Iowa, nor do we have any data about the relative smoking habits in Iowa and the other unknown location.

A frequent choice of strategy in rebuttal is the presentation of counter examples. If one side has given a spectacular example or case study to influence

Figure 9-1   "My speech is on the evils of stereotyping."

people, the other side can find an equally striking example or case to weaken credibility in the first one. For instance, if one side argues that marriages arranged for couples by their parents are longer lasting and happier than marriages agreed upon only by the partners, it is likely that an idealized picture of an Oriental couple's domestic bliss will be used as evidence. Rebuttal could consist of pointing out another couple—one in an arranged marriage which is miserable. It might also consist of the example of a happy couple whose marriage was not arranged in the usual way by parents. The device of offering equally appealing, or comparably believable, examples is probably one of the most often used for rebuttals.

Another powerful and common rebuttal device is offering at least one memorable example which contradicts some generalization held by the audience or offered by an opponent. If, for example, listeners believe that cats cannot be trained to do tricks on command, it is sufficient to produce one cat that has been so trained, or to produce evidence (photos, films, testimony) that someone has such a cat. If listeners believe that water always boils at 212 degrees Fahrenheit, all that you would need to do to refute this idea is to show that high altitudes affect the boiling point of water, as in Colorado, where water may boil at temperatures as low as 180 degrees. You could add a further fact, such as that it takes longer to prepare a hard-boiled egg in Denver than in Seattle, to emphasize your point.

You can often refute evidence by denying its importance. You can even concede the point in such a case: "Yes, refined sugar is indeed fattening, but its caloric value is so much smaller than everyone thinks that leaving it out of your daily coffee is utterly unimportant. If you use one spoonful per cup, at 18 calories per spoonful, three cups of sweetened coffee make only a trivial daily addition to a total diet of 1500 calories."

Similarly, you can show undesirable implications in some opponent's position: "If you give up sugar in your coffee, your sense of psychological deprivation may be more destructive to your diet than the few calories involved."

Another potent strategy of rebuttal is to direct attention to an opponent's possible motivations: "Of course Professor LeGrand is opposed to abolishing the foreign-language requirement at this University, for his job as a teacher of French to undergraduates would be jeopardized by dropping the requirement," a student might suggest. And Professor LeGrand might reply, "Of course Mr. Cochon opposes the foreign-language requirement; he has put off taking a language until now that he is a senior. Since he must still complete two years' study of a modern language, his graduation will be delayed." In this example, *both* imaginary speakers use the same device—namely, exposing the opponent's self-interest in the issue.

BUILDING CREDIBILITY AS A SPEAKER

To establish credibility as a speaker, you need to be aware of the variety of devices you can use to enhance the image of your personality and mentality as perceived by the audience. Note that you should try to present a favorable image as a responsible, thoughtful, reliable, and vigorous friend of the audience. There is never any guarantee that you will succeed. The best you can do is consider probable reactions to each statement and rely on generalizations about listeners: They tend to like people who are animated and committed to what they say. They tend to like clear organization. They tend to respond well to speakers who have the audience's best interests in mind. You are probably thinking, "How can an audience judge such matters?" The research on speaker credibility suggests that audiences make a judgment on whatever cues they have and then react holistically rather than on an issue-by-issue basis. That is, once they accept a speaker as credible, safe, reliable, and energetic, audiences are likely to accept the speaker's whole position rather than critically evaluate each point made. It thus becomes crucially important to build your image as much as possible to present the best conditions for persuasion.

The first step is to create commonality with the audience. If you can appear to be one of the group, sharing their ideals and experience, listeners are likely to respond favorably to your claims and beliefs. The problem, then, becomes not simply arranging and composing a message, but also presenting yourself. You must make judgments about how listeners will probably respond to various image-building strategies. Certain qualities seem to be held dear by audiences. Speakers who are cooperative, rational, moderate, and balanced in their views are more likely than zealots to dispose listeners in their favor. Confidence and enthusiasm are prized, but you should not jump to the conclusion, as some students have, that the whole secret of effective speech is confidence. A lunatic may be confident. So can be a terrorist or a criminal. Confidence is a valuable quality when coupled with stability, knowledge, humanity, and perspective. Further, attempts to pose or act out some role are likely to fail, for if you use them you have simultaneously engaged all the problems of the actor along with those of the public speaker. Attempting to "act out" a role that you suppose listeners want to see and hear is riddled with pitfalls. The merest suggestion that you are "acting" will shatter your credibility, even though the audience might thoroughly enjoy the "performance." Acting out the role of a persuader mastering an audience is really much harder than just persuading the audience masterfully.

Means of allying the audience with your position include the following strategies: You may tell about experiences that would evoke identification among members of the audience. For example, a prestigious professor addressing a commencement exercise might relate homely, common experiences shared by a sizable number of the listeners. Nostalgia is a powerful ally to speakers. Recalling the local beer halls and restaurants of bygone days, the peculiar wit of some lecturer, or the discomforts of some lecture hall familiar to listeners are all likely to admit the speaker to the hearts of the audience.

Among the most potent devices for establishing and building credibility is demonstration of the ability to keep control of an explosive, unstable condition. Audiences like someone who is calm in an emergency, able to see what is needed in a situation, and composed in the face of challenges and disruption of normal procedures. Qualities of courage, leadership, decisiveness, and integrity are all admired by people. Leaders often emerge from chaotic, threatening situations and take command of grateful followers. Those willing to take responsibility in unfamiliar and perilous situations often reap great rewards.

Probably the most influential personal quality of all is evident competence and expertise in the topic of a speech. When audiences believe that you are fully aware of all the implications in a speaking situation, including the views of the opposition, they are likely to accord you great respect and credence. Minor errors of fact and opinion may be forgiven, personal quirks and weakness in delivery may be disregarded, and every opportunity for success will be afforded any speaker the audience sees as genuinely authoritative. However, if you abuse their credence, listeners will reject you and any presented views, even valid ones, out of hand. It cannot be overemphasized that the single most important quality audiences demand in speakers is competence. You simply must know what you are talking about or no strategy at all will fool people for long.

SOME STRATEGIES
OF EMOTIONAL AROUSAL

A responsible persuader can sometimes use legitimate emotional arousal within the audience to improve conditions for persuasion. It is unfortunately true that charlatans can and do manipulate our feelings in such ways that we are more vulnerable. A student once informed a class that a man in a wheelchair visited the dormitories and sold the residents magazines that they really did not want, but they signed up for subscriptions out of pity for the salesperson. Later, the subscribers saw the same man on the street with no wheelchair and no disability. Fortunately, the law regarding cancellation of contracts within 3 days saved the residents from the outrageous sales ploys. This example shows clear fraudulence and manipulation. But what about arousing emotions in general?

In informative speeches, we try to arouse wonder, interest, pleasure, excitement, amazement, and laughter. We choose interesting examples and facts to "hold" or "grip" our listeners. Is the persuasive speech any less an appropriate place for the same strategy? We believe that a speaker responsible for his or her words is justified in actively using emotionally involving language as long as no fraud, exploitation, or advantage is employed. Sometimes there is a fine line between deciding whether our real motivations for persuading others are our own self-interests or truly selfless motives. For instance, most of us understand that salespeople make their livings on the profits on goods and services. Most salespeople certainly do not think of themselves as exploiters and frauds. They, too, buy goods and services. The ordinary commerce of the world requires competition, imaginative advertising, aggressive sales campaigns, and inevitably some emotionally stirring rhetoric. It is in this sense, of ethical and responsible persuasion, that we assert that emotional appeals have a justifiable place. From the earliest philosophers and rhetoricians we have derived the timeless advice to use emotion, logic, and speaker credibility as the foundation of rhetorical strategy.

Following are some specific strategies you can use to arouse emotion:

1. Use humor to cajole an audience and win its trust.
2. Use humor, satire, or ridicule to reduce an opponent's credibility or to lessen trust in an opposing position.
3. Promote a sense of belonging to a group or popular movement.
4. Promote a sense of being a specially knowledgeable insider and an initiate into some special or elite group.
5. Choose emotionally charged language rather than neutral words.
6. Arouse feelings such as fear, guilt, anxiety, pity, or anger, especially when they can be satisfied or resolved by your proposals.

You can, of course, use the devices listed simultaneously with several other strategies, such as particular kinds of organization, appeals to your own expertise and good will, and stirring examples.

The last group of strategies presented is not a prescription for speakers but a catalogue of everyday devices speakers use to avoid squarely facing issues or evidence. These suggestions may be familiar to you as logical fallacies, in some cases, but you should never forget that unscrupulous people make effective use of even the most transparent and illogical claims. Hitler claimed that the bigger the lie the easier it was to make people believe it. A frequent strategy in his propaganda was to avoid real issues and to choose his own substitutes.

HOW TO AVOID THE ISSUE OR POINT

1. State a claim in ambiguous language to avoid rebuttal.
2. Haggle over the definitions of terms.
3. Dwell on insignificant ideas so long that there is little time to deal with important and vulnerable points.
4. Extend the issue to such an extent that the original point is obscured and neglected.
5. Find someone as a scapegoat for a current state of affairs.
6. Refer to opponents personally rather than addressing the issues and objections they might pose.
7. Shift to the opponents or to listeners the responsibility for constructing the proof or logic of one's assertions.

A colleague once confessed that he deliberately lectured to his classes in vague terms because it forced them to listen carefully and to try to reconstruct whatever he must have meant. The confession sounds suspiciously like the last strategy just listed. It is true that within limits audiences will try to restructure and figure out what hazy and difficult statements mean. However, there seems to be little justification for being deliberately vague and confusing in most persuasive speeches. Speakers are fuzzy enough when they try their best to be lucid.

EXERCISES

1. Recall some occasion when one of the strategies discussed in this chapter was used against you unfairly. State whether you knew at the time that you were being manipulated or whether you discovered it later.
2. Do you consider some of the strategies listed in this chapter to be always offensive and unethical? Discuss which ones seem to you hardest to justify in everyday persuasion.
3. Assign one or more students to read further on the following terms and report to the class the most significant comments about them:

    ethos (ethical appeal)   *pathos (emotional appeal)*   *logic*

4. Modern terms for certain of the classical persuasive appeals are such words as "credibility," "charisma," "Macho," "straight arrow," "cool," and many more. Compile a list of personal qualities of people regarded in popular culture as highly credible or influential. Discuss the terms, paying special attention to any unique application or meaning. Example: "Honcho" suggests someone of great power and leadership.

5. In a classroom, some students build almost imperceptibly a kind of high or low credibility. Discuss how such "ranking" or "pecking orders" come about and what can be done to control one's place in it. Once a student is "placed" in that order, what efforts can change the place?

6. Report on some person you regard as highly persuasive. Each student in the class should name a person and the position held by that person, and then try to explain the persuasive strategies that person characteristically uses, even if unconsciously. For example, you might choose a former teacher, a principal, a bank manager, or an employer. Then describe any habitual strategies that person used, such as threats, anxiety production, "holier than thou" attitudes, and so on. The strategies need not be negative qualities. "Our principal worked us hard, and he always worked hard himself. His personal intensity was perhaps unconsciously his greatest persuasive strategy."

7. Make a private list of your own strategies. If you discover some unflattering weaknesses in them, try to substitute more effective and responsible ones. Do not become overly critical, for we all use some weak strategies from time to time. You can profit from changing just one or two habitual devices, such as shifting onto the audience the responsibility for clarity or overusing emotional terms.

8. Discuss the extent to which you think persuasive strategies, good and bad, carry over unconsciously into our everyday lives when we are not trying to persuade anybody. For instance, is there any correlation between someone's constantly "playing the martyr" and the strategy of evading issues or shifting responsibility? Is there a sense in which we are constantly persuading each other even when there is no apparent occasion for it? What strategies do people use to control others?

SELECTED READINGS

KENNETH E. ANDERSEN, *Persuasion: Theory and Practice*, 2nd ed. (Boston: American Press, 1983).

MONROE BEARDSLEY, *Thinking Straight*, 4th ed. (Englewood Cliffs, N.J.: Prentice-Hall, 1975).

RUTH ANNE CLARK, *Persuasive Messages* (New York: Harper & Row), 1984.

DOUGLAS EHNINGER, *Influence, Belief, and Argument* (Glenview, Ill.: Scott, Foresman, 1974), especially Chapter 7.

JOSEPH ILARDO, *Speaking Persuasively* (New York: Macmillan, 1981).

GERALD MILLER and MICHAEL BURGOON, *New Techniques of Persuasion* (New York: Harper & Row, 1973).

WAYNE MINNICK, *The Art of Persuasion*, 2nd ed. (Boston: Houghton Mifflin, 1968).

RAYMOND ROSS and MARK ROSS, *Understanding Persuasion* (Englewood Cliffs, N.J.: Prentice-Hall, 1981).

THOMAS M. SCHEIDEL, *Persuasive Speaking* (Glenview, Ill.: Scott, Foresman, 1967).

WAYNE THOMPSON, *The Process of Persuasion* (New York: Harper & Row, 1975).

chapter 10

Problem Solving in Small Group Discussions

Every day numerous problems affecting large groups of people demand examination and action. These problems are so complicated, numerous, and pressing that every educated person needs to understand the rudiments of group discussions in which people act together and try to solve problems effectively. How can a growing city supply its citizens with effective fire and police protection? How are we to dispose of the mountains of garbage that accumulate in every city? How are we to finance our schools and colleges to ensure an educated population for the future? All of these large-scale questions have to be answered. There is no evading them and leaving them for others to deal with. This chapter presents some ways to grapple with tasks that confront all of us, whether we are dealing with immense tasks, such as raising tax bills in a finance committee of the legislature, or planning how to finance a fraternity's annual budget.

In the range of tasks of every group of people trying to work out solutions to their problems there is, fortunately, some common wisdom about how any group can best produce sensible, effective outcomes. We explore suggestions for effective discussion procedures. Unfortunately, many pitfalls await inexperienced, impatient members of discussion groups, and it is easy to stumble into traps again and again. We examine those traps and show how best to avoid them.

All groups have more or less constant tasks to accomplish, regardless of what questions they deal with. We examine these and the roles of the group members. We consider how to improve the participation of each member so as to minimize friction and maximize effectiveness.

GROUP SOLUTIONS VERSUS INDIVIDUAL SOLUTIONS

Anyone who has been in a group situation in which numerous solutions to a troublesome, complex problem were discussed has felt the inevitable exasperation and impatience that result when someone impedes a discussion. Perhaps on some occasion when group action was needed you have said, "I would rather do the whole job myself than try to get this group to solve the problem. They go over and over the same stuff, get off the track and waste time, they don't carry their share of the workload, and they grate on each other's nerves." If you have ever felt these emotions, you have experienced the one dominant shortcoming of groups in purposeful action: inefficiency. If we think of efficiency as the speed and decisiveness of reaching a solution to a problem, say in a government, then we would favor a dictator over a deliberative body such as Congress, Parliament, or Knesset. However, there are other concerns which make group action more desirable than one individual's decision on how to solve a problem.

In simple problems, such as a decision to renew the contract of an employee who is both affordable and effective in the job, any supervisor can move quickly and just sign an authorization once the pertinent facts are known. When facing complex questions, such as whether to build new nuclear generating plants, no single individual is likely to do as thorough and effective job as a group. In spite of the jokes about a committee's stupidity and slow progress, group decision making in fact has several advantages over autocratic decision making.

Autocratic Decisions Versus Group Decisions

Imagine one very intelligent and powerful person, such as a dictator or king, who must decide whether to build up a nation's transportation system into a modern system or to leave it as it has been for decades, a primitive and almost negligible network of dirt roads in hot desert country. Now imagine the same problem presented to a group of about nine intelligent, experienced people: One is a highway engineer, one is a financier, one is a railway official from another country, one is a tax expert, one is an aircraft and engine mechanic, and another is a geologist. Which would be a better procedure, to let the king decide what kind of transportation system to build or to let the committee first study all conditions, needs, and terrain, and then make a proposal to the king? Just such a case actually arose many years ago in a small Mideast nation. The king decided everything. He decided that modern nations all had railroads. His nation, therefore, would have a railroad by royal decree. Before a few miles of track could be laid, however, the desert winds covered whole stretches of it under several feet of sand. Elsewhere, the wind blew the sand out from under the track and it hung in midair with no support at all. Since the nation had plenty of oil, great volumes of oil were poured onto the sand to anchor it in place in order to support the track. At enormous expense and with tremendous maintenance costs, a railroad was built and occasionally used, but enormous funds were squandered in buying track unsuitable for the desert, rail cars which could not function in the desert heat and sand, and, of course, in the oil itself, which could have been sold on world markets at high prices instead of being poured on the sand to anchor it. In this case, a group of experts was assembled and reached a decision—namely, that conditions were so severe that only air transport would make sense. They said a fleet of helicopters and planes would best meet the nation's needs. But the king overrode the recommendations. "There's going to be a railroad." There was. It was nearly useless, extremely expensive, unreliable, and buried half the time. The ancient method of travel by camel was faster, cheaper, and more dependable.

This true story summarizes the difference between autocratic and democratic decisions. The first depends on blind power, wealth, control of others, and perhaps luck (sometimes an individual is so bright that he or she can see far beyond what mere experts can envision). The group decision, by contrast with an individual's, is likely to be moderated by the experience of many different kinds of expertise. Even when no one in a group is an expert on some matters discussed, members still are much more likely to recognize their incompetence and need for advice (and then seek it out) than is an autocrat. History is full of stories of powerful leaders who were eventually overthrown because they would not listen to competent experience but depended on their own egotistical views. Adolf Hitler ignored his generals, his rocket technicians, his atomic scientists, and other experts who could have led Nazi Germany to victory in World War II. The mad dictator so depended on his own imagined genius that he destroyed his nation and himself while surrounded by technical genius enough to have thrust Germany into world dominance. Comparisons with Napoleon, Kaiser Wilhelm II, Kubla Khan, and many others might be made. The central point should be evident, though: Group decisions tend to be sounder than single individuals' decisions, for the following reasons:

> Groups have a greater range of experience than individuals. A wider variety of expertise can be brought to bear on a problem studied by a group than when one person studies it. In real life, few persons are expert in everything.

Even brilliant individuals tend to have blind spots in their perceptions of people, events, and facts. Groups have members who can from their varied viewpoints detect technical problems that an individual might overlook or minimize disastrously.

Members of a group tend to monitor and control the more unruly or irrational tendencies that can arise in decision making. An autocrat may begin to act as if directly responsible only to some supreme being; individuals tend to consider the opinions of their equals when stating conclusions on serious matters. For example, a convention of astronomers would not claim that the approximate alignment of planets in a straight line foretells the end of the world or the beginning of a new age of enlightenment, as some individual astrologers have claimed. In a sense, there is a safety in numbers, simply because the probability of a group's containing a rational, sensible, and tough-minded member is greater than the likelihood that one person will always make uniformly unemotional decisions on many matters.

Emotional excitement, exhilaration, personal ambition, or other powerful feelings might dominate one person. Such biased feelings can be avoided or at least limited by the sober, thoughtful judgment of a group, whose members may have no reason to be as excited as an individual might be. A controlled emotional atmosphere and stability of investigation is better than that prevailing when just one individual makes a decision.

The king described earlier has been presented as the leader of a large problem-solving group, in this case a whole nation. However, in many ways group dynamics apply just as well to small group discussions as they do to national policy study. A dictator or king is either self-appointed or by historical precedent the nation's leader. Moreover, delegates usually conduct the actual business of every government. The king or despot often consults with a cabinet of ministers or executives who actually run the country. Thus "small groups" may run nations after all by execution of all the details of policies decided upon. If those groups are wise and experienced, the nation may prosper. While *seeming* to be totalitarian, in fact a nation could enjoy the benefits of various skills and experienced advice.

APPOINTED LEADERS AND EMERGENT LEADERS

Usually a group assembled to solve a problem has been appointed by a larger group or an official. For example, a city council might appoint a committee to study a specific concern such as how best to establish and finance a modern fire department for the growing city. The mayor, city manager, or chairperson of the council might ask some prominent person to convene and serve as chair in such a committee. In some cases, in fact, the committee might begin its existence around a key figure chosen because of experience or skill to form such a group. In other cases, the committee might adopt as its first order of business the selection of one or more officers, including its leader.

An interesting phenomenon occurs when no leader has been appointed to a group or when it never occurs to the naive group to pick one of its members as a leader. One or more leaders may emerge quite easily and naturally without friction or without a word's being said about "choosing a chairperson." Evidently, what happens is that in many groups, especially those assembled willingly to deal with a project of common interest, the sense of cohesion develops quickly and the group takes on an identity of its own. The members seem to think and act with good spirits, cooperative attitudes which are always constructive, and harmonious ideals. When the great conductor of the NBC Symphony Orchestra, Arturo Toscanini, died after bringing the orchestra to great eminence, the players refused to have any other conductor at all and played many concerts with no apparent conductor. As a mark of respect and expression of their complete unity of ideals, they continued to play as Toscanini would have wanted and demanded. In this case, their leader's *memory* was their conductor; an ideal or spirit led the group with all the strength a real person might have had.

Further, when a group has no leader another effect often occurs. A single strong figure may "fill the gap" or informally step into a leading role toward solving the group's problem. Such a person is called a *task-centered leader* and seems to always keep an eye on accomplishing the task cut out for the whole group. He or she is the "whip" or guiding spirit that gets people back on track when they get confused or distracted, the reminder of where on its agenda the group is, and the identifier of what must yet be done to complete the group effort satisfyingly.

If two potential task-centered leaders begin to seek control of the group, a power struggle can ensue. The whole group can be disrupted and the task delayed while two or more people vie for dominance. Occasionally even when a leader has been appointed or elected, some other person may feel unrecognized and become, even unconsciously, a competitor to the leader. The result could be bickering, pot shots at the nominal leader, and bad morale within the whole group. Meanwhile, another kind of leader might emerge at the same time. This kind is called a *social-emotional leader* because of evident skill at easing personal tensions, encouraging harmony and dispelling ill will, and generally creating a constructive atmosphere. This kind of leader may not be particularly effective at advancing the group's task toward completion through research, insights, or discussion. However, he or she may be so valuable an asset by maintaining good morale that the lack of brilliant discussion skills is unimportant. A group might contain both types of leader using their respective talents at the same time. The task-centered leader moves the group onward intellectually while the social-emotional leader solves internal conflicts, ministers to bruised egos, and "strokes" those who need emotional reassurance. Needless to say, when a group has this kind of leader but not strong task-centered leadership, the group may feel very good but it may never get around to solving its designated problem. If there is no social leader, the task might be completed with some injured egos and feelings as casualties of the encounter. Sometimes—albeit rarely—both functions occur within one person.

STYLES OF LEADERSHIP

Specialists in group discussion have long noted that successful completion of tasks can occur under a great variety of styles of leadership. By style of leadership, we mean the personal choices exerted by a group leader in order to achieve the stated goals most effectively. The choices are centered on the leader's habitual, typical behavior during a discussion. We describe three such styles of leadership and comment on the merits and faults of each kind. The most appropriate style of leadership depends to some extent upon the nature of the topic, the people who constitute the task group, and the personalities of available leaders. A style appropriate for one situation might be totally useless in another.

Autocratic

The first style of leadership is called *autocratic*. In this style, a strong personality dominates the proceedings, tends to give orders rather than make suggestions, summarizes by selecting those points which support the leader's perception of the problem and its solutions, and rejects some ideas and data if they are not agreeable. The advantage of having an autocratic leader is speed and directness of confronting a problem. When the leader is intelligent, hard working, well informed, and honest, the eventual outcome may be satisfactory. The committee may have acted like a panel of assistants and may indeed have contributed much to the discussion, shaping and tempering the leader's heavy-handed approach. If everyone has the opportunity to be heard without being intimidated or ignored, this style of leadership can succeed. However, when the leader is so domineering that members hold back, clam up, refuse to contribute, or feel unneeded, the group effort is really a sham. "The boss just went ahead and did what he wanted to do in the first place, ignoring our participation." Curiously, many overbearing people do not believe themselves to be so, and what seems to others as domineering, even dictatorial style in running a group may be perceived by the leader as the necessary effort to get anything done in a group. However considerate and patient such strong-willed people try to be, they sooner or later give themselves away by giving orders, flatly denying or rejecting others' contributions, and sometimes losing their self-control in "righteous indignation" at the fallibility and slowness of others to see the "truth"—namely, their viewpoints. Still, in some situations, the heavy-handed dictatorial style works well.

Laissez-Faire

A strikingly different kind of leadership is also capable of success under certain conditions, but is generally not very effective. We call it the *laissez-faire* or "leave 'em alone" style. The leader is seen as a figurehead, ceremonial, or honorary official. Leaders may not be expected to do very much other than to recognize those wishing to speak, perhaps to summarize from time to time, and to ask a few questions. They tend to let the participants say whatever they wish without comment or reaction. (By contrast, the autocratic leader might dismiss an idea as irrelevant, out of date, or just stupid.) When the participants are indeed quite authoritative and strong personalities themselves, they might best be given a free hand in the discussion. However, the problems that can arise with this style of leadership are fairly serious. First, the group may have little respect for the leader and may make it plain. This attitude is not very healthy for a group as a whole and is certainly uncomfortable for the leader. Second, the group may flounder and wander off the topic with little strong-minded guidance back toward solving the problem. Such groups tend to drift and repeat ideas, wasting time and energy.

Democratic

A third generally recognized style of leader is the *democratic* one. This person has some qualities of the extreme types described earlier. Theoretically, this style of leadership is the most effective because it exhibits the strength of purpose felt by autocratic leaders and at the same time encourages full, complete, and uninhibited participation by everyone in the group. The best of both of the other styles is thus potentially available. The democratic leader says in effect, "I am here to recognize contributions and questions, to summarize, to probe further, to fill in gaps, to ask quiet members to share their thoughts, to mildly discipline those who talk too much, and to moderate clashes." This kind of leader never dismisses a participant's ideas or imposes selfish views. If discipline or control of an obstructive member is necessary, the leader uses the will and good sense of the whole group, rather than just personal authority, to control the troublemaker. The democratic leader tries to guide the group toward consensus but allows a minority to dissent and voice their own report, if they wish to make one in addition to the majority's.

FUNCTIONS OF LEADERSHIP

A leader, assuming that just one is appointed or elected, has certain fairly well-defined duties. These are discussed next.

First, the leader should keep the group's discussion on track, guiding those members who wander off the topic back to the main issues. "Jim, I recall that incident, but it really doesn't seem appropriate to apply it to our topic. Maybe I'm missing the connection. Do you have a point to make by mentioning that?" Such a comment from the leader gently but pointedly asks the speaker to get on with the discussion and either link his or her anecdote to the task or, by implication, not to impede the discussion.

Some participants may be just about to say something all through the discussion but are never quite aggressive enough to get a word into the proceedings because others are more aggressive or outgoing. The leader should be sensitive to everyone in the group and should guarantee that everyone has time to gather thoughts, make important points, and state values and beliefs without hindrance or pressure. Some people just think a bit slower than others; some people have good ideas but never articulate them in the presence of "chatterboxes." Further, one group may be patient, and permit each participant plenty of time to grope for words. Another group might be impatient, insightful, intolerant of its weaker members, and therefore hasty (even if brilliant) in reaching a conclusion. The leader should monitor the participants and decide when someone who wishes to contribute is being squeezed out. A good leader will ensure that everyone has an opportunity to contribute or challenge or question.

A good leader will also be able to sense when the group needs a summary of progress. When many persons talk, it is easy to lose track of the overall progress because of distractions. Different styles and rates of presentation, various individuals' peculiar emphases, and other factors growing out of the particular group's dynamics may make it necessary to stop and summarize the group's progress every now and then. The leader should decide when nonverbal cues indicate that an internal summary is needed.

The leader should recognize gaps and inconsistencies in the progress toward a solution and be ready to fill gaps in the information. If the leader does not have appropriate information, anyone could call attention to the need for it and invite contributions from those who might have the data. If no one has it, the leader might even delegate someone to search out further information the group needs. When hazy, ambiguous, or conflicting data have been presented, the leader might well question further those persons presenting them. The aim is to reconcile differences in reported data. For example, in a discussion of tax reform, different figures might be reported as the average income. One participant might report the figure of $14,500 as the average income in America, while another might report the figure as $18,000. The difference is great enough that serious doubts are raised about the accuracy. The leader might probe those figures carefully and reveal that one figure is the average individual income while the other is the average family income (where husband and wife both work). It goes without saying that the leader must be uncommonly alert to nuances of meaning and always ready to draw out details. The manner need not be challenging or insulting, but it should always be geared to securing greater precision and accuracy of statement. One participant, however well meaning, can by a slight misstatement of facts completely distort the findings of a group. The leader must be constantly on the alert for inconsistency and implausible reports from members. The assumption is that even if they are wrong, the members have faithfully (even if mistakenly) tried to discover valid information. A good leader probes and questions without insulting.

Inevitably some clashes of temperament and personality arise in a group addressing an important or emotionally charged topic. The leader must be ready to assume a peacemaker's role and try to iron out personal differences to the extent that they disrupt the group's work. The leader is not a psychiatrist, a big brother or sister, or a counselor. By definition, however, leaders do have some kind of superior qualities. In a group those might be tolerance, patience, insight, and breadth of vision. A person with these qualities is well equipped to moderate the passions of members who have less breadth and depth. Thus, a leader can assume the responsibility to *make the best of whatever the participants can contribute*, even if the various members tend to conflict with each other. A good leader rises above personality and synthesizes the contributions of everyone for the overall good of the group.

DYNAMICS OF GROUP PARTICIPATION

Communication Channels within a Group

Groups often exhibit peculiar behaviors because of the personal relationships established, or not established. For example, everyone may know the leader very well, but they may not know each other. Sometimes a group of people do not get along from their first encounter and then rarely or never speak to each other again during the course of the group's business. A sense of competition, poor personal relations, resentment, jealousy, misunderstanding, or any number of other causes can lead to erratic patterns of communication in the group. All along we have implied that good problem-solving groups are open, free, communicative, and responsive to each member. However, many groups do not exhibit this ideal behavior. Certain individuals speak only to specific other members of the group and to nobody else. Others might have friends with whom they converse and let the friends speak for them. Still others speak only to the group leader, either through arrogance or shyness. They ignore whatever others say and act almost as if they had not heard it, or as if they had read it somewhere long ago. Even when there is no obvious hostility within the group, there still may be channels of communication, or networks of people, all directing their remarks to the nominal leader. Diagrammatically, the connections between people might take some of the following forms, in which case some unique relationships and outcomes might occur.

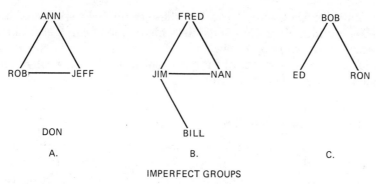

IMPERFECT GROUPS

Figure 10-1

Note that in the patterns shown some individuals may talk to the leader and anybody else, while in other patterns individuals may talk *only* to the leader or *only* to one or two other people. When this effect occurs, the intermediate group member who relays messages back and forth may feel extra pressure because the task is no longer just participation but also mediation between personalities. Sometimes loyalty to a friend might take precedence over the needs of the group. For example, suppose Bill says little in a group discussion to anyone but his friend Jim. Fred, the group leader, is uncomfortable with and not very friendly to Bill, but he gets along fine with Jim. Thus, Jim not only has to carry his own weight in the discussion, but he must also be alert to the friction between Fred and Bill, both of whom he likes. If an issue arises in which Fred and Bill differ, Jim then has to consider the risk of alienating one or the other of his friends as well as compromising his own

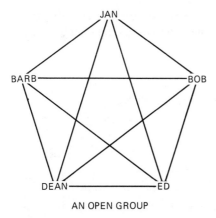

AN OPEN GROUP

Figure 10-2

personal opinion on the issue. Because of these complex interactions, it should be clear that the ideal situation is one in which anyone can feel free to speak either to the leader or to any other member without fear or recriminations. A group discussion can quickly turn into a conspiratorial hotbed when channels are not open among the participants.

Destructive Behaviors in a Small Group

It is unfortunate that people often cannot rise above their own narrow, selfish interests and act on behalf of everyone's best interests. When groups fall apart, fail to achieve their goals, or end in hostility among the participants, the fault may lie in some common destructive behaviors, which group members ought to recognize. Further, when it seems evident that such behaviors are beginning to emerge in a group, members should seek to avert the bad outcomes which may follow. Among the most common destructive behaviors are these:

Ill-prepared members or leader.

Poor attitude toward leadership or other members.

Sabotage.

Personal vested interests.

Nonparticipation.

Individual domination (excessive talking).

Getting off the track, irrelevancies.

Socializing rather than confronting the topic.

Constructive Behaviors of Participants

Benne and Sheats[1] have identified several convenient categories of group members' behavior. Their positive contribution is suggested by these observed behaviors:

1. Encouragers contribute by supportive comments to others.
2. Compromisers tend to ease friction during conflict.
3. Gate-keepers act as screeners of faulty information and pass on useful, constructive, accurate data.
4. Harmonizers help to reconcile differences, point out similarities of viewpoints, and find common grounds of understanding.
5. Initiators start a group toward solving its problem responsibly.
6. Elaborators are adept at explaining, expanding, and exploring ideas.
7. Standard setters establish a high aim for the group.

8. Group observers act as the conscience or commentators on the whole group's performance.

Clearly, each type of service to the group is valuable. In some groups, several of these functions are combined in one person. A group may successfully solve its problems without all of the listed functions' taking place, although most groups contain enough active, helpful members that most of the desirable roles are fulfilled.

AN AGENDA FOR GROUP DISCUSSION: REFLECTIVE THINKING

Once a group meets to discuss its charge, even if it has expert leadership and participants, it needs a rationale for its procedure. Growing out of the human thought process itself is a serviceable and reasonably efficient method of systematically studying a problem. In his book *How We Think*, John Dewey,[2] a philosopher-educator, wrote a five-step procedure that intelligent people use over and over to solve problems. Both individuals and groups can make use of the pattern, called the steps in *reflective thinking*. Many people have said that the steps are just plain common sense; they are. Nobody clearly and systematically wrote them down until Dewey thought to do so. To say that the rules are common sense, however, may invite you to underestimate their value and even sophistication. Most science and mathematics are common sense, but understanding and mastering them has come to humanity slowly and painfully. The point here is that students often have the illusion that something is clear or even obvious when it really is not. They feel insulted to discuss something so basic as thought processes until they realize that most people have not the faintest idea how (or whether) they think. Reflective thinking has that illusory quality which makes it seem familiar; yet, countless delays and failures in problem solving can be traced to the participants' stubborn refusals to proceed in rational, step-by-step fashions. Impatience to reach a solution, desire to avoid tedious details, unwillingness to search deeply into a topic, and irresistible urges to push one's own pet theories has ruined many a discussion.

To achieve success, then, a group should follow a carefully controlled procedure which consists of using applicable details from the steps of reflective thinking, outlined next. Of course, not every single detail will apply to every possible discussion question. A particular group will usually find it easy to reword the key details to make these steps fit their chosen topics.

  I. Awareness of a problem
    A. What is occurring to produce a problem? What symptoms are there?
    B. Is the problem getting worse? Will it go away in time, even without action? How extensive is the problem?

    C. Whom is it affecting? Where and when is it felt? How does it affect someone? Under what conditions does it occur?

    D. What present efforts to deal with the problem are there? What is being done to solve the problem and how are efforts working?

    E. What are the implications if the problem is not solved?

II. Analysis of the problem

    A. What primary and secondary causes led to the present difficulty?

    B. What are the criteria for a solution to the problem? What constitutes an *effective* solution? An effective action attacks the causes of the problem.

    C. What *limitations* must be imposed on the solutions? Any solution proposed must preserve insofar as possible the other values, such as social customs, laws, institutions, and rights of the people involved in the situation. Some solutions might be effective but create worse conditions than the original problem presented.

III. Exploring feasible solutions

    A. What precise actions are possible to solve the problem?

    B. What effects would each solution produce, including probable unintended effects?

IV. Proposing changes

    A. To what extent would each available solution strike at the causes of the problem?

    B. To what extent would each solution preserve other values in the overall situation?

V. Adopting the best solution

    A. Which solution proposed is the best remedy?

    B. How exactly can the solution be put into operation?

OUTCOMES OF DISCUSSION

Not all problem-solving discussions succeed. Sometimes the people involved are not able to deal with the complexity of the task. Sometimes the participants cannot work together and have to give the task over to another more harmonious group. Sometimes the problem so changes because of events that it is no longer timely. For example, a long-standing controversy between two states about ownership of a tiny island was settled decisively when a great flood changed the course of the river separating the two states and washed the island away. All the lawyers and commissions trying to solve the problem for years suddenly had nothing further to discuss.

Consensus

The most desirable outcome of any group discussion is *consensus*. This term means group agreement, and it indicates that the overwhelming sentiment of the participants is to adopt or recommend a clear-cut solution. Although it may sometimes be possible to reach consensus, as when we are voting to increase our own salaries, this ideal outcome of a group discussion is not easy to achieve. Most groups contain enough variety of opinion on just about any topic that something less than unanimity results. Even in the example about a group's voting to increase its own salaries, a unanimous vote is by no means certain. A few members of Congress repeatedly oppose raising their pay, either on principle or because they feel their political images will thereby be improved. Even though a group might feel frustrated by its failure to secure total agreement on an issue, there are other kinds of outcome that are nearly as satisfying.

Majority Recommendation

When full agreement is not possible, a group can report what the majority recommends and spell out in detail how its recommendation should be put into effect. If there is strong feeling against the majority report, a minority report fairly stating the differences of opinion and the recommendations of that minority can be attached. The net effect of such a procedure is to limit the effects of the majority's findings and to give the minority a fair hearing beyond the group. For example, a committee to study the closing of schools in a town might recommend 5 to 2 that a given school should be closed because of low enrollment, high costs of continuation, and remote location. The two members voting against closing might insist on a report which tells the community that they object to the closing because a whole neighborhood will be forced to bus its children long distances and that a neighborhood's identity will be damaged by closing the school. The minority report may be either a protest or only an alert to warn of future repercussions. For example, a minority may object to locating a new nuclear waste disposal site in the community not on the basis of radiation danger but on the grounds that acceptance of the site will establish a precedent and make the other towns in the state easier targets for future atomic-waste dumping sites.

Recommendation for Further Study

A somewhat disappointing but still honest outcome of a group's efforts is the admission that in spite of thorough, sincere efforts to resolve a problem, the group could not come to a satisfactory consensus or even a majority-minority report. Perhaps four quite different and mutually incompatible plans of action were all sought by various members, and nobody was willing to abandon a favored position on the matter. The report of the group might then state what general conflicts the group encountered, what the various recommendations were, and what the objections to each one were. Finally, the report might propose that a future group should continue trying to solve the problem. Sometimes this outcome means that the people in the group were not compatible, but it may also mean that not enough time or information was available. Often a problem is far more complex than it first appears. The group trying to solve it is saying, in effect, that with more time allowed for discussion and perhaps with a different kind of group membership, a good solution might be found in the future. This outcome should not be used as a cop-out for poor research, sloppy thinking, careless discussion, or laziness. It should be used as a last resort when honest differences in value systems, lack of critical information, incomplete data, or rapidly changing conditions may force a group to admit failure.

SUMMARY

Any effort by a group of people to solve shared problems requires them to accept certain duties, conveniently thought of as roles. One or more leaders can be appointed or allowed to emerge from the group. Although there are certain risks in having more than one leader, still sharing duties and exercising peculiar personal skills often make dual leadership effective and emotionally satisfying to the group.

Of several attitudes or styles of leadership, the democratic style is generally the best in the long run, although in some situations a more autocratic or a deliberately laissez-faire style might succeed. Some regular patterns of communication within a group have been recognized and understanding them can be useful to everyone in a deliberation. Successful problem solution requires the members to become informed on the topic, to participate actively and constructively, and to avoid certain destructive behaviors.

In addition, a group needs an agenda or plan of procedure which is economical in everyone's time and effort and which prevents floundering aimlessly. Dewey's steps in clear thought constitute a useful pattern for nearly all problems, and it should be memorized or at least made available to members of a group as they deliberate.

Full and open discussion leading to consensus is the ideal outcome of a discussion, but sometimes compromise is the best agreement possible in a complex situation.

EXERCISES

1. As a demonstration of whether group decisions are more sound than individual decisions, try this experiment: Bring to class a bag or jar filled with jelly beans, peas, or ordinary beans. Have each person in the class secretly estimate how many are in the container. Write down everyone's answer. Then divide the class into groups and have each group discuss how many items are in the container. Record the group estimates. Finally, compare the results of individual estimates with the groups' estimates. Is there a difference in accuracy? If so, how do you account for it? (Of course, someone must count the beans.)

2. Many games and variations of them are useful to demonstrate group dynamics. A favorite is a survival game. Imagine a lifeboat filled with everyone in the class. There are too many people in it, and all will perish unless three (or five, or some agreed-upon number) leave. Decide who will survive. One twist of this game is for you to assume the role of some historical figure of your choice and then try to persuade the class to let you survive. Still another twist is to assume that only *one* member can be saved, and the group's choice of that person must be accepted. You can, of course, volunteer to leave the boat yourself, and argue to save someone else of your choice. The point is, of course, to decide upon criteria for saving or ejecting people from the lifeboat.

3. Discuss what you believe to be the desirable personal qualities of a good leader in a problem-solving discussion group. Include whatever qualities you think are for the group's best interests, regardless of whether these traits are socially desirable.

4. If you were leader of a problem-solving group, which of the types of leadership would you most likely exercise? Do you regard personal harmony or getting the job done efficiently the higher value?

5. Not all group discussions are on problems. Sometimes a good discussion revolves around questions of shared *values*. Select five questions about the class's shared values which you think would be worthwhile topics for a group discussion. As a beginning, think about topics for which no particular *action* is required, but about which the participants' attitudes and beliefs are important. Examples: Honesty is the best policy. Those who reject public education deserve their poverty. It is better to give than to receive charity. Alliances with foreign powers are best avoided. Taxing the rich is just and fair. Learning a foreign language is culturally enriching.

6. Try to recall an actual discussion that bogged down or failed to achieve its goal (involving a committee to choose a play, hire a band, or organize a social event, for example). After having considered the group dynamics discussed in this chapter, can you account for the group's weaknesses? Can you recall a group project that succeeded particularly well? What accounted for the contrast? In your opinion, was the leadership or the member participation more important in the success or failure of the groups?

7. Discuss the merits and risks of having a group with no definitely appointed or assigned leader. Is there any advantage in allowing one or more leaders to emerge from the group? Could a group progress and succeed without a leader at all? Discuss.

8. What are Dewey's steps in reflective thinking? If a group skips over some of the steps, what is the probable result? How can a group which gets off the track in a discussion recapture the focus of the discussion?

9. What are the possible outcomes of discussion? List and discuss the relative desirability of each outcome in a problem-solving discussion on a topic of your choice, such as nuclear power plants.

SELECTED READINGS

RONALD L. APPLBAUM AND KARL W. E. ANATOL, *Effective Oral Communication* (Chicago: SRA, 1982), Part 3.

ERNEST G. BORMANN, *Discussion and Group Methods* (New York: Harper & Row, 1969).

BERT E. BRADLEY, *Fundamentals of Speech Communication* (Dubuque, Iowa: William C. Brown, 1981), Chapter 14.

DENNIS S. GOURAN, *Making Decisions in Groups: Choices and Consequences* (Glenview, Ill.: Scott, Foresman, 1982).

HALBERT E. GULLEY, *Discussion, Conference, and Group Process* (New York: Holt, Rinehart & Winston, 1968).

R. V. HARNACK, T. B. FEST, AND B. S. JONES, *Group Discussion: Theory and Technique*, 2nd ed. (Englewood Cliffs, N.J.: Prentice-Hall, 1977).

THOMAS M. SCHEIDEL AND LAURA CROWELL, *Discussing and Deciding: A Desk Book for Group Leaders and Members* (New York: Macmillan, 1979).

appendix A

Conducting Effective Interviews

One of the most demanding speech exercises you can face is an interview. The purposes of this form of specialized communication are varied, but all interviews share a great many features. This appendix deals with the fundamental events which must take place before, during, and after an actual interview if the overall effect is to be mutually satisfying and productive. Note that the word "mutually" is used. A common mistake is to suppose that an interview is solely a means of finding out information, getting a job, solving a problem, or airing one's grievance. Although all of these purposes are legitimate, you must remember that the interests of at least *two* parties are at stake. For either party to lose sight of the other party's interests and needs is to conduct an interview badly and to risk making the total situation worse than it was before the meeting. The fundamental premise, therefore, is that every interview is an exploration of mutual needs, information, and problems. But an interview is not a directionless, groping activity. To master it you need to envision an idealized outcome of understanding and harmony. Even if you do not realize that ideal outcome, your attempt to achieve it may give an interview focus and direction, qualities that interviews often lack. If you come away from an interview feeling that the session went off in totally unexpected, uncontrolled, and unproductive directions, you probably did not prepare for it adequately. Before examining ways to improve interviewing skills, we consider some examples of interviews which illustrate the mutuality of effort just described.

TYPICAL KINDS OF INTERVIEWS

Job Interviews

A job interview is not simply a chance to beg for a position. It represents not only someone's quest for a job that is satisfying, interesting, and rewarding, but it is also a device for an employer to search for a productive and harmonious worker to advance the company's needs. Because of the complex mental and emotional processes which take place during a job interview, there is much potential for misunderstandings to arise. Skillful self-presentation and readiness to furnish useful information are necessary on both sides of an interview of this type. Preoccupation with "getting the job" or playing games during an interview are sure to create many problems later. An interviewee who is excessively concerned with hiding weaknesses and inflating strong points is only laying traps which will be painful for both parties later.

Because there are numerous ways job interviews can go wrong, and because nowadays this type of interview is so important to students, useful guidelines and suggestions for conducting employment interviews are presented in detail later in this appendix.

Grievance Interviews

Inevitably, employees find themselves in situations in which they feel imposed upon. Policies adopted by a company may offend people in matters they regard as personal business. For example, you might feel harrassed because you have a beard, long hair, or unusual dress in a job for which a dress code is either explicit or subtly enforced. Matters of job procedure, conflicts with immediate supervisors and coworkers, or slow advancement are sources of dissatisfaction among employees. Again, your willingness to solve a shared problem in a grievance interview will help to maintain open communication, whereas sole concern with getting your way is sure to worsen the situation by alienating those who could perhaps remedy a grievance.

Information-Gathering Interviews

A common use of the interview is to collect unique views and data from some unusually competent person, a particularly interesting public figure, or someone catapulted into the limelight by disaster or fortune. A sweepstakes winner, a movie actor, an astronaut, a neurosurgeon, or a senator might catch your attention and grant an interview. You need a particular set of skills in questioning and maintaining rapport and interest to conduct this kind of interview. In a corporate setting, interviewing departmental supervisors or heads to discover attitudes, work progress, or plant needs are all occasions when you would use the information-seeking interview.

Exit Interviews

A conference with someone who is quitting a job, or who has perhaps been fired, can be both an unpleasant and a helpful event. A company can find out why one person and perhaps other employees perceive unhappy working conditions. The employee can air gripes, possibly point the way to improving conditions for other workers, and perhaps discover some useful, if painful, insights about mistakes he or she made while employed with the company. An exit interview is a chance for an employee to examine future career prospects and to make some judgments about where to seek more compatible employment.

When skillfully and sincerely conducted, an exit interview illustrates particularly well the mutuality of needs described earlier. The company can learn better ways of holding employee loyalty and satisfaction while the employee can express objections and learn why companies adopt certain policies and do not always adjust to what seem like legitimate complaints. For instance, companies do not always reward loyalty and may consider a very loyal employee insufficiently aggressive to advance in the company. One's willingness to do a job steadily without complaint or demands for salary increases could be interpreted by the company as complacence, even though the employee considered any demands for an increase to be unseemly. One who cultivates competitive offers may, by contrast, be seen as a go-getter, one to be held and promoted by the company. A loyal worker could understandably be outraged at the advancement of such a "pushy" and self-serving worker who seems to spend most of his or her time seeking good offers and is then promoted over the hard-working loyal employee. It is bitter to discover the company's attitude at an exit interview, but the realities of managerial responsibilities can sometimes be made clear in this situation better than in any other. Each party has much at stake and the frequently uncertain, ambiguous status of a given person in a corporate structure is quickly clarified. The company must make a decision whether to offer redress to some grievance, perhaps increase a worker's salary or benefits, meet another company's offer, or merely to allow the person to leave. Of course, the company may have a policy of allowing disgruntled employees to leave, regardless of the reason, because the company can then employ new people at less cost. More commonly, however, a company finds that training new people is expensive and that salvaging an experienced employee who is threatening to leave is worth some effort. The exit interview, therefore, has considerable value to a firm. Sometimes it results in productive workers' being retained. Even if it fails to dissuade a key person from leaving,

it may reveal recurrent personnel problems which top management has ignored.

Coordinating Interviews

Sometimes an interview is used to synchronize the operations of two division heads, two departments, or two individuals whose work is intertwined.
For example, an art director needs to confer with a stage director in producing
a Broadway play, and the work of the two artists might be handled in conference or interview to ensure harmony of design. A salesperson might need
to interview the director once every month because the work keeps him or her
traveling most of the time. A middle manager might need to interview either
the boss to present a status report or a subordinate for a similar purpose. The
giving and gathering of full, accurate, and often complex information is the
common denominator here. Further, any changes in the assumptions underlying policy, market conditions, or attitudes can be revealed confidentially and
accurately by an interview. This type of interview is, of course, similar in many
ways to a conference. The main difference is that it more like a conversation
than a public discussion.

PREPARATION

Regardless of the type of interview, participants must make sure that the
whole purpose of the event is not thwarted by some failure to prepare for it
or by some extraneous factor. Following are some general principles to consider
in the preparation stage.

Personal Appearance

Even if your dress and grooming do not seem to have much to do with
an interview, they in fact often make the difference between success and failure. It is important to consider the situation and the person you will interview
with the same care you use to assess an audience in a public-speaking situation.
The fact that one person is the whole audience does not lessen in any way the
demands upon you to present a case or a series of coherent questions. Often
students have the illusion that they function well in one-to-one conversations
but cannot give public speeches. Although stage fright is a very real emotion
in a public presentation, its absence in an interview may be false comfort. You
are just as much on display and under examination while seated informally
in a chair across the desk from another person as you are on a podium. Thus,
you should consider every detail of careful dress and grooming appropriate to
the situation. If you are seeking a job as a manicurist or hair stylist you should
ensure that dirty fingernails, unkempt hair or beard, or unpleasant breath do

not betray personal qualities that in the actual job would turn off clients. An interviewer will certainly notice any carelessness in those matters and might deny you a position on the grounds that the intimate personal contact inherent in such a position requires unusually careful grooming. On the other hand, if you are seeking a job as a welder or gardener you might be suspect if coddled hands gave absolutely no evidence of your having done a day's rough work. It is usually enough to make sure that you are decently dressed, not offensive in any way, and appropriately groomed for the situation. For instance, if you know that an employer has a dress code and that he or she frowns on beards, your seeking an interview while flouting the customs is likely to waste everyone's time. On the other hand, many companies once considered conservative now permit beards and informal dress on the job. Find out before you seek a job. In addition, even if the interview is just to get some information, it is wise just from the standpoint of avoiding any negative impression to conform to the standards expected. If you irritate someone you interview, and that person has the power to give or withhold information, you have in effect subverted your effort.

Manner, Manners, and Composure

A person's attitudes are often revealed by manner, manners, and composure. Manner is a general bearing one reveals. It may be confident, fearful, arrogant, diffident, furtive, or bland. Manners, however, are conscious efforts to ease the social interaction. People with good manners are polite, responsive, and friendly even when passing the time, and they are ready to make conversation easy and open for others. Manners are often artificial procedures deliberately chosen to make introductions graceful and comfortable. Most people would rather talk and deal with those they know than risk meeting new people they may not like or trust. Manners are the civilized practices such as handshakes, smiles, greeting forms, and little actions (such as holding doors open, standing aside for others, and rising as a gesture of respect for elders or superiors). Finally, composure is self-possession and alertness to a situation. The ability to adjust gracefully, to control emotions, to fit in socially, and to respond comfortably even in tense, unexpected situations are all evidence of composure.

All three of these just-described terms should concern you. A positive manner tends to make others like and respect you. Good manners make you durable, easy to be around, and open to communication. Sound composure makes you seem tryout worthy, dependable, stable, and reliable. If you are weak in any one of these qualities, an interview is likely to turn sour. Attention may be diverted from the content and purpose of the communication to wondering about your personality defects. If you have a fearful, withdrawn manner, the interviewer may lose respect and wonder, "Why is this person frightened? Is there something to hide?" If you have rough or uncouth manners, such as coarse language or behavior, the interviewer loses sympathy, saying, "Why should I help this slob? This person won't fit in here. I'll be glad to finish this interview. I don't like to be around loud, uncouth people." Finally, if your composure is shaky you may create pity, rejection, or even amusement. The interviewer might think, "Wow, this person is sure jumpy. We can't have her around here. She's so spooky she would get on everyone's nerves. This person surely wouldn't create a very good image to represent our company."

Timing

Often the difference between quite an adequate communicator and quite an inept one is a sense of time. Impatience is common in our pressure-laden world. People all talk at the moments of their own choosing. If a particular chosen moment is not convenient for someone trying to listen to something else, irritation and poor communication can result.

A classic situation portrayed in cartoon and story is the tired husband coming home from work and being met at the door by his wife enthusiastically relating the events of her day and his children exuberantly trying to tell all their deeds. Social and business situations often present the same dilemma—one person wishes to spill out many details when the intended receiver (whom we might call the victim) is just not ready yet.

A considerate interviewer has a sense of time and timing that inwardly reveals when others are ready to respond. This sense of timing includes several skills:

1. The sense of when someone else is attentive or not.
2. The sense of when someone is receptive to a particular idea.
3. The sense of the order of information another will find acceptable.
4. The sense of how much time one is using and has used so far.
5. The sense of when to terminate the interview.

Presenting information or questions before a listener is ready to pay attention is almost certain to muddle the picture you want to create. For example, an interview interrupted by phones, intercoms, people sticking their heads in a door, and so on, is likely to remain a hazy event in the mind of the interviewer. If you are able to control the situation, it is best to wait until the environment is calm and then begin. If interruptions occur, it is wise to briefly summarize the interview if the respondent seems to need the prompt. However, it is easy to insult someone who does not need the review. You might have to arrange another time if the interview is too hectic. In a few circumstances the pace of interruptions and work is typically fast and furious, and the person interviewing just has to face up to that fact. A big city newspaper, an airport tower or radar room, or service agencies which must process many people all day are likely to be more or less frantic most of the time. On a Friday night, a big hospital emergency room is hardly the place to gather information for a term paper.

Sometimes when you prepare an interview you may have one or more key ideas or crucial questions which are awkward but with which you must deal. To present them too soon can be offensive and may result in a failed interview. An obvious example is if you are interviewing for an entry-level trainee position, and you want to know the salary and benefits before you discuss the nature of the position being offered. Another example would be your premature laying out of unpleasant options to an employee if it turns out that none of them is necessary. "Unless sales improve next month, we will have to respond by laying off personnel, retiring those nearing eligibility, discouraging lagging sales agents by small advancement, and not filling vacant positions. If sales improve by 6 percent, these steps will not be necessary." To begin an interview with "We are concerned with lagging production schedules and suspect that either you or some higher ups are deliberately delaying manufacture" is hardly likely to endear you to anyone, worker or manager. Concern with production is the proper focus, and explanations or proposals may render the threats totally unnecessary.

We might draw an analogy here between a festive party and an interview. Too much of even the best of things becomes a bore. Knowing when to stop a party is said to be the secret of having a successful one. Everybody leaves at the height of interest and just before boredom sets in. The result is that memory of the last things that happened is vivid and pleasant. Because we tend to remember most vividly events that are first and last in a long sequence, rather than those which occur somewhere in the middle, a positive image remains of the party or an interview that ends on a high note of interest.

You should be sensitive to how long you have talked and how much time you can rightfully demand of the interviewer. If it seems clear that you have gleaned all the data you can, or that you have either failed or succeeded soundly, then you must bring the interview to a timely conclusion. You should finish decisively but not abruptly. No matter how much positive affect there is, do not dawdle. You might thank the person conducting the interview for the time granted and the favor given you. Then leave gracefully.

Anticipation

Predicting approximately what will happen in an interview is usually possible. In a job search certain questions are almost a certainty. If you anticipate them, you can give smoother and more complete answers than if you are unprepared. In other types of interviews, there is considerable uncertainty about what questions to ask. For example, in a highly technical industry you may not know enough to ask intelligent questions but the interviewer cannot know what information you are seeking until you make a query. When this dilemma arises, you should do enough research to formulate sensible, pointed questions to prevent a wandering, indecisive, or vague response. In yet other kinds of interviews, you usually have an inkling of what is to come. If you are a worker and you have decided to quit or you have been fired and have been given an exit interview, you should not just brood and pout but you should formulate some clear, constructive advice or explanation of the mismatch with the job. A departing worker can at least help others by presenting grievances, assuming they are shared by other workers. If you just want to move to a better climate and have no particular gripes, you might try in advance of the interview to imagine how the company might improve its product, service, or policies, and seek to leave on a pleasant and cooperative note. If you are remembered kindly, your recommendations may reflect warm memories. All of these examples point to your need to foresee the results of your behavior and, within limits, to control the outcome of interviews. At least you can have the satisfaction of avoiding a sense of being a victim of fate.

In some interviews you might need to bring charts, lists, data, samples, polls, and the like. A part of anticipation is the readiness to produce needed information in understandable form. Compilations or digests, if needed, would be a thoughtful and impressive aid to the interview. For instance, if you knew you were being considered for promotion, you might bring a summary of data you had compiled to demonstrate your mastery of the duties and skills needed for the new position. Too much information can be presumptuous, however, and you might decide not to use all the data you have. If you reveal a little too much you might injure your chances by overeagerness. However, you should not be caught short of information you need.

PRESENTATION

So far we have considered getting ready for the interview and in imagination we have projected ourselves into the process. Now we need to consider some of the dynamics of the actual interview. Because every interview is unique in purpose, participants, and procedure, we examine the forces at work and the specific behaviors you can practice to influence the outcome. Surveys of numerous businesses and agencies have yielded a clear, definite pattern of what is desirable and undesirable behavior in an interview. We turn now to the constructive forces that can help an interview succeed.

Language Economy and Precision

Nothing is so revealing as your choice of word and idiom. If you reveal ignorance, insensitivity, coarseness, or selfishness when the opposite qualities are needed, others will tend to reject you and your requests. We all know coworkers or students with whom we have no close bonds and share no interests. We do not snarl at them, but probably get along pleasantly. Yet we do not want to get to know them any better, perhaps because of some thoughtless slur or jocular profanity. Some unguarded breach of our standards produced a barrier.

To avoid these unwelcome barriers in important conferences with someone who has the power to aid or hinder your career, to accept or reject you as a cooperating worker, or to choose you as friend or just an anonymous worker, you need superior command of language. As stated elsewhere, a gigantic vocabulary is not necessary to impress others, but a precisely used one is essential to be clear and to prevent misunderstanding.

Almost as important as choosing the exact word or phrase to express your thoughts is the habit of economy. Eschew verbiage. Generally, a brief, clear statement is better than a loose, roundabout one. You can be too clipped and parsimonious, but there is little risk of that fault. Our highly verbal culture encourages excessive, repetitive, extraneous, superfluous, unnecessary, and redundant language.

Directness rather than roundabout expression is a quality to cultivate. Precise diction saves time, creates a lively mood, reveals an acute intelligence instead of foggy thought, and creates confidence. You should seek the most direct way of speaking. Directness, however, is not the same as brevity. A sentence or thought can be quite long, even though it is direct. Government publications tend to be long and indirect. Income-tax forms remain, in spite of years of effort to clarify them, obscure and hard to read. In any case, directness and clarity are hard to achieve. Just try to rewrite a few paragraphs of the tax-instruction booklet, and you may discover how difficult it is to be clear and direct.

One way to be direct is to cut out excessive qualification: "It seems to me," "In my considered opinion," "It seems to be," and "hopefully" are all examples of expressions we freely inject to appear fluent. However, often these expressions just pile up words without adding any content. Who is hoping in the following sentence? "Hopefully no new taxes will be imposed next year." A direct statement made from that hazy one would be, "I hope no new taxes will be imposed . . . " or "We all hope. . . ." Consider this sentence: "I would hope that all employees of this company would be free of worries about medical aid in emergencies, either for themselves or for those legally dependent on them." What is the imaginary applicant trying to say? Which of the following sentences would you regard as equal or superior to the inquiry on medical aid?

1. "What would happen if I or, perish the thought, one of my kids were sick or injured in an accident?"

2. "I regard a comprehensive insurance plan as essential in any position I accept."

3. "What coverage in the way of insurance have you got?"

Although all of these questions grope toward information about how extensive and specific company insurance coverage is, only the declaration about insurance coverage's being *essential* really asserts anything about how the prospective employee feels. It says that accepting employment *depends* on adequate insurance. All the other sentences are feeble inquiries. In the direct statement the speaker has chosen to take a stand and has moved the interview forward. While asking for details about the company's insurance coverage, the applicant helps the interviewer to determine information about the applicant's expectations.

SUMMARY

Interviews are frequent and useful types of speaking. Although they are not usually conducted as public speeches, interviews require some of the same personal mastery of self, information, and situational analysis that public speeches do. The forms and purposes of interviews vary, but all of them pose the responsibility for careful preparation, appropriate personal grooming and dress, and sensitivity to the mutual needs of the parties involved. During all actual interviews, control of timing, emotional composure, manners, and language are important.

EXERCISES

1. Have pairs of students in the class invent typical interview situations and conduct them before the class, which overhears them. Then have the class critique the interviews. Was everything needed brought out in the interviews? Did one person dominate each session? Was the language effective and direct? Did both parties show good will and cooperation in the effort?

2. Have each student present in detail an interview situation that might realistically occur in the next few years—job seeking, termination, and the like. The best of these situations can be used for *other* students in the class to pair off and conduct interviews. If one member of the pair knows more than the other one, some interesting situations can be revealed. The teacher might, for example, tell one member of the interviewing pair much more than the other and watch to see whether and when the hidden information is brought out. Sample situations: A job interview for a job that is very undesirable. A job interview for a position which requires special schooling at the applicant's expense. A job interview for a job which expects part of the pay to be given back as a tithe or for a job that is partly a religious duty. A terminal interview in which management really wants to talk the employee into staying on.

3. Discuss what happens when one party in an interview mistrusts the other. Assume the role of a person being interviewed just for discovery of facts, but pretend the person suspects a police investigation or fears a lawsuit if he or she tells too much about an accident witnessed earlier.

4. Apply the tests of effective discussion from this Appendix to television interviews seen on local television. Do media people consistently violate any of the "rules"? To what extent is the power of editing TV footage an advantage? A disadvantage?

5. Set up a job-seeking interview in which several students in turn are interviewed for the same job, for which they might really be qualified and in which they might really be interested. Have at least three candidates interviewed before the class, but exclude the competing candidates from hearing those who precede them. Have the class "hire" the best applicant.

6. Establish a real reason to conduct a brief interview with someone in the community. Conduct the interview, remembering always to avoid wasting other people's time. For instance, if you really are considering a career in finance or investment, interview a banker or broker. Prepare your questions carefully to make the interview meaningful. This will help you avoid trivial questions and lead you to discover information of genuine use. Sample situations: Interview a dean and find out how widespread cheating is. Confer with a minister or rabbi about the preparation needed for ordination in your church or synagogue if you have an interest in the clergy. Talk to a college director of graduate study about qualifications and requirements needed to pursue an advanced degree. Talk to salespeople about a major investment, such as buying a computer system for your home. Shop for a car or boat. Talk to a bank officer or a broker about how to invest in gold, how to build a portfolio of stocks, or how to finance a house.

7. Watch a talk show and write a critique of the host's interviewing technique. Do the participants have entertainment responsibilities? If so, does that fact change the conduct of interviews in any way? If so, how? Make an oral report on such a show of your choice to the class.

SELECTED READINGS

Ronald L. Applbaum and Karl W. E. Anatol, *Effective Oral Communication for Business and the Professions* (Chicago: SRA, 1982), especially Chapters 15, 16, and 17.

Randall Capps, Carley Dodd, and Larry Winn, *Communication for the Business and Professional Speaker* (New York: Macmillan, 1981).

Cheryl Hamilton, Cordell Parker, and Doyle D. Smith, *Communicating for Results* (Belmont, Calif.: Wadsworth, 1982).

Charles J. Stewart and William B. Cash, *Interviewing: Principles and Practices*, 3rd ed. (Dubuque, Iowa: Wm. C. Brown, 1982).

appendix B

Sample Student Speech: Responsibility for Misuse of Handguns

by Tracy R. Kaplan

Last Sunday morning, a family who had formerly lived in my home town was found dead. They had been killed by the father of the household using a handgun. After he killed his wife and three children, he then committed suicide. These five deaths are just a few of the hundreds of thousands of handgun deaths recorded in recent years.

With the rate of violent crimes rapidly increasing in the United States, any method of gun control is worth a serious trial. Crimes of armed violence have grown until drastic measures are needed. Just how extensive is this problem? Among the 220 million people in the United States there have been 340,000 cases of violent crimes committed with the use of a firearm.

If we compare data from other countries, it is easy to see that a crackdown on handgun sales is necessary in the United States. For example, in West Germany, where there are 70 million people, there were less than 300 violent crimes in a recent year. Similarly, in Japan, which has 151 million citizens, there were only 171 crimes. Great Britain has only one-tenth of the murder rate that the United States has. In fact, guns have finished off more Americans since 1963 than did World War II, which lasted from 1941 through 1945. Handguns accounted for 400,000 deaths since 1963.

This speech was given in partial fulfillment of requirements for the basic course in public speaking at the University of Illinois. Used by permission of the student and edited by the author.

These statistics have a sobering effect on us when we consider how control of handguns is related to violent crimes. Our ideals do not match our actions. We say we want safe streets for our citizens but we do not control the manufacture and sale of guns. The latest Gallup Poll finds that 62 percent of Americans want stricter laws governing sales of handguns, but sales of guns are brisk. In fact, one gun is sold every 13 seconds, which turns out to be over 6000 a day. It seems clear that any effort to control the sale of guns might produce a substantial reduction in violent crimes. Even if we cannot approach Great Britain's rate of one-tenth our rate, any reduction at all would be worth the effort in lives saved and misery avoided.

In order to reduce the number of handgun deaths and violent crimes in the United States, the manufacturers, the people who profit from the sale of weapons, should be held financially responsible for the damage they cause. Although this proposition may seem extreme, there would be immediate effects that manufacturers of Saturday Night Specials would prefer to avoid. They would have to pay very high rates for liability insurance, because no insurer would want to risk paying out enormous sums in case of successful lawsuits against a weapons manufacturer. To protect themselves, the insurance companies would immediately pass on the costs to the manufacturers. In addition, the gun makers could lose their insurance coverage altogether if costs of insurance soared or if lawsuits began to make coverage impossible. Companies routinely cancel policies of stores, plants, or even homes where the risk of damage and loss are very high. In the long run, a manufacturer would have to keep a tighter control on gun sales or get out of the business altogether when it was no longer profitable.

From the standpoint of concerned citizens, the results of accepting the proposal in my thesis would be just the ones we want. Manufacturing and sales of handguns would decline when people became aware of the arguments I will present. First, the major task for those of us asking for restrictions on guns is to prove that small-caliber, short-barreled guns of three inches or less, lightweight, inexpensive weapons costing $50 or less are designed, manufactured, and distributed principally for shooting people. These easily concealed weapons are ideal for the purpose, but little else. They are not accurate or reliable enough for sporting use, shooting vermin on a farm, or police and military purposes, or even for self-defense. These properties therefore make the gun "defective" by design, and since they have no purpose other than to kill and injure people, they are of no benefit to society. Furthermore, selling of handguns creates an unreasonably dangerous situation with a very high risk of harm to society.

A common means of deciding about the desirability of something controversial is to balance the risks of a product or policy against its usefulness. Thus, we keep poisons like mercury and arsenic in everyday products such as thermometers, medicines, and insecticides because they are very useful and, properly used, not very dangerous to anybody. When a product is highly dangerous and not very useful, we rid ourselves of it. When it is both useful and dangerous, we put stringent controls on it, as we have done with weed killers, lead-based paints, and certain drugs like opium products. In the proposition urged here, the risk versus utility balancing test is a key factor in holding manufacturers of handguns responsible.

The risk of injury posed by the design of the product is weighed against the benefit to society. As I said earlier, there is no benefit and high risk in possession of a cheap handgun. If we balance the known and demonstrated risks from handguns against their utility, then their destructiveness must argue against them and brands them as a menace to public safety. The risks? An average of fifty people a day are killed by them. Hundreds of thousands of injuries from assaults, accidents, and design flaws cost the public millions of dollars in medical expenses.

The proposal to make manufacturers responsible for the destructiveness of their product might be compared to action against the Corvair and Pinto automobile manufacturers. Ford paid a lot of money in damages and defense costs when lawsuits claimed that the Pinto exploded when rear-ended. The suits made the public more wary of buying Pintos, and because of the bad publicity there are no more Pintos on the market.

Another key factor in gun control is the soaring insurance costs to a manufacturer when society makes its liability for damages high. This rise in insurance cost may in fact be the most powerful strategic tool to use against the handgun industry. If full responsibility for damages is clearly placed on handgun makers, it may not be necessary to engage in prolonged litigation to ban or restrain manufacturers. It will be the enormous and continuous financial risk which will shut down makers of cheap guns. Insurance companies will probably have to reissue policies, charge much higher rates, and put the manufacturers in a special ultra-high risk liability pool. This pressure from insurers will make gun makers cut back marketing of their cheap weapons to reduce their liability. They might even stop making Saturday Night Specials for their own financial good.

No plan for so complex a question is completely foolproof, however. Objections of several kinds are sure to arise. But these disadvantages of making manufacturers liable for the harm done by their product can be endured. First, any proposal for gun control is going to meet strong opposition from the National Rifle Association. The NRA is the most effective lobbying organization in Washington. Their position is so adamant that one might think they consider the sacredness of human life less important than the pleasure of owning a gun for sport. Of course, the issues are more complicated than I can present here, and the legalities of the proposal are intricate. Still, the proposal has strength in two areas where other attempts to regulate handguns have bogged down.

My proposal avoids the usual constitutional argument—namely, the issue of the right of citizens to bear arms. Further, it calls upon the courts and Congress to support the citizen's right to legal redress in cases of loss or injury. It reaffirms the value of human life more strongly than past policy has done. If the end result of adopting this proposal were to be reduction, however slight, in the number of violent crimes, the effort would be worthwhile.

The proposal would also tend to remove the contest between advocates of gun control and their opponents from Congress and put the struggle in the courts. Here, proving liability is less likely to be influenced by pressure groups and lobbyists. Judges and juries cannot be so easily influenced as legislators have been. Practices such as getting big contributors to political campaigns to influence legislators may hide the real source of pressure on Congress, which again and again defeats gun-control proposals. Although there are in fact numerous state and local ordinances which try to prevent the selling of guns to just anyone, they are ineffective and hard to enforce. Their lack of effect and the high rate of violent crime make more restrictive laws necessary. Right now anyone with $10 in cash can find someone to sell him or her a used or stolen handgun. The enormous supply of such guns has an even more sinister effect. With so many guns distributed through the underworld, crimes committed tend to be more severe than they would be without guns. A criminal intending to rob a store in a petty theft unintentionally turns the crime into armed robbery or even murder when armed. Youths made bold by the cheap handgun in a burglary or robbery can be killed or maimed themselves when they go up against police armed with heavier, professional arms.

I believe that holding manufacturers responsible for the product liability, much like other industries are held, is a necessary change in policy. The change would help reduce violent crimes, discourage the escalation of minor crimes into major ones, and increase our concern for human life. My proposal would meet the problem head on by discouraging the manufacture of cheap guns in the first place, by making the sales of such guns to a mass market less attractive and profitable, and by forcing makers to face up to responsibility for violence against society through the use of their product.

I concede that setting up the details of a workable plan needs careful thought and ask you only to consider the urgency of our need for such a proposal. It is important to you, directly, for your home or bank or store or friends may be next. Do you want to take a chance on being the next victim of handguns? If you think the threat is small, remember that while I have spoken, 32 handguns were purchased today.

Like you, I went home last Wednesday for the holiday, expecting to spend a happy time with my family. I planned to relax and enjoy the vacation from school. I didn't expect to be told when I walked in the door that an old high-school friend had been murdered along with his whole family. You never think tragedy will come close or happen to you personally. That's what I thought, and probably that's what Jim thought.

BIBLIOGRAPHY

Isaacson, W., "Duel over Gun Control," *Time,* March 23, 1981, p. 33.

Kratscoski, P. C., "License to Kill?" *USA Today,* July 1981, p. 70.

"More on Gun Control," *Commonweal,* April 10, 1981, p. 197.

Morrow, L., "It's Time to Ban Handguns," *Time,* April 13, 1981, p. 51.

Nagy, D., "Saturday Night Specials . . . " *US News and World Report,* April 13, 1981, p. 29.

Reese, M., "Guns Out of Control," *Newsweek,* April 13, 1981, p. 57.

Weiss, E. F., "Guns in the Courts," *Atlantic,* May 1983, pp. 8–16.

COMMENTARY ON TRACY KAPLAN'S SPEECH

Although the delivery of Tracy's speech cannot be reproduced in print, the content, organization, language, and strategies chosen can be. Accordingly, this critique is primarily about them. The actual presentation was straightforward, controlled, and affecting without being overly dramatic. The language is clear, moderate (given the topic), and idiomatic. The audience was evidently kept in mind as Tracy wrote her speech. Divisions of the speech are clearly marked and transitions lead the audience from idea to idea smoothly. The problem-solution order is unobtrusive. The topic is somewhat routine, in that it is repeatedly debated in the mass media and speech classes, but this speech holds our interest well. The introduction establishes extraordinary involvement in the topic, warns of the grim personal commitment of the speaker, and foreshadows the powerful emotional conclusion.

Although personal involvement was high and the statistics were well placed throughout the speech, Tracy never mentions the sources she used and thereby weakens the believability of some of her data. The strikingly high figures would have even more impact if their sources were identified briefly. It would not be necessary to give a long, detailed citation. Because the author's checking the sources revealed that Tracy depended rather heavily on the organization and data in one source, Tracy should have given credit to that source in her oral performance—it is not enough just to cite the source in the bibliography. As commonly happens in research, the information in the listed sources often overlaps and is sometimes identical. Any speaker should comment succinctly on the relative use of the sources. For example, this speech needs a statement such as "*Time* and *Newsweek* both contained articles the same week on this problem and cite similar statistics on the number of deaths in recent years." To give due credit, Tracy might also have said, "Writing in *Atlantic* this year, E. F. Weiss has the best overview and guided my organization," or at least she might have cited Weiss often enough to show his article's relative contribution to her speech. It would also have helped to state briefly the qualifications of the sources used or quoted. Did the FBI or Department of Justice release the data? Whose idea was it to take the issue into the courts?

Another weakness which listeners noted in Tracy's speech was the rather hazy definition of just what they are being asked to do. Are they being persuaded to do something or are they merely being asked to accept a viewpoint? Are suggestions to move the issue out of the Legislature and into the courts explained adequately? Is it in our power to do anything along those lines? An improvement in the speech, if it were to be given again, would thus be to select a more specific statement of just how the audience is expected to react to the speech. If Tracy is really saying, "We are going to have to provoke a test-case lawsuit and win it to establish once and for all the responsibility of gun makers," she should say so.

The examples, statistics, and supporting material of the talk are both sufficient and pertinent. The alarming data along with the subdued outrage are affecting. The speech illustrates a balanced use of emotion, personal credibility, and evidence. The readings are extensive enough to show adequate research, and even though they are not cited in detail, their impact is felt. Tracy does not overuse statistics, but inserts them right where they are needed. The overall effect is a sense of completeness, importance, and urgency. The personal loss reaches into the audience and gives unusual force to the speech without displaying excessive emotion. The speech still provides for serious gun enthusiasts to pursue their interests with high-quality firearms.

Reference Notes

CHAPTER 1

1. Thomas M. Scheidel, *Speech Communication and Human Interaction,* 2nd ed. (Glenview, Ill.: Scott, Foresman, 1976), p. 42.
2. For a discussion of the implications of this phenomenon, see Bert E. Bradley, *Fundamentals of Speech Communication,* 3rd ed. (Dubuque, Iowa: Wm. C. Brown, 1981), pp. 46–48.
3. C. W. Sherif, M. Sherif, and Roger Nebergall, *Attitude and Attitude Change* (Philadelphia: W. B. Saunders, 1965), p. 24. See also C. A. Kiesler, B. E. Collins, and N. Miller, *Attitude Change* (New York: Wiley, 1969), p. 248.
4. For a discussion of the relationship between attitudes and behavior, see Nan Lin, *The Study of Human Communication* (New York: Bobbs-Merrill, 1973), pp. 95–100.
5. J. Mills and E. Aronson, "Opinion Change as a Function of the Communicator's Attractiveness and Desire to Influence, *Journal of Personality and Social Psychology,* 1 (1965), 173–177. For a recent survey of the concept of credibility, see James C. McCroskey, "Ethos and Credibility: The Construct and its Measurement after Three Decades," *Central States Speech Journal,* 32 (1981), 24–34.
6. WGBH, Boston, 1983. This was the second program on Dieting in America in the NOVA series.

CHAPTER 2

1. Ralph G. Nichols, "Do We Know How to Listen? Practical Help in a Modern Age," *Speech Teacher,* 10 (1961), 120. See also Stuart Chase, "Are You Listening?" *Reader's Digest* (December 1962), p. 80.

2. Gordon Allport and Leo Postman, *Psychology of Rumor* (New York: Henry Holt, 1948), pp. 55, 100, 135. The mechanism is not fully understood, but evidently we remember selectively, and we enhance some data to make them complete and consistent with our beliefs and language.

3. Nichols, "Do We Know How to Listen?" p. 120.

4. Larry Barker, *Listening Behavior* (Englewood Cliffs, N.J.: Prentice-Hall, 1971). p. 71.

5. Although it seems obvious that listening requires less physical effort than speaking, writing, and reading (turning pages), an informal study attempted to show the differential calorie consumption among the four activities. Compared with sitting quietly, listening showed no measurable increase in calorie consumption. Speaking used the most calories, and writing the next most.

6. Richard F. Whitman and Paul H. Boase, *Speech Communication* (New York: Macmillan, 1983), pp. 104–106.

7. Emerson Foulke and Thomas G. Sticht, *The Intelligibility and Comprehension of Time Compressed Speech,* Proceedings of the Louisville Conference on Time Compressed Speech. Louisville, Kentucky, 1966, Chapters 2 and 3.

8. Raymond Ross, *Speech Communication,* 5th ed. (Englewood Cliffs, N.J.: Prentice Hall, 1971), pp. 86–87.

9. Charles F. Diehl, Richard White, and Paul Satz, "Pitch Change and Comprehension," *Speech Monographs,* 28 (March 1961), 65–68.

10. Stafford H. Thomas, "Effects of Monotonous Delivery on Intelligibility," *Speech Monographs,* 36 (June 1969), 110–113.

11. D. W. Addington, "The Relationship of Selected Vocal Characteristics to Personality Perception," *Speech Monographs,* 35 (1968), 492–503.

12. This concept is controversial. For interesting discussions of crowd behavior, see Gustave LeBon, *The Crowd* (New York: Viking Press, 1960), p. 26. Cf. Roger Brown, *Social Psychology* (New York: Free Press, 1965), p. 760.

13. Carl H. Weaver, *Human Listening, Processes and Behavior* (New York: Bobbs-Merrill, 1972), pp. 99, 105.

CHAPTER 3

1. Plato's two dialogues, *Gorgias* and *Phaedrus,* reveal his misgivings about rhetoric and his admission that the skill might be useful and ethically employed.

2. See Joseph A. DeVito, *The Elements of Public Speaking* (New York: Harper & Row, 1981), pp. 89–90. See also Howard H. Martin and Kenneth E. Andersen, *Speech Communication: Analysis and Readings* (Boston: Allyn & Bacon, 1968), pp. 252–253. This is an adaptation of work in Irving L. Janis and Carl Hovland, *Personality and Persuasibility* (New Haven, Conn.: Yale University Press, 1959), Chapter 11.

3. A good discussion of the variables involved is found in Bert E. Bradley, *Fundamentals of Speech Communication,* 3rd ed. (Dubuque, Iowa: Wm. C. Brown, 1981), Chapter 8. This chapter has unusually full documentation of studies which show *why* each recommendation is made. Another good source is Appendix B in Douglas Ehninger, Alan H. Monroe, and Bruce E. Gronbeck, *Principles and Types of Speech Communication,* 8th ed. (Glenview, Ill.: Scott, Foresman, 1978).

4. A. H. Maslow, "A Theory of Human Motivation," *Psychological Review,* 50 (1943), 370–396. See also Maslow, *Motivation and Personality* (New York: Harper & Row, 1954), Chapter 5.

CHAPTER 5

1. Darrell Huff, *How to Lie With Statistics* (New York: W. W. Norton, 1954).

CHAPTER 7

1. De Vito, *The Elements of Public Speaking,* pp. 337–345.
2. Foulke and Sticht, "The Intelligibility and Comprehension of Time Compressed Speech," Chapter 3.
3. William R. Tiffany conducted an in-class experiment challenging students to read a two-minute passage of moderately difficult prose at their normal rates and then at half their normal rates. All of the subjects tested in the experiment reverted to their habitual rates within less than 30 seconds. Even stopping students and reminding them to slow down had only a brief effect.
4. S. A. Beebe, "Eye Contact: A Non-Verbal Determinant to Speaker Credibility," *Speech Teacher,* 23 (1974), 23–24.

CHAPTER 8

1. The issue of fear-arousal's effects is by no means settled. Much recent research suggests that fear-inducing speeches may be effective if they present means for avoiding the threats described. See Bert Bradley, *Fundamentals of Speech Communication,* pp. 355–358, for his conclusions and advice, and a list of studies on p. 371. The present author believes that low to moderate fear stimuli are all one needs to make a point forcefully and that there are some risks that fear-inducing stimuli will backfire.
2. A. A. Lumsdaine and I. L. Janis, "Resistance to 'Counter-Propaganda' Produced by One-Sided and Two-Sided 'Propaganda' Presentations," *Public Opinion Quarterly,* 17 (1953), 311–318. See also C. A. Insko, "One-Sided versus Two-Sided Communications and Counter-Communications," *Journal of Abnormal and Social Psychology,* 65 (1962), 203–206.
3. James C. McCroskey, *An Introduction to Rhetorical Communication,* 4th ed. (Englewood Cliffs, N.J.: Prentice-Hall, 1982), p. 72.
4. R. G. Smith, "Effects of Speech Organization upon Attitudes of College Students," *Speech Monographs,* 18 (1951), 292–301.
5. Kenneth Burke, *A Rhetoric of Motives* (Englewood Cliffs, N.J.: Prentice-Hall, 1950), p. 55.
6. Norman H. Anderson, "Likeableness Ratings of 555 Personality-Trait Words," *Journal of Personality and Social Psychology,* 9 (1968), 272–279.
7. H. Leventhal, "Findings and Theory in the Study of Fear Communications," in *Advances in Experimental Social Psychology,* vol. 5, ed. L. Berkowitz (New York: Academic Press, 1970), p. 120.
8. Ronald B. Adler and George Rodman, *Understanding Human Communication* (New York: Holt, Rinehart & Winston, 1982), p. 370.
9. I. L. Janis and S. Feshbach, "Effects of Fear-Arousing Communications," *Journal of Abnormal and Social Psychology,* 48 (1953), 78–92.

CHAPTER 10

1. K. D. Benne and P. Sheats, "Functional Roles and Group Members," *Journal of Social Issues,* 2 (1948), 41–49.
2. John Dewey, *How We Think* (Boston: Heath, 1910), pp. 68–78.

Index

Italic page numbers indicate an endnote reference. Boldface page numbers indicate an illustration.